DEDICATION

To Dad, the best storyteller I know.

Acknowledgements

It goes without saying that this book would not have been possible if the fine group of interviewees you're about to meet had not willingly given up so much of their time to discuss their craft, often under very hectic circumstances.

And behind every one of them was an assistant, secretary or PA who found themselves harassing their respective bosses on my behalf. My thanks to all of them, particularly Jennifer Horton, Deric Hughes, Elisabeth James, Lorraine Garland, Eric Stillwell, Sue Binder and Jamie Turner.

Thanks also to those at Titan: my editors David Barraclough, Adam Newell and Jo Boylett, and designer Martin Stiff, for accepting the countless delays, explanations and excuses that generally accompany a project of this nature. Their unflappability was much appreciated, although there are now undoubtedly a few holes in the office walls of Titan Towers bearing my name.

Finally, much thanks to my wife Sheelagh, who as usual, had to live through every step of this book, whether she wanted to or not. Yes, it's finally finished. No, really, it is.

Joe Nazzaro

The publishers would also like to thank Stephen Thompson at *The Onion A. V. Club*. www.theonionavclub.com

CONTENTS

INTRODUCTION

'I hate television, I hate it as much as peanuts. But I can't stop eating peanuts.'
— Orson Welles

'I write when I'm inspired, and I see to it that I'm inspired at nine o'clock every morning.' — Peter De Vries

This book came about, as many ideas often do, in a fairly simple way. I'd been reading Mark Salisbury's excellent *Writers on Comics Scriptwriting* (also published by the good folks at Titan Books, incidentally), when I thought, what about a similar book in which writers of fantasy and SF television discuss their work? Having spent the last decade or so covering various genre programmes, I'd always been fascinated by the process by which a script was created and produced. Where do the ideas initially come from, and how do they become words on paper? What makes a good script or a bad one? How does a writer find the 'voices' of his characters? But I also wanted to know about the craft itself. How did some of these writers break into television in the first place? What were the best ways of finding old scripts to study before the Internet? Did the 'rules' of the game differ from the US, to the UK, to Canada? Inquiring minds wanted to know, or at least this one did.

Before I talk about some of the people who provided their insights for this project, let's take a few moments to look at the process of writing for television. This is by no means a complete account, but it should explain a few of the terms that will be used in upcoming chapters. I should also point out that this is primarily the US model we're discussing here, based on conversations with a number of American writers over the last several years. As you'll see, the UK way of doing things is somewhat different.

Okay, let's say you're a would-be writer trying to get started. First, you need to know about the mechanics of writing a script. There's always film school if you've got the time and money (and several of the interviewees went that route), but it would also be helpful to track down some old scripts for study; there are plenty on the Internet — try www.scriptcrawler.net. Books about scriptwriting are easily available now (an excellent one to start with is *The Complete Book of Scriptwriting* by a certain J. Michael

Straczynski) and so is software that will give you the basic format for writing a script, such as *Final Draft*.

Once you feel confident about your abilities, you can try writing a script 'on spec', as an example of your work. A good spec script or two will help you get an agent, and give them something to send out on your behalf. You'll need an agent, by the way; most unsolicited scripts sent directly to a production company are either returned unread or simply dropped in a bin. Until recently, the various *Star Trek* series were home to just about the only people in Hollywood willing to read an unsolicited script, but since the advent of the latest *Trek* series, *Enterprise*, that's no longer the case (at least for the time being), so don't bother!

Generally speaking, the rule of thumb is, if you want to write for *Xena*, don't write a *Xena* script; write a spec script for a different series, that will show you have a range of abilities, and can write good drama and good action. And if you want to break into the drama market, it's probably not a good idea to write a comedy spec.

If those spec scripts show some merit, the agent can send them around, and hopefully get you a meeting to go in and 'pitch' on a series. In a pitch meeting, a freelancer will present several ideas for possible episodes to the show's producers. It's usually a good idea to work up a number of ideas, because in all likelihood, the producers have A) heard every story idea under the sun, B) already done that story, or C) have a script in the works based on that idea. Also, many series are essentially staff-driven, which means that most episodes are written by the in-house writing staff, and only two or three slots for episodes to be written by freelancers are left open each season. Nevertheless, producers are always looking for new and different ideas, particularly after a series has been on the air for several seasons.

Should you be lucky enough to come up with that one magical spark of inspiration, the producers may commission you to write a detailed outline of your proposed script. If it's worth developing further, they could buy the story idea from you and have one of their staff writers tackle the script. Or they could bring you back in to 'break' the story, a process by which the writers sit down in a room together and map out (sometimes literally, on a blackboard) the major plot points of an episode. Those points can then be made into a 'beat sheet', where the story is broken down act by act (the 'acts' being each chunk of the episode between ad breaks). From there, it's on to the script. If you've been given the assignment to write a first draft, most rewrites are generally done in-house. This is not uncommon, nor should it be taken personally; on *Buffy* for example, virtually *every* script gets a final polish from series creator Joss Whedon before going into production. So you're in pretty good company there.

This explains why the writing credits on TV episodes can be quite complicated, often with separate 'Story by' and 'Teleplay by' credits. Without going too far into this difficult area, suffice it to say that if a staffer rewrites a freelancer's script, and believes they've made substantial changes to it, both versions can be submitted to the WGA (Writers Guild of America, the writers' union, a powerful body that has rigid codes of practice, and minimum terms of payment for particular types of screenwriting) for arbitration, a final decision on 'who wrote what'. Because the final credits determine who will get residual payments for that episode when it is repeated, it can be a some-what contentious issue. Some producers prefer that the original writer gets full credit regardless of how much rewriting is done. Other productions, such as the *Star Trek* series, will go to arbitration, which is why you'll sometimes see a number of different writing credits on an episode (usually those credited for the 'Story' are the freelancers, and the 'Teleplay' are the staff writers who rewrote the script). Ask five different writers about this subject, and you'll probably get five different opinions on how such things should be dealt with.

Getting back to the matter at hand, even if the producers don't buy your pitch, all is not lost. I've heard of freelancers who had every one of their pitches shot down. It turned out that most of their ideas were already in development, which meant they were very much in tune with the tone and direction of the series. They were then given a script already in development to try and rewrite, or a brand new premise to go away and develop.

If a freelancer proves to be adept at writing for a particular series, he may be asked to join their writing staff. Becoming a staff writer on a show is, as *Star Trek* veteran D. C. Fontana points out in her interview in this book, the 'lowest of the low in the roster of positions'. Essentially, a young staff writer will start out with simply writing their own scripts, but if they progress up the ladder, they will gradually start to rewrite other peoples' scripts, and acquire more and more responsibility on the production side. There are different titles depending on the responsibilities for each job, ranging from story editor (who will rewrite scripts), to the slightly more senior executive story editor, upwards to anything with 'producer' in it, from co-producer, to producer, to supervising producer and so on. Writers who have reached this level will have increas-ingly more to do with the day-to-day running of the show, not only choosing stories, commissioning scripts and rewriting them where necessary, but sitting in on casting, working with the costume and art departments, and discussing the editing of an episode. The bottom line is that they are a 'writer employed in additional capacities'. Then there's the job at the top of the tree (the position that most of the interviewees in this book now find themselves in) — the executive producer, or 'show runner'. More often than not, the show runner is also head writer, and is responsible for com-missioning scripts and putting together a writing staff. The show runner also knows the tone of a series better than just about anybody else, and will probably be the person doing the final polish on a script before — and sometimes even during — shooting.

If the show runner also created the series, he's probably the person with a long-term plan locked away in his head. Whether or not that plan is set in stone depends on the writer; Joe Straczynski knew how *Babylon 5* would end right from the beginning, and so does Paul Donovan on *Lexx*. Others, like Robert Hewitt Wolfe on *Andromeda*, know the broad strokes of their story, but are more willing to see how it evolves over time.

And just how tightly should those story threads be woven together? While most writers would probably like to create a novel for television, there are other factors that frequently come into play. Networks aren't too keen on multi-part episodes as a rule, because when a series is eventually sold into syndication, its new masters want to be able to break it up in whatever manner they see fit. *Farscape* is a notable exception, where current show runner David Kemper claims the Sci-Fi Channel has encouraged him to experiment with the format as much as he likes. It's a luxury that most show runners don't enjoy.

As I pointed out above, that's essentially the US model (which is pretty much the same in Canada). In the UK, the system is usually a lot simpler, with no in-house writing staff as such, just a script editor who commissions scripts from freelancers, rewriting them if necessary when they are delivered. The interview with ex-*Doctor Who* script editor Terrance Dicks reveals more about how this system used to work at the BBC in the 60s and 70s, although these days the process is becoming closer to the US setup, with some series (especially ones made by independent production companies) experimenting with US-style writing staff.

That should cover some of the general areas we'll be discussing in the coming pages. I should point out that it was not my intention to write a dry, step-by-step 'how-to' training manual about screenwriting, although you will learn many technical details of how a script is put together from reading these pages. As a journalist, it was more my intention to give you a glimpse into how a genre series is created, and what it's like to work on one, day-in, day-out.

And that brings us to our next point: how did I decide which writers I wanted to interview for this book? Well, just as a show runner will put together a staff of people he wants to work with, I began by making a list of people I've gotten to know over the years, and a few that I've always wanted to talk to.

The first couple of choices were obvious ones. I met Rockne O'Bannon back in 1993, when *Farscape* was still called *Space Chase*. Nearly a decade later, the series is about to go into production on its fourth season, with no sign of slowing down. Rock has turned over the day-to-day responsibilities of running *Farscape* to his old friend David Kemper (who is doing a marvellous job) in order to concentrate on new projects, but his love of and commitment to the series hasn't waned. It's also interesting to hear his thoughts on a possible *Farscape* feature film.

There's a scene that was cut from the final episode of *Babylon 5*, in which a struggling Joe Straczynski is seen being wheeled down one of the station's corridors on a gurney, a computer keyboard still tightly clutched to his chest. I sometimes think that scene is more autobiographical than anything Joe has written to date. The first time I interviewed JMS was after seeing a rough cut of the *B5* pilot, before the final sound mix had been done. It was dark and gritty, but definitely had a lot of potential, and it soon became my personal crusade (no pun intended) to try and get this project a little more attention. In those early days, it wasn't easy. Some eight years after that first conversation, Joe agreed to take some time from shooting his new series, *Jeremiah* (and he'd been putting in twenty-four-hour days to get the production up and running), to talk about creating *Babylon 5*, its spin-off series *Crusade*, and the possible *B5* revival, *Legend of the Rangers*.

The first time I spoke to Robert Hewitt Wolfe, he was still a struggling staff writer on that other space station series, *Deep Space Nine*. He's now executive producer on *Andromeda*, which carries on the Gene Roddenberry legacy, taking it in a somewhat different direction. Robert had run into some last-minute production problems, but managed to make some time to talk just a few days before the final chapter of this book was to be handed in. Better late than never, I'm very happy to say.

Also representing the Roddenberry contingent are two writers who hail from very different parts of the *Star Trek* universe. Dorothy Fontana was involved with the original series from day one, as well as overseeing the animated series and writing episodes of *The Next Generation* and *DS9*. Although she's become well known for her many SF credits, she's written for just about every genre on television. Michael Piller came aboard *The Next Generation*, staying on to co-create *DS9* and *Voyager*, as well as writing the big screen outing *Star Trek: Insurrection*. Michael is also responsible for the marvellous but short-lived series *Legend*, and I'm hoping his pilot for *The Dead Zone* has been picked up as a series by the time this book sees print.

Strictly speaking, Rob Tapert is the only non-writer represented in these pages, but it was his creative vision that helped create *Hercules* and *Xena* (he was executive producer on both shows), as well as reviving the long-moribund female action heroine genre. Rob has always been frank and self-critical about his work, a far cry from the usual hype that most producers indulge in.

On the international side, Terrance Dicks is one of the writers most identified with the myriad incarnations of *Doctor Who*, both as a long-running script editor, and now novelist. Rob Grant and Doug Naylor I spent several months working with when I was writing *The Making of Red Dwarf* back in '94, and was always fascinated by their strange gestalt creative process. The two have since gone their separate ways, but our conversation from before the split shows just how close that relationship was. A few years later, I was back in London for the filming of *Neverwhere*, interviewing its writer Neil Gaiman for a possible making of book that never got off the ground. Ironically, while the show arguably became an exercise in how *not* to do fantasy for television, Neil's novel of the series later became a major best seller, and is now in development as a feature film. The interview featured herein should provide some idea of what

Gaiman originally had in mind, and gives some intriguing hints of what we might have seen in a second season, had it ever been made.

From Canada, Paul Donovan discusses the creation of *Lexx*, one of the most delightfully perverse SF series ever. It's perhaps no surprise to discover that his story ideas usually come from meetings that involve 'lots of beer'! Jonathan Glassner talks about his work on *The Outer Limits* and *Stargate SG-1*, both of which were shot in the wilds of Vancouver. Jonathan has returned to LA, where he worked on *The Invisible Man*, and I have no doubt that we'll be seeing his name attached to a new genre project before too long.

Then there's *Buffy the Vampire Slayer* creator Joss Whedon, who is a difficult man to pin down, since he's usually pretty busy tackling roughly two dozen projects at the same time. Therefore, I'm delighted to be able to present (courtesy of *The Onion A. V. Club*) one of the longest — and most candid — interviews he's ever given. Plus, Whedon's long-time collaborator David Greenwalt also happily had time to talk about the early days on *Buffy*, and gives some fascinating insights into the creation of the spin-off series, *Angel*.

I wanted this book to give a sense of the different stages of the life of a genre show, from the earliest days of development, to a show runner looking back at a successful seven-year run. So, along with the likes of Rob Tapert and Michael Piller recalling their experiences as executive producer on shows that have now passed into legend, I've included a few conversations with writers just starting out on a new series. Especially intriguing here is an interview I did with Chris Carter during the early days of *The X-Files*, before the mythology began getting too complex, in which he outlines his hopes for the (then) future of the show. It's rather interesting to compare what he said then to what actually happened... To bring things right up to date, I've also included interviews with the creators of two of television's hottest new genre shows. Charles ('Chic') Eglee discusses his collaboration with movie legend Jim Cameron on *Dark Angel*, and comic book veteran-turned TV writer Howard Chaykin talks about the superhero action adventure, *Mutant X*.

But enough of introductions; it's time to sit down with some of the finest writers and producers working in genre television today. With any luck, you'll discover a few things about your favourite programmes that you didn't know before, and get to know a lot more about the people who created them.

Joe Nazzaro
New Jersey/London
November 2001

Here are two excellent 'first stop' websites for aspiring script writers:
UK: The BBC 'Writers' Room', www.bbc.co.uk/writersroom
US: The Writers Guild of America, www.wga.org

GLOSSARY

While not exhaustive, this brief glossary acts as a handy guide to the main terms and expressions you'll come across in the following pages.

back-story   background to a character (or series), not necessarily depicted on screen

beats   the major plot points into which a story can be broken down. These can then be arranged on a 'beat sheet', which maps out the story act by act

bible   a document, usually written in the early stages of the development of a series, in which all the important details are set down, summarising the characters and their back-stories, the world of the show, background mythology and so on. This helps a show to avoid inconsistencies (and can be a source for story ideas)

breaking   the process whereby the writers sit down together and map out the major plot points of an episode

dailies   the film which has been shot over the course of a day, which is then watched in its raw form to gauge progress

freelancer   a non-staff writer who is hired on a temporary basis, possibly on the strength of a 'spec script', to work on a particular script or story-line

mythology   pivotal incidents, recurring themes and subplots which form the background fabric of the fictional world against which each episode is played out

network   a channel with national coverage, on which a show airs at the same time on the same day regardless of which region of the country the viewer is in

outline   a synopsis of a proposed story/script, usually written without dialogue

pilot   an introductory (often double length) episode made for a proposed series to showcase it to the public, or sometimes just the network or syndication executives. Usually introduces the set-up and characters

pitching   when a freelancer presents several ideas for possible episodes to a show's producers, with a view to being commissioned to write a detailed outline for a script

producer   the more senior of the 'writer employed in additional capacities' titles, they have increasingly more to do with the day-to-day running of the show, including choosing stories, commissioning scripts (and rewriting them where necessary), sitting in on casting, working with the costume and art departments, and discussing the editing of an episode

show runner   usually the executive producer – the most senior position on a show – and head writer, who is responsible for commissioning scripts, putting together a writing staff and, largely, for maintaining the tone and general direction of the series. They will probably also do a final polish on each script

spec script   an unsolicited (or 'speculative') script written by a freelancer as an example of their work. Sent into a show by the writer (or preferably their agent) with a view to being asked in to pitch

staff writer   the most junior writing position on the staff of a show, who usually starts out simply writing their own scripts, but will gradually start to rewrite other peoples' scripts, and acquire more and more responsibility on the production side if they progress up the ladder to a 'writer employed in additional capacities' producer position

story arc   a story-line which runs (as a main or subplot) for several episodes or even a whole series

syndication   a show is shown in syndication if it is not produced for a network, but sold to local stations. Consequently it may air at different times and on different days (or not at all) depending on which region of the country the viewer is in

WGA   Writers Guild of America: the powerful American writers' union, that has rigid codes of practice and minimum terms of payment for particular types of screenwriting, and to which writers go for arbitration in disputes over writing credits

ROCKNE S. O'BANNON

ockne O'Bannon's name is now indelibly linked with his most famous creation to date: the outrageous space series *Farscape*, which arrived in 1999 with all the force of a bucket of cold water in the face, shocking SF television out of its complacency. O'Bannon was no stranger to SF and fantasy, though. Coming from an industry family, he started his scriptwriting career working with the likes of Harlan Ellison on the 1980s incarnation of *The Twilight Zone*, before going on to write the original *Alien Nation* feature film, and introduce *seaQuest DSV* to the world. But *Farscape*, about a wise-cracking US astronaut who flies through a wormhole and ends up on a living ship with a group of escaped alien prisoners, has really been pushing the genre envelope. Regulars have come and gone without warning; the lead character has spent an entire season having an internal monologue with the show's main villain; and the crew has even been split up for several episodes, going their separate ways with different adventures. Much of the show's success can almost certainly be attributed to the wildly imaginative writing staff, now led by executive producer David Kemper. At the beginning of each season, Kemper and O'Bannon sit down together to map out the broad strokes of their story arc before production resumes in Sydney. Although O'Bannon took a step back to executive consultant at the end of *Farscape*'s first year, he still writes some of the major 'arc' episodes for each season, and as this interview demonstrates, he's not about to step away from the series any time soon…

How did you originally break into television as a writer?

I slept my way in! Actually, I come from an industry family. My father was a gaffer, a lighting director who worked for Warner Bros for forty years. This was in the 1960s, and he would bring home armloads of scripts for me to read — features that were being shot, and old television shows. That's how I learned the structure and the template for screen writing. Every opportunity I had to visit the studio with him on holidays and summer vacations, I would go in to work with him and hang out. Since he was a gaffer, we were always on the sets, which is a far more interesting place to be, but we'd go past the office buildings where the writers and producers were, and I was always intrigued by what those people in there might be doing. It was obviously quite a thrill for me to finally make that transition and become a professional writer, and get to hang out in those offices. I soon realised that what goes on in offices like that is a lot of banging of heads against desks and slapping of foreheads.

When I graduated from high school, my father got me a job in the mailroom at Warner Bros where I delivered mail and did tours for a couple of years. I then got a job as a production assistant/Xerox boy at Lorimar Productions, which is when they were doing *The Waltons* and a show called *Apple's Way*. It was a great opportunity to finagle my way in and talk to writers, and I was doing spec stuff of my own, trying to break in, and would do anything. I had an interest in SF and fantasy and that sort of thing, but I was writing spec *Magnum P. I.* episodes, anything to try and break in. I remember reading in the trades that ABC was going to do an anthology show titled *Dark Room*, with James Coburn as the host. Peter Fischer, who went on to co-create *Murder, She Wrote*, and Christopher Crowe, who later created *Seven Days*, were the two guys running the show. It sounded like it was going to be a sort of *Twilight Zone* anthology, so I wrote two short spec scripts, sent them to Peter Fischer and got a very nice note back saying, 'These are terrific, but I've left the show, so I passed them on to Chris Crowe.' Shortly thereafter, the show was cancelled and never heard from again. I put the scripts in the drawer. But a couple of years later — after I was able to get an agent, who'd also started Stephen Cannell [*The Rockford Files*, *The A-Team*] many years earlier — we heard that Steven Spielberg was doing this show called *Amazing Stories*, and that CBS was bringing back *The Twilight Zone*. So I dusted off these spec scripts written for *Dark Room* and submitted them to both places, and they reacted very positively. But while *Amazing Stories* was working its way up the hierarchy to get to Spielberg, Phil DeGuere at *Twilight Zone* called me in. I pitched some other ideas, and he put me on staff immediately. So that was how it all began. I later wrote an *Amazing Stories* for their second season, but *The Twilight Zone* was my home for a year and a half, and it was an incredible experience. I was working with Phil DeGuere, a top television creator who came out of that Universal family, Jim Crocker, who's done a lot of SF stuff, Harlan Ellison who's just a kick and Alan Brennert, a terrific talent. There were five

ROCKNE S. O'BANNON

Date/Place of Birth:
1955, Los Angeles, California, USA

Home Base:
Los Angeles, California, USA

Education:
Entered the Warner Bros. mailroom straight out of high school

First TV work:
The Twilight Zone: 'Wordplay'

TV Career highlights:
The Twilight Zone, *Amazing Stories*, *seaQuest DSV*, *Farscape*

of us on staff and I was the puppy, the little story editor, who absorbed everything I could. It was a wonderful introduction, the fact that my entrée into the business could be *Twilight Zone*.

You actually did a tongue-in-cheek story called 'Personal Demons', in which a writer named Rockne O'Bannon has these strange little creatures torturing him while he's trying to write!

It was truly the most bizarre idea I ever had, and a testament to the show that Phil said, 'Let's do it.' I can go to my grave with the claim that Martin Balsam has portrayed me on screen. The thing that pisses me off is when the show went into syndication, the people who were syndicating the show didn't get the gag. We specifically went to the Writers Guild for permission to put the writing credit at the end of the show, rather than the beginning, because the whole point of this episode is, this guy Rockne O'Bannon is troubled by these little creatures. At the end, he says in desperation, 'How do I get rid of you?' and they say, 'Just write about us and you'll never see us again!' So he sits down and starts to write, and the credit comes up: 'By Rockne O'Bannon.' The intent was to break down the fourth wall, and have people say, 'Oh shit, does this guy really have these little creatures hassling him?' One of the conditions Phil had in let-

HARLAN ELLISON

Described by no less than the *Washington Post* as 'one of the great living American short story writers', the inimitable Harlan Ellison has been a force to be reckoned with in the world of SF and fantasy for over fifty years. His work is devoured by fans who often enjoy what Isaac Asimov described as 'his gifts for colourful and variegated invective' as much as his dazzling fiction (which includes such classics as '"Repent, Harlequin!" Said the Ticktockman' and 'I Have No Mouth, and I Must Scream'). His SF television work spans from the original, award-winning script for *Star Trek*'s 'The City on the Edge of Forever' to, more recently, his position as conceptual consultant on *Babylon 5*. In the mid-1980s Ellison acted as creative consultant for the revived *Twilight Zone*, working on several scripts for the show, including 'Paladin of the Lost Hour', which earned him Hugo and WGA awards. For the young Rockne O'Bannon, working with him was a rewarding relationship. 'Harlan read 'Word Play', which is the script that got me the job,' he remembers, 'and he really liked it. There's a paragraph he wrote on 'Word Play', long before he ever met me, that says, "Not a single misstep, this is amazing, what bush has this guy been hiding under?" Harlan either loves something or he hates it, so he was obviously very effusive in his praise.'

ting me do the episode, was that he didn't want the writer to be attractive at all. I said, 'I'll make him old, I'll make him quadriplegic, I don't care what he looks like!' So we compromised on an older guy who's on the skids. Considering I was a young guy with my first job, it was kind of a kick, having Martin Balsam playing me.

After *Twilight Zone*, you did a script based on *Lucifer's Hammer*, Larry Niven and Jerry Pournelle's novel about a comet hitting Earth. Why did that end up not getting produced?

That was for Paramount Television. It was December, past the season when pilots are commissioned, and they hadn't been able to find a writer to do it. I wrote a one-hour pilot script called 'Stronghold', based on this rather long, elaborate book, and the tone was obviously something the network wasn't going to go for — but I got so much heat off of that script! I remember going to a meeting with some studio, and hearing people in the hall saying, 'He's the guy who wrote 'Stronghold'!' I'd never had that happen before, so it had obviously been passed around a lot. At around the same time, there was interest in my writing original ideas for series, and I went around and essentially pitched *Alien Nation*. I pitched it as a television series first, but nobody quite got it, so it didn't sell. This was the spring of '87, and I was prepared to wait until May when staffing season began, so I wrote *Alien Nation* as a spec feature instead.

What made you think *Alien Nation* would work better as a feature than a TV series?

I just thought it was a great idea, and maybe I wasn't pitching it well, but I liked the idea of an alien story that wasn't about spaceships. I didn't want to go on board a spaceship, and I didn't want it to be anything hi-tech like that. I specifically made them a slave race so they didn't bring the technology with them. It was a totally automated ship they were on, so they had their own culture, but they didn't come down with devices that would suddenly totally change Earth's technology, where they could apply the mechanics of an alien device and make cars that run without fuel, or whatever. I wanted it to be about the clash of cultures and the new immigrants, that sort of thing. Maybe that sounded too 'soft', but TV didn't go for it. But I loved the premise, so I wrote the movie script. I was prepared for it to be just an exercise, and then I'd go back to being on the writing staff of a television show in May. But lo and behold, we sold it to [producer] Gale Hurd and Twentieth Century Fox on Easter Day, and they started shooting in September, so it was very quick.

Having pitched *Alien Nation* for television in the first place, what was your reaction when Fox decided to spin the movie off into a TV series?

Obviously there was a certain amount of evil glee in that it took a whole movie to get people to come around and realise hey, maybe it *is* a series! I had a meeting with Fox about the series, and it was all very pleasant, but I'd already sold *Fear*[*], the movie I

---

[*] *Written and directed by O'Bannon, Fear (1989), starred Ally Sheedy as a psychic detective hunting a killer who is also psychic.*

was going to direct, so I wasn't available. At that point they had Ken Johnson in their back pocket anyway. I've never spoken with Ken Johnson, or had any dealings with him, but I was very pleased with the reception the television series received.

It was after you'd finished directing *Fear* that Steven Spielberg's Amblin Television approached you about developing *seaQuest*, wasn't it?

Yes. They had several ideas in house, and one of the ideas they wanted to pursue was a futuristic submarine show, but they didn't quite know what they wanted to do, if it was 500 years in the future or five years. They'd already made inroads to Roy Scheider, who had expressed some interest, but obviously wanted to know what the show would be. So I sat down with the people at Amblin, and then went away and came up with the basics of the series.

One of the big attractions for you must have the chance to collaborate with Spielberg. How much input did he have?

Unfortunately, I had very few meetings with him. I obviously would have loved to spend more time with him, but he was in a very fertile period. When we first started

THE TWILIGHT ZONE

More than four decades after it was first broadcast on US television, *The Twilight Zone* is still widely regarded as one of the most influential anthology series of all time. It was created by award-winning writer Rod Serling, who had grown tired of the restrictions of writing for network TV, and decided to create a series by which he could use fantasy and metaphor to tell powerful stories about the human condition in a way that conventional dramas could never hope to match. Serling wrote many of the episodes himself (as well as appearing in the show's trademark on-camera introductions), and was joined by such frequent contributors as Charles Beaumont and Richard Matheson. The original series ran for five seasons, ending in 1964. In 1985, CBS revived *The Twilight Zone* as a lavishly produced one-hour series, with episodes directed by a number of Hollywood's top directors, including Wes Craven, William Friedkin and Joe Dante. Although it was a critical success, viewing figures were less than spectacular — partially because of its poorly positioned Friday night-time slot — and the series was cancelled after just two seasons. A thirty-minute syndicated version soon followed, combining brand new episodes with those from the previous incarnation, but that lasted just one season and *The Twilight Zone* once again returned to television limbo.

meeting on this project, he was prepping *Jurassic Park,* and then was shooting it while I was writing the pilot. I shared my office with the line producer of *Schindler's List,* which they were prepping, so Steven was a pretty busy puppy at the time. What was interesting in my meetings with Steven was that anything he said goes. I hadn't been in the room with genius people before, but he really has an amazing ability to immediately get to the heart of a project and come up with wild stuff. He'd come up with extremely wild stuff, which you just couldn't do in a TV episode, but I quickly learned that it's better to stay fluid and open to everything, as opposed to being pragmatic. If you let him spin, you really get the advantage of the brilliance, and obviously the Amblin people would just nod with a little grin on their faces!

So, I'd come up with the basics, and there were three elements that sold the show first to Steven, then to Roy and ultimately NBC, none of which bore fruit in the series, but they were part of my initial concept. Again, they didn't know if they wanted it set five years in the future or 500, so I said, 'I want to place it twenty-five years in the future.' I wanted it to be an accessible future that with health and luck, our audience would be there to see someday, and more importantly, it was the world our children were going to inherit. When Amblin pitched the idea of a submarine show to me, one of their notions was, maybe mankind has polluted their continents so much that they have to retreat into the ocean. I said, 'That's exactly what I *don't* want to do.' So number one was a positive view of twenty-five years from now. Number two was the character of Nathan Bridger. I didn't want the typical jut-jawed Captain Kirk hero. I wanted a guy who was flawed and very damaged, maybe not as dark as Captain Nemo, but with a Nemo-type quality. He was someone who really had to scramble to be sociable and pleasant, who other characters would have to work hard to get close to, and that's something that Roy Scheider sparked to in a big way. Here he was, making his first foray into television, and the idea of being the captain of the *Seaview* in *Voyage to the Bottom of the Sea* was not appealing. This idea is what got him on board, and was part of the pitch to Steven and to the network.

The third thing that sold the series to everybody was the dolphin. I wanted the dolphin to be Mr Spock, in the same way that Gene Roddenberry said, 'Among this crew of the *Enterprise,* there should be an alien. He's not Kirk's buddy or man servant, but a ranking officer in Starfleet, who happens to be an alien.' I wanted to do the same thing with a dolphin. My conceit was the technology developed within those twenty-five years would be able to take those clicks and whistles and body motion, and translate it into language. But it shouldn't be 'Ma Loves Pa' like they did in *The Day of the Dolphin.* He should speak very articulately; maybe in an unusual way with unusual syntax and a wildly exotic point of view, but I wanted it to be complete sentences. I also wanted it to be a very articulate voice, and suggested that maybe we could get a classically trained actor to do it. And the dolphin would be a naval officer, an ensign in the navy, so we were using another species from our planet. This was highly imaginative and they loved it, so those were the three ideas I wanted to write into the pilot script. But the series didn't follow through on any of them.

Were you disappointed that the series turned out very differently from the one you'd imagined?

That's why I didn't leave *Farscape*, and will never leave another series I created during its first year while we're getting it on track. With *seaQuest*, it just became a futuristic submarine show, as opposed to any of the subtler and potentially interesting stuff that I had in it. For example, take the character of Lucas Wolenczak, who I put in at Steven's request as a younger person on board. The background for Lucas was that his father invented the technology that allowed the dolphin's thoughts to be interpreted and spoken aloud, and the dolphin was raised along with Lucas. Well, from his father's point of view, having a dolphin that can communicate is something that nobody on the planet Earth has ever done before, and that was his life's work. Having a son isn't as remarkable as the dolphin, so I set up this real sibling rivalry between Lucas and the dolphin. There was grist there to play, but it wasn't part of the show that I ever saw. When I finally got a cut of the show, the dolphin was talking baby talk, plus it was Roy Scheider's buddy from the island, as opposed to him being part of a navy-training program. I wanted to have Bridger come in and say, 'Holy mackerel, you built the ship I designed way back when, and you've actually got a dolphin on board, which was something I'd conceived but didn't think was possible!' and then let him develop a relationship with the dolphin.

Mind you, we went through the same thing on *Farscape*. SF shows are so incredibly difficult to mount, to get people to understand. If you're doing a doctor show or a lawyer show, everybody understands that world. In SF shows, at least the ones I've created, you're inventing a whole new world.

It wasn't long after *seaQuest* that The Jim Henson Company got in touch about *Farscape*, was it?

I finished on *seaQuest* in February of '93, because I remember taking my wife to Hawaii for a month to get away. We went to the hotel on the big island that had the 'dolphin encounter' — so I couldn't get away from it all; everyone else was digging the experience, and I'm the one trying to slap the dolphins! I think I met with the Henson people in October or November of that year, and wrote the pilot in December. My wife and I went down to the Hotel Del Coronado for New Year's, and I sat on the beach doing hand-written notes for the final draft of the pilot script. The whole thing was a great experience. I really enjoyed working with Hensons, and having this wonderfully free tapestry to work with. The other thing was that *Space Chase* (which is what *Farscape* was originally called) was the first time I tried to be funny. I had moments in *seaQuest* and *Alien Nation*, but it was more of a conceptual humour, as opposed to actual jokes. There was a lot of humour in the *Space Chase* pilot that didn't come to fruition, because it was just too expensive and we had to cut it out.

In creating *Farscape*, did you basically look at what was already out there, to avoid what had been done already?

That's generally the way I work anyway. I look at what's already been done and what's out there, and say, 'What can I do to twist it and make a difference?' But also ideally, to try and come up with something truly original. The first meeting I had was with Brian Henson, and then Alex Rockwell who was their head of television, and I dealt with her most of the time after that. They had one page which they had come up with in house, which I've still got it buried in a drawer, somewhere. I think it was about a cargo ship that was populated with various aliens, none of which are the aliens that you see on the show. There was a lifter-loader, a big lumbering thing, and the captain of the ship was a blind woman. I don't know how they planned to make *that* work. I get things like that all the time, where people say, 'We want to develop this,' and I read it and say (never aloud, because I'm not an idiot) 'I wouldn't put something like this on paper and show it to anybody, for fear that they would lock me away!' This one-page idea had some bizarre things that you could conceivably make a SF novel out of, but a blind female lead is a tough one to sell to the network...

So I thought about what kind of show I wanted to do. The primary thing I came up with, which I think is the nucleus of the series, is the notion of a man from our time, one of us, dropped into a *Star Trek/Star Wars* kind of world. Part of my pitch was the notion that this doesn't take place 500 years in the future, or a long time ago in a galaxy far, far away, but is absolutely today. Our guy John Crichton is out there right now in some other part of the universe, trying to get back to us. John Crichton can return home, and tonally, that was very important to me. The other thing I really appreciate about the series is that it does have that sense of humour. It can get as bizarre and out there as it possibly can, but always adheres to its own reality.

Once you had your core idea, what did you do to surround it with characters and situations?

The initial plan was for Moya to be populated by literally hundreds of prisoners. It was a prison ship, so taking a leaf from the *Star Trek* book, there would be so many characters on board that we could have entire stories take place on the ship, with new characters who we've never met before. But once we got into the production reality of it, we realised there was no way we could do that. We wanted everyone to be alien-looking except for Crichton and the Sebaceans, and Hensons was saying, 'We love that idea, but we've got to do it judiciously. We can't have them walking down a passageway and have alien characters wandering around, because there's no way we can produce that,' and they were absolutely right. Then it became a matter of coming up with the core family of characters. My first thought was to populate it with archetypes. The initial conceit of the show is that John Crichton is dropped into a *Star Trek/Star Wars* world. So, on one level, he should think he's bumped his head and he's kind of fantasising this whole thing. In which case, the characters he comes across would be representations of icon characters from other movies and TV shows, that sort of thing. The other concept I was trying to service was to come up with a really good mix of looks and tones and genders, so that the puzzle pieces would fit, and they'd all complement each other. If you look at the pilot script or the first episode, there are shadings to all the characters, but they're also icons. Zhaan is the peacenik, you've got D'Argo who's the brutish warrior, Aeryn the good soldier, and Rygel, the little self-important potentate. Obviously the intent was always to broaden them and colour them in, but for the initial conceit to work, I felt they had to be identifiable icons.

Is the *Farscape* that eventually began on the Sci-Fi Channel in 1999 substantially different from the one you pitched to Twentieth Century Fox in 1993?

It's not radically different, but has certainly evolved into something different. That's a direct result of the fact that we're on the Sci-Fi Channel, which is run by very bright, hip people, who want the show to be as out there and unconventional and odd as possible. That's something that the Fox Network, being one of the 'big four', would never have gone for. The original script for the show was more whimsical; it never quite broke with reality but it came awful close. In the original pilot script, I did several joke scenes that I was very proud of and I think helped sell the series. They were examples of the sense of humour that I wanted to give the show, but weren't things we ultimately realised, and I think for the better. One of the things that makes the series work is, even though John Crichton is always making Earth references and all that, it's never us winking at the camera. I had a couple of important discussions with Keith DeCandido, who was writing the first *Farscape* novel, about this. I think there was a reference he'd made to a planet, or planetary system or something, that was from *Doctor Who*, and there was another reference to *Star Trek*. It wasn't Crichton's thing, it was Keith fooling around and saying, 'I'm going to put the name of a *Doctor Who* planet in this, and I'm going to use a *Star Trek* reference over here.' I called him up and said, 'No, never again!' because the world that John Crichton finds himself in *really exists*. It isn't a jokey place where there's something named after *Doctor Who* or *Star Trek*. It doesn't share names with those fictional entities, and whether people realise it or not, I think that's one of the things that has really kept the show satisfying to the audience, that it's true to itself and not jokey. We can do the wildest episodes, where the characters really lose it — like 'Crackers Don't Matter' [from season two] — and I hope they will be wild and funny, but the series is grounded in its own reality. We did an episode in the third season ['Revenging Angel'], in which a third of the episode is animated. It's very weird and very funny, and probably this year's 'Won't Get Fooled Again'[*], arguably one of my favourites from the second season. Crichton gets cracked in the head, and is lying there half-conscious, so this animated world is how his mind deals with it. But again, the situation is borne from that, it isn't just Crichton going down to a planet and finding that it's a Roger Rabbit-style animated world.

How difficult was it to find writers who 'got' the show?

Starting out, it was incredibly difficult, not only from the writing point of view but from production as well. We weren't doing *The Next Generation*, where they at least

---

* Set largely inside Crichton's hallucinating mind, the episode features such outrageous highlights as the menacing Crais in high heels, carrying a small dog.

had the original *Star Trek* as a template of some sort. They might have veered off that template, but at least they had a starting point that they could explain to people. We didn't have that, so in the early days, we used to get scripts from some of the free-lancers we first went to, and they had Crichton essentially as the captain of the ship. They'd see some threat out the forward portal of the ship, and it was Crichton giving orders. We'd say, 'No, that's not the show. This guy knows the *least* of what's going on!' He has no knowledge about how the switch in front of him on Moya works, so the one thing he brings to the party, which I think is pretty inherently human, is wild abandon. Even if somebody drops into some snake-filled pit at the bottom of Moya, he's the one who's willing to dive into that pit to get the keys. The one thing he's got to offer is this wild abandon, and in rewriting the early scripts, I worked very hard to bring that aspect to it, so people weren't turning to Crichton and saying, 'What do we do?' It's exactly the opposite, he's turning to other people and saying, 'What do we do?', but we still had to keep him heroic. That was tough to do, and tough to get other people to understand. Ricky Manning was one of the first people who came in and really got it. Ricky has a really wicked sense of humour, and like David Kemper and myself, he had a real knowledge base of all the SF shows that came before *Star Trek*. He was our real big find right at the beginning. You'll see a lot of names on screen in the first season — consultants and people like that — and you'll notice that most of them are gone now. We got to the middle of the season, and Justin Monjo came in and did a really good job on 'The Flax'. It wasn't quite there, but he got the

DAVID KEMPER

With Rockne O'Bannon turning much of his attention to new projects, *Farscape* is in the hands of executive producer David Kemper, who's been taking the series in ever more outlandish directions with every season. 'One of the things we're trying to do,' explains Kemper, 'is to be shocking and outrageous — not gratuitously shocking, but we always want to sur-prise the audience. We don't want to do an episode where halfway through it, they're able to say, "I know how this is going to end!"' Kemper is a veteran of genre television, having written episodes of *The Next Generation*, *The Outer Limits*, *Voyager* and O'Bannon's creation *seaQuest DSV*. Both writers were sharing an office when O'Bannon invited Kemper to work on a series he was developing for Fox, called *Space Chase*: 'They wanted four back-up scripts in something like two months, so Rock and I wrote those scripts, which were good enough for Fox to say, "We'll pick you up." But they'd only pick us up for thirteen episodes, and Hensons couldn't afford it, so the series languished for a while. But eventually Brian Henson called Rock and said, "Get Kemper; we think we sold it to Sci-Fi" and back into the fire we went!'

show very quickly, and Justin is now one of the most visionary people we've got on the show, because he really thinks outside the box.

One of the most intriguing aspects of *Farscape* is the way new characters are always being introduced, some of whom become series regulars. Do you bring a character in specifically to keep them around, or do you 'try them out' first to see how they fit in?

Both. We introduced Gigi [Edgley, as Chiana] in the hope that she would be staying as a regular, but we built it in so we could have easily got rid of her if we wanted to. It turned out that Gigi was a dream, so we chained her to the set; we weren't going to let her go! Stark was a one-shot character in the two-parter at the end of season one, and off he went. It was rather abrupt, because we bought him on board our ship, and we'd written a moment where we made mention of the fact that we'd given him a pod and he'd left. That line didn't make it into the final edit of the episode, so Stark suddenly disappeared, which was a point of humorous consternation to fans on the bulletin board, who would also ask me about it at conventions. I used to say, 'He's still on board the ship, he's just wandering around.' So Stark was just a character at the end of season one, and we thought the character had some play in him, but it was the actor [Paul Goddard] that we really liked. It's been kind of a struggle finding something for Stark to do, and how to make him a really effective part of the mix. The good new is, Zhaan's exit in season three gave Stark that healer, spiritual person role.

Speaking of which, how did you feel about the loss of Zhaan when Virginia Hey left the series early in the third year?

Obviously I have a lot of affection for the original family of characters. I was very pleased with the way we were able to mix different types, and in my mind, they're different facets of the human character. Losing Zhaan was like losing one of those aspects, but it didn't faze me that much. I knew the practical reasons why Virginia wanted to go, and believe me, I respect her for putting in the two years of shaved heads and eyebrows and that incredibly heavy make-up on a daily basis, and I'm really pleased with what she gave us in those two years. I think you definitely miss her leavening influence in season three because it's a darker season, but to answer your question, it's just part of the game.

It must be difficult to bring in an actress like Tammy McIntosh, who plays Jool, and not have her perceived as a replacement for Virginia.

Jool was not brought in with the intention of being a replacement for Zhaan. When David conceived of the character and wanted to bring her in, it was going to be in a two-parter at the beginning of season three. When the whole thing with Virginia occurred, my suggestion to David was, 'Look, here's a great opportunity to really pay for the return of Aeryn. At the end of season two, we've got this big, emotional funeral for Aeryn, and we're asking the audience to really give themselves over emotionally, to the fact that this beloved character is completely dead. Obviously we're going to resurrect her in season three, but if we just wave our magic wands and make her reappear, the audience will be less inclined to go to that emotional place again the next time, because we've very easily brought the character back. Here's a situation where Virginia wants to leave the show, and we've agreed to that. Why not let Aeryn's return be paid for by the loss of another character that *doesn't* suddenly reappear?' I thought it was a great opportunity in terms of the integrity of the show. The Jool character was always intended to come in around that time anyway, but it gave the impression of a revolving door, where Zhaan went out and Jool came in. When we introduced Chiana in episode fifteen of the first season, and she stayed, people on the bulletin board were saying, 'Who's this new person? Why is she here, we don't need her!' so it's always difficult when somebody new moves into the house. But if we removed Chiana now, I think people would riot!

Do you find that with each season's cliffhanger, you and David have to set the bar a bit higher?

That's generally true of anything you do. At the end of season one, we sat there and looked at each other and said, 'Gee, it's been quite a year.' If you look at the last episodes of season one, we went on board the Gammak Base, this huge environment with huge production values. And then the final episode is much smaller and more emotional, with Crais stealing the baby Talyn, and Crichton and D'Argo essentially sacrificing themselves to destroy the Gammak Base. So there's all this wonderful big emotional stuff and heartfelt goodbyes among the characters. If you look at that episode, there isn't a lot of action, but from what everybody says, it's very compelling stuff. So I'd say we set the bar pretty high at the end of season one, and then we hit another at the end of season two, so how do we top that with three?

Looking at the third season of *Farscape*, it's almost a completely different show from season one, isn't it?

The show is definitely growing. One of the great things about the way *Farscape* has evolved, is that John Crichton and the other characters aren't just in the same place, with a set adventure every week. I think season three is a much darker season. If you look at the first season, Crichton is a lot like Tom Hanks in *Cast Away*; he's thrust out there and has to figure out how to survive in that environment, and the relationships are all fairly tenuous. By the end of season one, you've established a rapport with those characters, and in season two, some of it's the same, but he's obviously far more effective in that world. In season three, he's effective in that world, but also struggling against it. He's now part of that environment and having to struggle, so it's a natural progression for this series. As we get into the next season or two, I think it will start to come around to where Crichton is really working diligently again with this knowledge to try and get back to Earth. I'm really quite pleased with the way it's uncompromising in that regard. In the past, television tended to just have the same premise and the characters stayed in the same place. They would have new adventures every week, but the characters stayed where they were emotionally. That certainly isn't the case with this show.

There have been mixed reports about a possible *Farscape* feature film. Where do you stand on the subject?

The Henson Company is very passionate about doing a movie, but they don't quite understand just how incredibly difficult that is to do in the midst of also producing a television series. When we wrapped our third season, everybody was absolutely fried and we were all looking forward to a couple of months off before starting up that hellish schedule again. The notion of fitting a movie in between the two is a frightening proposition, so that's obviously an important issue. The other problem is trying to do a movie based on a series that changes as often and radically as our series does. Where do you place a movie? Chris Carter did it with *The X-Files*, but he created a movie that fit in between two seasons of the TV show. When I went to see the film, I hadn't watched *The X-Files* ardently during the set-up season, so I really didn't know what the hell was going on, and for me personally, it wasn't all that satisfying. I'm kind of loath to do that with our show. It also begs the question: *when* do you place the movie? Does it have Zhaan in it? Does it have Stark in it? Which characters are in and which aren't? If I was to sit down and write a movie based on the *Farscape* premise, I would write about a human astronaut who goes up in a one man module, goes through a wormhole and ends up in this other environment, where he meets these other characters for the first time. But I can't now create a movie with that premise, I'm not going to start with him on Earth and going to that place. I have to set it as though he's been there a couple of years and he already has established relationships with these characters.

Now if you're doing a feature film, you're obviously hopeful that it will draw in a new audience that doesn't have the Sci-Fi Channel or hasn't seen the TV series. But you're also presenting a story about this character John Crichton who has been in this other part of the universe for two or three years already. As a moviegoer, I'm thinking, okay, I'm obviously watching something that's ongoing. So the movie becomes a big episode of the TV show. You can get around that if you do something like *Star Trek* does, which is wait until the series is concluded, and then do the next big adventure of the show as a feature. One of the things I wrestle with is trying to figure out how to make a movie in the midst of production on a TV show, that doesn't just come off as a bigger, slightly more expensive episode of the show. Like I said, the production difficulties alone might be such that a movie isn't going to be possible. But the Jim Henson Company is really passionate about getting something up and running, and believe me, I'm all for it. I'm just trying to figure out how to make it work.

In an ideal world, how long would you like to see *Farscape* run?

I think its longevity will come from the fact that it is constantly changing and grow-ing. The blessing is that we're on the Sci-Fi Channel here in the States, where we're the top-rated show and well thought of by the audience and by critics. We're always the 'smart and sassy *Farscape*, the thinking man's sci-fi', so for the Sci-Fi Channel, it's a really wonderful calling card. If we were on some other network, obviously our rat-ings would not sustain enough for them to keep us on. To answer your question, the fact that we have this interesting, occasional revolving door on the show, that allows new characters to come in and be there for a while and then go off, keeps it fresh and interesting and challenging. I'm hoping it will go beyond five years. And once the series goes off, I'd love to keep it going as a movie and books and that sort of thing.

Is it true you're also trying to get a new anthology series off the ground?

Look, I've done an outer space show, I've done an undersea show, and I'd really love to do my own anthology. It's just a matter of getting people to buy into an antholo-gy. People I've talked to have said, 'Great idea, but not for us,' so I'm not that bummed by it. I always tell writing classes, the great thing about spec scripts and story ideas is they can go up on the shelf and they don't dissolve, they don't turn into dust — at least in your own lifetime. So I'll just put it aside for the time being and pursue it another time. I'm also working on a potential series idea with David Kemper, and I've been meeting with another director about some TV stuff. We've got a thriller TV idea that we might flesh out and see if we've got something there. Other than that, I'm working on stuff that I want to start directing again.

So you've got the itch again?

It's never really gone away, but I've put creams on it to keep it suppressed! After the last directing gig, the TV series started to come up and kids came along, so I got fair-ly distracted, but it's something that really interests me, the notion of following my own stuff through. You can do that in one of two ways: you can do it in episodic tel-evision by being the show runner, therefore it's your baby, or you can do it in long form, whether it's TV movies or features as the director, so that's what I'm pursuing for the moment. ∎

CHRIS CARTER
ON THE X-FILES

he truth is out there. When those five words flashed on screen back in September of 1993, no one, least of all writer/producer Chris Carter, knew just how much *The X-Files* would become a part of popular culture worldwide. Carter, a journalism graduate who began his career writing for *Surfing* magazine, had started out in TV as co-writer and producer of such innocuous fare as Disney's *B.R.A.T. Patrol*, going on to create and produce *Brand New Life*, an updated version of *The Brady Bunch*. But then came his long-cherished 'scary show'. Since the *The X-Files'* début, the weekly adventures of two FBI agents — one a believer, the other a sceptic — investigating cases of the paranormal have been widely imitated, often parodied, but never duplicated. What was it about *The X-Files* that struck a chord with the public? The chemistry between David Duchovny and Gillian Anderson, who played agents Mulder and Scully, certainly didn't hurt. Neither did the top-notch production values, the atmospheric direction, and a bestiary of bizarre monsters and aliens the likes of which had never been seen in weekly television. But it was the show's so-called 'mythology' episodes that helped build a loyal core viewership. During the first season, Carter began weaving a complex web of alien abductions, government conspiracies and clandestine scientific experiments. Small wonder that another catch phrase, 'Trust no one', soon became equally popular. This interview with Carter was conducted just after *The X-Files'* first season finished airing in America. Considering the show's evolution over the next several years, it's interesting to look back at some of his comments from the very beginning...

Is it true that one of your big influences on *The X-Files* was *The Night Stalker*?

I can only remember about two scenes and those scenes only vaguely, but I remember it being something that I just couldn't get enough of. I've actually taken no specifics from it; I never went back and researched it. I just took it as something that appealed to me. I knew that the biggest pitfall for them was that they had turned into a sort of a 'monster of the week' show, and that was something that I didn't want to have happen. I knew there was a bigger world out there, of the paranormal, weird science and so on, and I wanted to explore those things with two interesting characters.

Where did the FBI connection come in?

I figured there are lots of reports of the paranormal in the news, and I had seen an FBI agent on *Larry King Live* on CNN, whose beat was investigating reports of people involved with satanic cults. I thought, 'Hey, this is what he does; this is his thing. Who are the people who investigate paranormal phenomena?' and it took off from there.

How responsive was Fox to the idea?

There are two entities we're speaking of here. Twentieth Century Television was the company that hired me to create TV shows for them, and they were very responsive to the idea immediately. I went in with Peter Roth, the president of the company, to the Fox Broadcasting Corporation, and we pitched the idea to them, and they turned us down on the first pitch. Because Peter and I both believed in the idea, we went back in and re-explained it, maybe making them see some things they weren't seeing, and they bought the idea on the second pitch. I wrote the script, they liked it a lot, and then I had to do a little bit of selling in order to commit the money to make a pilot.

We made the pilot, and it was extremely well received. I think I showed it to the network brass on a Tuesday, and by Friday they'd ordered thirteen episodes. And now they're behind it one hundred per cent.

How much discussion did you have about the casting?

The two characters I had created, Mulder and Scully, had been written off-centre. I wanted fresh, new faces; I didn't want the Barbie and Ken of classic network television. I wanted two smart characters, who could deliver smart lines, and that's what I got. What happened was that I found two people for whom there was chemistry as well, and that's something you can't manufacture. You can only hope it happens, and we got lucky with David Duchovny and Gillian Anderson.

How did you get some of your ideas for stories in the early days? Would people send you clippings about unusual events they had heard about?

CHRIS CARTER

Date/Place of Birth:
1956, Bellflower, California, USA

Home Base:
Los Angeles, California, USA

Education:
California State University

First TV Work:
The B.R.A.T. Patrol ('Disney Sunday Movie')

TV Career Highlights:
Midnight Caller, *The X-Files*, *Millennium*, *Harsh Realm*, *The Lone Gunmen*

Not as much as you would expect. There are a lot of people who are interested in writing spec scripts now, but I haven't read many of them unless I've had reason to. All the ideas and scripts you've seen thus far on *The X-Files* came from us. We get those ideas from journals, magazines, newspapers, and just out of our twisted imaginations!

Do you have any self-imposed limits on how outlandish the premise can be?

I have this operational phrase, which is, 'These stories all have to take place within the realm of extreme possibility.' The secret is — and this is the only way these stories will ever be as scary as I want them to be — they have to be real. If they don't feel real, they're not going to be scary. Pulling back is actually the difficult part. If we let our imaginations soar, we can come up with a lot of crazy, unbelievable stuff, but part of the ingeniousness of our storylines has to do with the way we make them believable.

So it goes back to the old saying, 'Truth is stranger than fiction.'

Oddly enough, even when we do things that I think are a little farther than what I had intended doing, we'll see a news item that validates or confirms what we had dramatised.

KOLCHAK: THE NIGHT STALKER

Chris Carter has often mentioned that one of his major influences when creating *The X-Files* was the 1974 supernatural investigation show *Kolchak: The Night Stalker*. Created by Jeff Rice, the series, which span off from two highly-rated TV movies, starred Darren McGavin as Carl Kolchak, a rumpled reporter whose explorations into the unknown brought him into contact with a wide range of bizarre creatures. Most episodes of *The Night Stalker* would begin with Kolchak investigating a series of gruesome murders, usually against the wishes of his editor Tony Vincenzo (Simon Oakland). The perpetrator was eventually revealed to be some sort of creature: a werewolf, vampire, zombie or swamp monster, perhaps. One story even featured a modern-day headless horseman: the decapitated, motorcycle-riding gang member, Chopper. More often than not, by episode's end, the monster had been destroyed without witnesses, leaving Kolchak without any proof to support his outrageous claims. More than two decades after *Kolchak*, Chris Carter, who had long hoped to book McGavin as a guest star on *The X-Files*, finally got his wish. The actor finally appeared not as a reporter, but as a former FBI agent whose unresolved case comes back to light, in the fifth season episode 'Travelers'.

Like that news story about a person brought into the hospital with toxic crystals in their blood?

I used that as an element in the season finale. What I'll do is, when I see a big story like that, which people will immediately recognise as *X-Files*-like, I won't do an episode on it *per se*, but I might incorporate it into another kind of story.

Was there a perception early on that you would be doing a lot of UFO stories?

It wasn't fair, but I think that's what people expected. I think they expected alien abduction/UFO of the week, and indeed, if you look at the first and second episodes, that's what you might think, but it was never my anticipation. I knew the show had to be more than that in order to gain a wider audience.

What did it feel like to get such an enormous groundswell of support from the fans of the show?

That's been a big surprise, and I can't explain it. I never anticipated the hardcore audience who would feel this attached to the show. It's very satisfying and rewarding. It also heaps a tremendous amount of responsibility on me, which I feel every day. I don't want to let them down. I want to keep giving them the good stuff, and I want to keep topping myself. That's a good thing, in that it keeps you from resting on your laurels. The fans, who I have direct contact with now, through the on-line services, let you know if you falter.

Has the feedback been constructive in terms of where you wanted to go with the series?

I think when you get an astute, reasoned and critical evaluation from a fan, which is what I value most, you will look at it and say, 'You're right.' In fact, I can think of one letter I received that was quite disturbing, because I felt this person had looked at the show in a very accurate and critical way, and it actually changed the way I looked at the show. I thought about it, and realised this person saw what worked best and what worked least and called me on it, and I took that person's criticisms to heart. It changed the way I now come up with my own stories.

Your actors also seem to have built up a big following among FBI agents, haven't they?

Indeed they have. David, Gillian and I took a trip to their offices, and I have to say that they really rolled out the red carpet for us. Of course they can't make an official endorsement of the show, but according to people in the FBI, they think it reflects very well on them.

Do you make an effort to be accurate in terms of FBI procedures?

The show is only as scary as it is real, and only as believable as it seems accurate, and we really make a great effort to be accurate. Of course when you go to the FBI, they'll tell you there are certain things we do that they just wouldn't do. For example, when you have an agent going into a structure that he thinks might be inhabited by a dangerous person, it might take them forty-five minutes to get up those stairs, using a two-man team covering each other. We go charging up those stairs, because we've only got forty-six minutes per story, so there are certain things we do that are not by the book. If we did an entire show about Mulder and Scully climbing a stairwell, I don't think it would make very good drama...

Are you trying to keep the number of main characters to a minimum?

I'll add characters as I see fit. We do have one character who's sort of ongoing now, and that's assistant director Skinner. There's been no calculated or conscious number of regulars.

What sort of response did you get after killing off Mulder's mysterious source of information, Deep Throat, in the first season finale?

People were very upset, but big things have to happen in drama. If they don't happen, you get a series of little things and you get predictability. When that shot was fired, I think it said to all the hardcore fans that everything is up for grabs. Anything can happen, so they'd better pay attention!

Does it annoy you when viewers ask if you're going to bring a character back?

I think people become attached to characters, and they don't like to see them disappear. That's not to say there won't be someone who appears in Deep Throat's stead.

How resistant have you been to pressure about a relationship between the two main characters?

It's the audience's prerogative to ask for these things. It's our job to give them surprise, and good stories well told, and that's what I'll continue to do. I don't see that Mulder and Scully having a romantic relationship would benefit anyone, from the characters to the stories to the show. People still ask the question, but I think they know my answer now.

Do you agree with the 'Moonlighting principle', that a series starts to go downhill once you cross that line?

I think shows proceed on the strength of that flirtation, and then after a while, I think the audience as well as the writers and producers feel that flirtation has reached the point where people have to act on their feelings. On our show, there may be some sexual tension between them, but it's not the show, whereas with *Moonlighting* and *Cheers* for example, that became a big part of the reason for those shows.

What about creating an outside love interest?

I may be using this word wrong, but I've resisted the need to 'domesticate' the show. I'm not primarily interested in Mulder or Scully's personal lives, so to put those things ahead of our stories, which are really little mysteries each week, would be working against ourselves. We wouldn't be giving our audience what they're tuning in for the most, which is to see a good scary, unexpected mystery.

Were there a lot of problems dealing with Gillian's pregnancy?

In fact we hadn't written the scripts that she was going to be in when we learned of her pregnancy. It was a problem to be addressed and solved. That's what writers and producers do: they solve problems. It was a larger problem than we had anticipated having to solve at this point, but I think we worked around it and turned it into a virtue. We shoot around her pregnancy. We don't show it, we don't feature it, and hopefully you'll watch the show and never know she was pregnant.

What stories do you feel worked and didn't work in your first season?

I'm very proud of the first season, and I wouldn't do a post mortem as much as a 'happy birthday' look back at the year. I can talk about the episodes I'm most proud of, but I think it would be unfair to talk about the episodes I feel didn't work as well. The episodes I'm most proud of would start with 'Beyond the Sea', which guest-starred Brad Dourif. I thought it was an episode that succeeded on all levels: writing, directing, acting performances, special FX and the realisation of a terrific production. I'm really proud of that show. I'm also proud of our season finale, 'The Erlenmeyer Flask'. I just watched it again the other night, and I liked it very much. I think 'Ice', about the Arctic worm, was a terrific episode. 'Conduit' was different; a little softer for us, but it was a very effective and emotional episode. The two episodes involving the character Tooms, 'Squeeze' and 'Tooms', about this man who fed on livers and awakened every however many years to take five victims; those were both effective and very well done. I'm very pleased with 'Deep Throat', which was the episode I directed, and I was very happy with the pilot. There were some episodes I thought were less successful, and the audience has showed that they think so too. There's one, 'Space', where I tried to do something, but given the demands of time and maybe even the concept, I think it was one of our least successful shows.

Is it difficult to direct when you've got all these scripts in different stages of development?

We're always doing five things at once, on a practical level. You are writing a script, prepping a script to be produced, producing and shooting a script, editing a filmed episode, and then you are doing sound and music on that episode. Every day that you get up and put your clothes on, there are always five or six things that you are doing. Beyond that, you have interviews, you have Standards and Practices, which is the censorship wing that you're dealing with on a regular basis, you're dealing with the network who are giving you notes on your work, the studio that is giving you notes, and various and sundry other things. It is a mind-boggling job.

Especially when you're directing as well!

Some say that I'm a glutton for punishment, but it was an opportunity for me. A director had dropped out for that episode, and I thought, 'What do I do? Do I hire a director I don't know and I've never worked with to do this work, and have to communicate to him in very specific terms what I want? Or do I just bite the bullet, do that extra work that I wouldn't normally have to do and get what I want?' and that's what I did.

What do you want to do in upcoming seasons that you haven't done before?

I'd like to do a 3D sequence in some future episode; not the whole thing, but I have an idea about how to use a brand new 3D effect, which I think would be an interesting

BEYOND THE X-FILES

Thanks to the unexpected success of *The X-Files*, it wasn't long before studio executives at Fox began talking to Chris Carter about developing other projects for the network. To date though, none have been able to duplicate the unique popularity of Mulder and Scully. In 1996, Carter created *Millennium*, a much darker piece than *The X-Files*. It focused on Frank Black (Lance Henriksen) a former FBI profiler, who moves his family to Seattle only to become involved with the mysterious Millennium Group, who are trying to combat evil as the next millennium approaches. Although production values on the series were high, many of the stories were downbeat and humourless, and *Millennium* was cancelled in 1998. Carter's next two series were even less successful. *Harsh Realm*, loosely based on the comic book series of the same name, followed the adventures of a young soldier (Scott Bairstow) who volunteers to test the army's new Virtual Reality training machine, and finds himself trapped in the nightmare world of Harsh Realm. The series lasted just a handful of episodes. Most recently there's been *The Lone Gunmen*, featuring that popular trio of hackers from *The X-Files*, but their tongue-in-cheek spin-off ran for only half a season before being deleted from our screens.

thing to do*. I don't know… just taking advantage of the expanding digital FX technology, and maybe do a couple of FX that we haven't done before. Beyond that, I'm just going to tell very good scary stories, and make them believable.

Any talk about going to film in different locations, perhaps to widen the show's international appeal?

We'd anticipated maybe going to Russia for an episode, but we put that aside when we realised the hardship of that idea, and the difficulty in shooting there. And I don't think setting an episode in Hungary, for example, is going to make the show any more popular in Hungary. The show is going to be as popular as it is good. It's already playing in forty countries, so we have a very big international following, but you can always do better. You can always have more and better, and build on those things, but I don't think there's any correlation between where we shoot the show and how popular it's going to be. Some people may suggest it, but I have plenty of reasonable arguments against it.

Are you happy to have created a series with a cult following?

This show is perceived as a cult show, and that's a label I really like. It makes it seem that we're doing something underground, offbeat and eccentric, which is something I believe we're doing. It should be the most popular cult show on television. I believe there is a wider audience out there who have not yet sampled it, and I'd like them to come in and make this something they sit down and do on a regular basis. I'd like nothing better than to build my ratings and get the show to more people, because it's worthy and deserving of it. I think the people who liked *The X-Files* will continue to come back, and I hope they'll help spread the word. ∎

---

* This intriguing idea never came off, but future episodes did play with format, using black and white ('Post-Modern Prometheus') and *Cops*-style documentary handheld camerawork ('X-COPS').

HOWARD CHAYKIN
ON MUTANT X

Howard Chaykin is a veteran comic book writer and artist, best known for hard-hitting, adult-themed titles such as *American Flagg* and *Black Kiss*, neither of which feature comics' usual staple diet of superheroes having escapist adventures. He may therefore seem a strange choice to be the head writer on *Mutant X* — a superhero TV series for the 21st century. In fact, Chaykin is no stranger to superheroic television fare, having previously worked on *The Flash*, still widely regarded as one of the rare examples of a character to successfully make the leap from comics to live action TV. Although mutant superheroes have been at the forefront of popular comic books for years, they've only recently been successful on screen. Thanks largely to the success of Twentieth Century Fox's long-awaited *X-Men* movie, Hollywood has finally begun looking at their commercial potential. But *Mutant X*, the latest project to move from page to screen, has encountered more than a few bumps along the road. Loosely adapted from the Marvel comic of the same name, it was originally to have followed the adventures of a group of super-powered mutants, code names, colourful costumes and all. However, following a well-documented legal dispute with Twentieth Century Fox, various aspects of the series underwent a rethink. Interviewed while *Mutant X* was in the early stages of production, Chaykin gives a preview of the series, outlining his aspirations for the show during that nervous period when he just had to hope that the viewing public was going to like what he and his fellow writers were developing...

Having spent the last couple of decades staying well away from the world of mutant superheroes in your comic book work, what made you decide to work on this series?

If you know my background, you know how weird it is for me to end up doing this sort of material. To give it to you in a nutshell, if you know comic books at all in the context of Hollywood, both in television and film, comics are perceived not as a medium but as a genre. That tends to mean if you come out of a comic book background, they're going to presume you're good with 'comic book' things. My first job in television was on *The Flash*, which again, is something I'd never done in comic books, but I understand the sensibility. Plus, I've worked for [*Mutant X* production company] Tribune before. I did a season on *Earth: Final Conflict* for these guys, season three, which I'm told is referred to by *cognoscenti* as 'the good season'. Praise with faint damns, but I'll take what I can get. And then I was in development on another series with these guys when *Mutant X* came along, so they shunted me from that to this. The fact is, I'm familiar with this material because I came up out of the ranks of the comics fanboys, and by the time I became a professional, I'd sort of shucked off a lot of my fanboy ways, but I still knew the material backwards and forwards. Gil Kane[*] is the archetype; Gil is a guy who outgrew the sensibilities of the work he was drawing and writing many years ago, but he was still able to produce more than credible work in that context. By my standards, I wouldn't be particularly interested in doing this material in comic books. But I love doing this stuff in a television universe, because it's an opportunity to impose my will on material that is not the sort of stuff I had done in comics. But I bring my own peculiar sensibility to it, and I think that's exactly why I was hired and why they want me here.

One of the things you learn translating this sort of material into a television marketplace is that you have to find a narrow line to dance on. You're satisfying the people who know the jargon and sensibility, having grown up reading this sort of thing in comic books for years and years, but at the same time you're also interested in addressing an audience that has never given a damn about the comic book. That's the audience that's more important. One of the reasons I believe I'm here is that my sensibility is able to transcend the comic book aspect. Someone once wrote a really snively, dismissive crack about my stuff in one of the comics magazines, referring to my work as 'public transportation dialogue'. While they were sort of smacking me with it, frankly I took it as a great compliment, because too much comic book dialogue sounds like expository bullshit. My feeling is I was able to tell stories in language that was recognisable as people's patois if you will, and that's what I'm trying to do with *Mutant X*. To a great extent — and this may sound bizarre — it's like going right back to square one, to what [the legendary comic book writer] Stan Lee did in 1961. When Stan Lee set out with the *Fantastic Four*, he originally wanted to do a comic book in which there were no costumes. He and [artist] Jack Kirby were dealing with the human problems that came out of having guys who had super powers in a real world. It ultimately evolved very quickly into

HOWARD CHAYKIN

Date/Place of Birth:
1950, Newark, New Jersey, USA

Home Base:
Los Angeles, California, USA

Education:
Tilden, Queens, New York

First TV Work:
The Flash

TV Career Highlights:
The Flash, Viper, Gene Roddenberry's Earth: Final Conflict, Mutant X

---

[*] *Veteran comic book artist, who was also Chaykin's mentor in the industry.*

much bigger, fantasy-based material, but its original conception, from Jack and Stan's position, was to do pretty much what I'm doing here: people with enhanced abilities, coping with the problems of having those enhanced abilities in a real world.

How much of the concept of *Mutant X* was handed to you when you came in?

That's open to discussion. Many of the characters have come through similar to what they originally wanted to do. But the character names and the back-stories are all different, and they've evolved in completely different directions. There are a number of characters that are entirely different, because as I pointed out to a lot of people, certain character abilities, although they sounded really good on paper, when you actually acted them on a weekly basis, they made no sense. So what I did was, I named all the characters, developed their back-stories, and created a thirty-five-page series bible that reflected where I wanted the show to go. They approved all that stuff, and then we went running with it.

What is the basic premise of the series?

Sometime in the last third of the century, a company called Genomex, which is secretly a front for the US government intelligence services, engaged in illegal and covert genetic experimentation on approximately 1,000 children prenatally. The result of the experiments was totally unexpected. Those 1,000 children were born with enhanced abilities to one degree or another, which developed over time as they matured. They were born with these abilities, and like learning to walk and talk and everything else, they had to learn to command them. Ultimately, one of the people who was responsible for this project broke free of it. Seeking his own redemption, he found four of these so-called 'children of Genomex', and formed a group called 'Mutant X' that was intended to combat the security division of Genomex, the Genetic Security Agency. Our stories are about the secret covert operations between these two groups. Both groups are seeking to find new mutants. Our heroes are looking for new mutants in order to rescue them, and put them into what is our equivalent of a witness protection program. Genomex is trying to find new mutants so they can put them in stasis pods, experiment on them, and use them to develop covert operatives and assassins, which was their original intention.

With a premise like that, were you looking for writers who were good with drama, SF, comics or all of the above?

Interestingly enough, I actively avoided looking at comic book people. One of the problems I've always had working with comic book talent in the TV universe is that they have no grasp of structure. They don't know how to do what is done on the comic book page within the weekly confines of a show that shoots in eight days, that has a specific and finite budget. A few times, I've actually considered bringing in comic book people, and they've tanked on me because they've given me stuff that is much too story heavy, all plot driven. Plots are great for movies, but television is a character-driven medium, and most comic book people have no grasp of how to do the scale of the stories we're talking about in a structure that is literally a pre-credits teaser and five acts. My core staff comes out of network episodic television. They're people who can handle a story, who are strong in the room and can work as a group, who are gifted with writing action and structure, who know how to present stories, because so much of what we do is based on holding and grabbing the audience. It's knowing where to put your buzzes, your action beats, your energy, how to tell a story without being too expository, and again, always working within the constraints of the budget we've got.

Did you map out most of the first season in advance?

Not really. I obviously shape every story premise that comes through the house, but when we started the show, we were looking at the distinct possibility of a massive writers' strike, and the pledge we made was to basically deliver ten scripts in advance of that. So what we did was sit down the first month we were here, and we developed those ten scripts right from the bottom. We knew we had to do certain episodes that would be character revealing and set up certain structural elements in the characters'

EARTH: FINAL CONFLICT

Loosely based on concepts by the late *Star Trek* creator, *Gene Roddenberry's Earth: Final Conflict* made its syndicated TV début in 1997. Sometime in the early 21st century, the Taelons, an androgynous alien race, come to Earth, calling themselves the 'Companions.' They promise to help rid the planet of war, illness and famine by sharing their advanced knowledge, but some people remain skeptical and form a resistance movement. Enter William Boone (Kevin Kilner), a former Special Forces soldier turned cop, who rescues North America's alien overseer Da'an, and becomes the Companions' Earth-Taelon liaison. But Boone is also working for the resistance movement, trying to discover the aliens' true motives, which may not be what they appear. When Boone was apparently killed early in the show's run, his role was largely taken over by Robert Leeshock, who played Liam Kincaid. Also playing important roles in the complex story-line were Lisa Howard as Boone's long-time associate Lili Marquette, Richard Chevolleau as the genius hacker Augur, and Jane Heitmeyer, playing resistance fighter Renee Palmer. After four seasons which even the show's producers admit have varied greatly in quality, the series entered its final year with the promise that major shake-ups for the characters were on the way...

back-story, while also telling a front-story that was exciting and fun. And we succeeded. Then of course the strike didn't hit, so we were okay. But then we made some major adjustments in where we were going to go with these characters, so it hasn't really been a vacation.

I still always want to stay five to seven scripts ahead of shooting. Right now, I've got the script for the episode we've started prepping this week in front of me. I've delivered the script that preps after that already, I'm about to deliver the script that preps after *that* at the end of this week, and I've got a freelancer coming in today. I've also got three more scripts in-house, so we're always moving forward.

Are you a fan of the long-term story arc?

Beyond being restrictive, it's also very difficult to do in the context of a syndicated series, as *Mutant X* is. For example, you have no idea when you're airing shows, and you can never do one-offs in syndicated television. Network shows always do one 'holiday' episode a year, either a Hallowe'en show or a Thanksgiving show or a Christmas show, because they know when episodes are going to air, but you don't see that in syndicated television. There's a generalised arc, and you usually have a season finale of some sort, but overall, it's very difficult to even think about serialisation. In our fourth show shot, we had some amazing chemistry between one of our leads and a guest star, and we may bring that character back in some way or another. When we

THE FLASH

Still considered as one of the best TV versions of a comic book series, *The Flash* raced onto the small screen in 1990. John Wesley Shipp starred as Barry Allen, a police scientist who is caught in a lab accident that gives him the ability to move at super speed. In true superhero tradition, he quickly dons a colourful costume and goes off to rid Central City of criminals, evil scientists and supervillains. The series also featured Amanda Pays as research scientist/possible love interest Tina McGee (who knew of Barry's dual identity) and Alex Désert as Barry's lab assistant, Julio (who didn't). Following the success of Tim Burton's *Batman* in 1989, studios and TV networks soon began looking for comic book properties with equal potential. By all accounts, *The Flash* had a good chance of success. CBS gave the series a healthy budget, which allowed for some impressive visual FX and a bit of interesting stunt casting (including *Star Wars'* Mark Hamill). Sadly, despite some excellent episodes by comic book veteran Chaykin and his partner John Francis Moore, many of the other stories were formulaic, and *The Flash* was cancelled at the end of its first season.

see characters like that, that really pop out, where there's blow-off-the-screen chemistry, that's where you find your arcs. In a general sense, we know where we're going for the first two seasons. I have a broad idea of what the first season finale is going to be. It's not something that pushes the show into a dramatically different direction, but it sets up a problem for the second season that has to be solved.

What lessons did you learn about superheroic television from working on *The Flash*?

That was an extremely expensive series, so we had a lot more money there than we do here. We also shot mostly on the Warner Bros lot, which was a great lot to work on. If you remember the show at all, the Central City Police Station was the first building they'd built on the Warners lot in about ten years, and it's now used as the front of the hospital on *E.R.*. So we had access to the lot, which meant there were all sorts of different variables: we had a controlled space where we could do special FX gags and stunts, for example. We also had a lot of support from both Warner Bros and CBS in terms of pushing that envelope. We're much more finite on *Mutant X*, so we're still playing with that.

But hasn't visual FX technology really come along since then?

Absolutely, but in realistic terms, on *Mutant X* we're dealing with four regulars with special enhanced abilities, plus, generally speaking, a mutant of the week, perhaps two! The idea frequently for us is to also play against the possibilities of drama with these characters, or go for comedy as well. So we rob from Peter to pay Paul. We find places to use this material knowing that we're going to be sacrificing other elements.

Are you at the point in the series where you can start writing your lead characters specifically for the actors who have been cast in those roles?

We were very lucky in the sense that we got to meet all the actors before we started. One of the things that happened during pre-production was that we found there were certain characters we were writing in one direction, but when we met the actor, we made major scene changes. Shalimar Fox is the best example. Vicky Pratt is sharp-witted, and very kittenishly flirtatious and funny, so we found ourselves writing that for Shalimar, and it really paid off big time. Victor Webster, who plays Brennan Mulwray, is wonderful to write for because he's got a wise guy sensibility that really plays beautifully. Forbes March, who plays Jesse Kilmartin, has a bad boy quality that's perfectly in line with the character, who grew up as a poor little rich boy. Lauren Lee Smith is such a cutie pie, and so smart and so funny and so flirtatious that again, we found ourselves writing for these qualities in her character Emma deLauro. With John Shea, I always visualised Adam as a retired Samurai, and John has stepped up to the plate on that. He's sensational. And Tom McCamus is going to be the revelation as our primary villain. He's truly terrifying as Mason Eckhart, and we've got some great stuff with a great deal of humour, without ever losing the jeopardy.

Let's talk in a bit more detail about how the show's main characters were developed, starting with Adam.

John Shea plays Adam, a guy who was part of the Genomex team and who ultimately saved the lives of these 1,000 people. When he discovered exactly what was going on in this company that he thought was doing innocent work, he left and started his mission. Adam made his millions as an early investor in what eventually evolved into the Internet, and has a mountain stronghold called Sanctuary, where he basically runs an underground railroad for new mutants, protecting them from Genomex. The great thing about John is that he has found all the humour we hoped he'd find in the material. He's got a great sensibility and a great presence. Besides *Lois & Clark* [in which Shea memorably played Lex Luthor], I was aware of his work from a wonderful series called *WIOU*, which few people have seen, but I loved that show[*].

How about the villainous Mason Eckhart?

When you see the confrontation between Adam and Eckhart in the second half of our season opener, they are phenomenal together. We're shooting an episode right now where they have to work on a truce, but we're also developing an episode in which the two of them literally team up to solve a common problem, that is sort of *The Defiant Ones* meets *Die Hard* in Genomex!

Is it a challenge to make sure your villains don't become formulaic?

I make it a point to make sure our heroes are pretty sharp too. All of our guys get some serious zingers in. My feeling is it's important to have heroes who are smart asses as well.

Moving back to our heroes, there's Victoria Pratt as Shalimar, who has both human and animal DNA...

Victoria's very happy to be here, and we love having her. Her husband T. J. Scott[†] directed a couple of our first episodes. He did our 'Shalimar in love' episode, which is just unbelievable. Vicky and I have spoken a number of times about Shalimar, and frankly, she's a kittenish and funny woman, so we've really written that into the character. She's also an athlete and a gymnast, and she steps up to the plate on everything. One of the things about our show that we never stint on is action. There's movement, it's fun and it really works. As I said to our staff the day we saw the cut of the first episode, it's really wonderful to be on a show that you have no apologies for. The work speaks for itself, and that's really important.

Shalimar is our physical character, she's our muscle, and our stunt staff has managed to find some really funny gags to do with her. Trust me when I say that she brings a

---

[*] *WIOU* (1990-91) starred John Shea as Hank Zaret, the news director at a small TV station. Despite lavish praise from critics, CBS cancelled the drama after thirteen episodes.
[†] Who directed numerous episodes of *Hercules* and *Xena*, as well as Pratt's previous series, *Cleopatra 2525*.

comic sensibility, without ever stepping away from the jeopardy, to every action moment she's involved in. Paul our stunt co-ordinator is just unbelievable. He knows comics pretty well too, so when we discuss the idea of posture and posing and striking attitudes, he's really on the money.

Then there's Victor Webster, a character with electricity-based power. What's his back-story?

Victor is a reformed hoodlum and wise guy who used his powers from the time he was a kid to disarm alarms and hot wire cars. He was a thief, who's found a way to redeem himself through our group. He's sort of a wise guy with the heart of a poet. He's a major fan of nineteenth century poetry, and early twentieth century fiction. In the middle of his wise guy-style dialogue, he'll throw out literary references completely out of context, so that's the kind of guy he is.

Emma DeLauro is a 'telempath'. Does that mean she's a mind reader?

She's not a mind reader *per se*, but she can get a sense of how you're feeling. She can also manipulate the way you feel, and we've set it up that, before she joined the group, she denied that she had these powers, but at the same time, she knew she had them all too well. The point of view she receives is frequently symbolic, and what she transmits is also symbolic, in comic ways and in jeopardy-filled ways. At one point, she makes a crack about the fact she used to be a salesgirl in the misses and petites department and used her powers to manipulate customers — so we try to really bring stuff to a common ground with the viewers. Emma and Victor are the characters that are brought in during our opening two-parter. Shalimar and Jessie are already in place, so the two-parter is about our group coming together as a team.

And that leaves Jessie Kilmartin. What was your intention in creating his character?

As a matter of fact, we're developing Jessie's back-story in an episode right now. It's a real out-of-the-box episode, and we're really excited about it. Jessie is a poor little rich kid who's found a family with our group that he's never really had in his home. Jessie and Brennan are basically the worst possible combination of tricksters and troublemakers, and they have great chemistry together. It's sort of a 'Can you top this?' kind of thing.

How does Jessie's ability to alter his density work?

He can go phase and go mass; he can become a moving intangible or utterly impermeable. One of the challenges we've had is to find fun ways to play with that. What we want to do is whenever these guys use these powers, they also use their physicality with them. For example, we've developed the use of wire work and a lot of flipping to go in tandem with these abilities, so that's where the fun comes.

Who was the first person cast?

We actually signed up Brennan, Vicky and Forbes the same day, and then Lauren and then Tom, and then John. We'd seen a lot of people, but ultimately there were certain people that no one else came close to. With others, there were one or two people in line, and we had to choose, but we were really happy with our choices. One of the things about our show is we're in a very lucky position of having a cast that's physically beautiful and can also do the job. Very often you find a cast that looks this good who can't do shit, but these guys really go for it and kick serious ass.

Are there built-in sources of conflict within this group of characters?

We're not really dancing on that issue in our first season. We're developing ourselves as a team. There's conflict, but it's small. I don't want to get into that breast-beating, angst-ridden 'I hate you!' stuff, at least not this soon. I want our audience to get to know the characters before we start playing with that aspect of them. All of our characters make mistakes. They have human foibles, and they make problems for each other, but going right back to Stan Lee 101, we're not talking about the Thing and Johnny Storm [the constantly squabbling half of the *Fantastic Four*]. That kind of sensibility is not appropriate for us. Down the line, we'll have a lot more conflict between our characters, but I think you have to get to know them a little more before you can understand why there's conflict.

What sorts of mutants have you and your writing team created for the first season?

One of the premises of our show is that Mason Eckhart's number two, his lieutenant, his second in command, is always a mutant, a guy who has sold out his kind for the sake of order, and the conceit is that they change every week, because they disappoint him. In our opening show, our mutant is a telekinetic, a blue-collar guy who looks like a monolith, who doesn't look like he needs telekinesis to move anything! In the episode I'm working on right now, we've got a character who absorbs energy, who is frail and weak except when she absorbs electrical energy; then she turns into this absolutely breathtakingly beautiful doll. My next episode involves a supermodel who's gifted with Superman-like strength, whose real abilities boil down to being an incredible marketing and manipulative advertising genius, who's working with Eckhart to develop a campaign; things like that.

Why do you think so many comic book projects turn out so badly on screen?

Because there's a happy medium that has to be found doing this kind of material, and that's difficult to do. You just can't approach it with a kind of love, or utter worship of the material, as if it was graven in stone. Bu at the same time, you can't approach it as if you're making fun of it, either. You've really got to find a way to look at it that's a new perspective.

Is the next *X-Men* movie making life difficult for you in terms of the comparisons?

Not especially. My model for this show is much more to do with *Mission: Impossible* and *The A-Team* than anything else. I'm more interested in reaching an audience that doesn't care about comic books. I want to reach the guy or gal out there who, if they have read a comic book, it was years ago, and is looking for a way to spend an hour with some fun people, doing some fun stuff. Bear in mind, our guys aren't spandex and masks and capes. It's an action-adventure show.

Can you see yourself doing this series for several years?

Your lips to God's ear. We've got a commitment upfront for forty-four episodes, so I'm hoping to be here at least another year and a half. Look, a lot of network shows start with just a six-episode commitment, so where do you go from there? As I've said, this is the first thing I've worked on, in my memory, where I've got no apologies to make. This is terrific stuff, and we're really thrilled by the material. We spent yesterday at Tribune going over where we stand, and there was genuine feedback of 'This is great stuff!' so we're very happy. ∎

TERRANCE DICKS

lthough there have been many writers associated with *Doctor Who* over its long and tumultuous history, there's no one who's written for more of the various Doctors, in different permutations, than Terrance Dicks. After beginning his TV writing career by working on early episodes of *The Avengers* with his friend and mentor Malcolm Hulke, Dicks joined *Doctor Who* near the end of second Doctor Patrick Troughton's tenure, staying on as script editor for five seasons with Jon Pertwee. As a freelancer, he wrote Tom Baker's first story, as well as several other episodes, including the twentieth anniversary special 'The Five Doctors' in 1983. Add the stage plays *Doctor Who and the Seven Keys to Doomsday* in 1974, and *Doctor Who: The Ultimate Adventure* in 1989, as well as an unmatched string of *Who* novelisations and original novels, and you've got one pretty impressive body of work. Not that Dicks' output has been restricted to our favourite Time Lord of course. In the mid-80s, he produced the BBC classics serials, including critically acclaimed adaptations of *David Copperfield*, *Oliver Twist* and *Vanity Fair*. After leaving the BBC, he continued to write for television, but also began to further his career as a successful author. Today, Dicks is one of the UK's most respected and prolific children's fiction writers, but as this interview attests, he's not about to forsake SF or *Doctor Who*...

How did you get into the business?

By writing TV and radio scripts in my spare time, more or less. Radio was certainly an easier market in those days [the early 1960s], because they didn't pay much money, so they had to use new people! I simply wrote a radio play and sent it in [to the BBC], and they accepted it, so I started doing radio work after that. I did a couple of other plays, and also a comedy series, so that was the radio side of it. The television really happened because I'd changed my lodgings and moved into a house that was owned by Malcolm Hulke as an investment. He had a great aunt that he was looking after, and the rest of the house was let. So I met Mac, who was sort of my landlord, and we became friends. One day, he mentioned that he'd been asked to write for *The Avengers*, but hadn't really got any ideas. I said, 'I've got lots of ideas!' and Mac, being a really generous man, collaborated on one of them with me. I think we co-wrote two or three *Avengers* together[*], so that was really my first step into television.

---

[*] *Dicks and Hulke co-wrote 'The Mauritius Penny' and 'Intercrime' for season two, and 'Concerto' for season three.*

Did he teach you how to write a television script?

To an extent. I already had a fair amount of experience in radio, and television isn't all that different, other than layout and stuff like that, which is easily picked up. The advantage was that Mac was an established television writer, and his name made it much easier for me to sell stuff that was linked to him, because at that time my name was not known in television.

But before you got that far, how had you worked out the format for a radio script in the first place?

There were plenty of books around that explained that kind of thing. It's not difficult to write a radio script, but television can be a bit more complex. Mac certainly helped me with that because he was an experienced television writer, but he was really good about it, treating me as an equal, and we split the money fifty-fifty. I would have done it for nothing, for the glory of getting into television! According to cop novels — which I read a great deal of because I'm very fond of thrillers — in the police force you need what's called a 'rabbi', which is an older, more experienced person who looks out for you, helps you along, gives you good advice and points you in the direction of opportunity, that kind of thing. Mac was certainly my rabbi in my first years in television, and was a great help to me.

Once you got your foot in the door and understood the process, did it become progressively easier?

It's very much a matter of one thing leading to another. Through Mac, I got recommended to *Crossroads*, which was a soap opera, and during those days in English television, it was one of only a few soap operas. Now there's nothing on but soap operas, but at that time, I got on to *Crossroads* and did quite well. I became a regular writer, and a story-liner as well, which is the person who writes the plot lines that are then handed out to the writing team. While on that show, I met Derrick Sherwin. He was then the script editor on *Doctor Who*, but wanted to get away from it because he'd been offered another job, which he wanted to do more. I chatted to him about it, and one day, he rang up out

TERRANCE DICKS

Date/Place of Birth:
1935, East Ham, London, UK

Home Base:
Hampstead, London, UK

Education:
Downing College, Cambridge

First TV Work:
The Avengers 'The Mauritius Penny'

TV Career Highlights:
The Avengers, Doctor Who, Space: 1999, Moonbase 3, Shakedown (video)

of the blue and said, 'How would you like to be script editor on *Doctor Who?*' so it was as simple as that. In this business, you need a few lucky breaks, but you also need to come up with the goods. If I hadn't been able to come up with good ideas, I wouldn't have been able to go on working with Mac. If I hadn't been good at soap opera, I wouldn't have stayed on *Crossroads* very long, and if I hadn't been able to cut it when I got onto *Who*, I wouldn't have stayed there, so it's not all luck. Mark Twain once said, 'The harder I work, the luckier I get.'

Didn't you once compare your new assignment on *Doctor Who* to being captain on the *Titanic*?

Yes, though not even the captain, but the cabin boy! The show had been having trouble with scripts, amongst other things. The ratings were beginning to drop, Patrick Troughton was thinking of leaving, and it was beginning to look as if maybe that might be the end of it. They'd had three years of Bill Hartnell and two years of Patrick, so five or six years was a good life for a television show. But Patrick did another year and then other things happened: Barry Letts took over as producer, the show went into colour for the first time (which shows you how long ago it was!), and Jon Pertwee took over as the Doctor and became a great success after Patrick finally left. Plus, I took over as script editor. So all those things together gave the show a boost, and it took off from there, really.

What were the responsibilities for a script editor back in those days?

It involved getting the scripts in; it's as simple as that. You're responsible for finding the writers, commissioning the scripts and nursing them through the script process. I used to rewrite a lot, because in my time on *Who*, we never abandoned a script once it had come in. I always reckoned that if I'd commissioned it, it was my responsibility to make it work. The BBC department concerned with write-offs once called me up and asked, 'How many write-offs have you had this season?' and I said, 'None, we don't do them on *Doctor Who!*' I'd go through a couple of drafts with the writer, but I'm not a believer in putting the writer through endless rewrites, because it comes to a point very quickly where he's not getting better, he's getting worse. What I would do is get a first draft, discuss it with the writer and the producer, and the director if he was available, get the writer to do a second draft, and that was it. I never asked for more, and then after that, it was my business to make it work. Some of them were fine, but there's always something, because when you take a script into the production process, there's a location you can't use, it's running too long or running short, or something emerges that doesn't make sense, and it's the script editor's job to fix that. That's what he should be doing as part of his job, and at the same time, he's also getting in the scripts for the next show and the one after that. If a script just didn't work for some reason, and it wasn't any good, I would rewrite from beginning to end if necessary. Sometimes that happened, but as you find better writers, and get to know your writers, it shouldn't happen. I'm not a believer in the script editor writing the show, unless there's an emergency and you're faced with disaster.

Some of the American writers interviewed for this book didn't necessarily agree about whether or not they felt comfortable about putting their names on somebody else's script.

I think the American Writers Guild is much stronger than ours is! The only job I ever did for an American company was an episode of *Space: 1999*[*], which was made in England. I went to see the producer, Fred Freiberger, who discussed what they were looking for, and I said, 'Okay, I'll go away and think up some ideas and send them to you.' He looked horrified and said, 'For God's sake, don't put anything on paper, because if you do, I'll have to pay you! If you get a good idea, ring me up.' What you do in English television is write a storyline, either short or long according to taste, and you're prepared to do that on spec because it's all part of the game. If they take it forward, they'll pay you, but it might just be effort wasted. Apparently in America, if you set typewriter to paper, they've got to pay you. So what happened in this case, I let it drag on, because my agent had said, 'Nobody has sold these people a story yet, they're only throwing it open to English writers because they're legally obliged. They don't actually want any English writers, but they're going through the motions, so it's no good, you won't sell them anything.' But I came up with an idea, which was basically

SPACE: 1999

When *Space: 1999* began in 1975, it appeared to have a lot going for it: a respected cast, big name guest stars, and the high-quality model work that has always been a trademark of a series from Gerry Anderson. Much like the inhabitants of the show's Moonbase Alpha though, the series never really seemed to find a definite direction. In *Space: 1999*, the Moon is torn apart by an atomic explosion resulting from a build-up of nuclear waste. The surviving half, carrying Moonbase Alpha's crew of 300, is hurled out of Earth's orbit and off into space on a series of adventures. The group included the base's commander John Koenig (Martin Landau), medical officer Dr Helena Russell (Barbara Bain, Landau's real-life wife) and scientist Victor Bergman (Barry Morse). While the series featured excellent sets and FX (the latter provided by *2001*'s Brian Johnson), performances were often less than captivating, with little chemistry between the lead characters. For the second year, former *Star Trek* producer Fred Freiberger was brought in to revamp the series, introducing some new characters, notably Catherine Schell as alien shape-changer Maya. It was too little too late, and *Space: 1999* came to an end after just two seasons.

---

[*] *'The Lambda Factor', for season two.*

for Koenig the captain [Martin Landau] to be haunted, and he couldn't go to sleep, because whenever he does, he's haunted by these ghosts. I liked the idea of doing a ghost story on a brightly-lit space station instead of a gothic castle. I phoned Fred Freiberger, and said, 'Look, you've probably forgotten seeing me weeks ago, but I do have an idea,' and he said, 'Shoot.' I think I pitched this idea to silence at the other end of the telephone, and when I finished, there was a little pause, and the voice said, 'Okay, we have a deal,' and he put the phone down, which was unique in my experience.

Are you saying there's more of a gentleman's agreement for British writers?

A certain amount, and I think it's a jolly good system. Because American television and film tends to mess people about a bit more, they probably need better protection. But good for them, I'm all for it.

When you began working on *Doctor Who*, were any scripts already in development, to get you started?

No, but what I did have, and this was an oddity, was that Derrick didn't actually get the job that he'd hired me to replace him for, so for a while, both of us were around. That was very useful for me, because it gave me a year's training period rather than being thrown in at the deep end. I was working with Derrick, so I had a longer chance to pick things up. Eventually, Derrick and Peter Bryant, who was the producer then, went off to make a show called *Paul Temple*, the first of those location shows that shuffled all over Europe. When they left, and Patrick left, Barry Letts became producer and I took over as full script editor. But by then, I had a year of experience behind me, which was most useful.

Did you commission scripts from writers you already knew, or would freelancers contact you as script editor?

A little of both. When it becomes known in the business that a show is looking for scripts, people would send in ideas, but at the same time, you might go to someone who you knew. Obviously I went to Mac Hulke, who wrote a lot of *Who* scripts. It's difficult to explain. There's a saying that 'It's not what you know, it's who you know', and that's too cynical, but what *is* true is that 'It's what you know *and* who you know'. In other words, contacts are very important. If I hadn't got to know Derrick when we were both working on *Crossroads*, and then he subsequently went to *Doctor Who* and then wanted to move on, if we didn't get on and he didn't think I was fairly capable, he wouldn't have come to me. Although Mac was a good friend and I owed him for all his help at the beginning, I wouldn't have gone to him unless I was confident that he could write a good *Who* script, because otherwise that was going to reflect on my reputation. You can't employ a no-good writer just because he's your friend, but if there's a series of good writers to choose from, it's quite likely that you'll choose one who's your friend first, because you know you'll get on with him and you'll work well together.

What kind of people did you have coming in?

Robert Holmes sent in an idea that had been rejected by a previous script editor, Gerry Davis. When he heard there was a new script editor, he thought there was no harm in trying again, so he sent in what I think was pretty much the same idea. As I recall, he came in and we talked things over, and we finished up doing not that idea but another one. Sometimes you might go to people, as I went to Mac, saying, 'Would you like to do it?' Or perhaps somebody might come in or send in an idea that impressed you, or as with Bob Holmes, the idea might not work out, but the writer would impress you. The weirdest one was Bob Baker and Dave Martin, who started a bit later, and also became semi-regulars. One day, a script arrived on my desk, which was a comedy about young recruits in the army. So I read this script and it was very good and very funny, but it was nothing to do with *Doctor Who*. I kept wondering when the Doctor was going to turn up, but I read the whole thing through and he didn't. The script had simply been mis-routed; it was intended for the light entertainment department and landed on my desk by mistake. But I liked the script, so I sent for Bob and Dave. They had several goes at coming up with something for *Doctor Who*, because they were bright but undisciplined, but after many attempts, where I think we were all nearly driven to despair, they eventually came up with a storyline, which became 'The Claws of Axos' [during Jon Pertwee's second season]. After that, they wrote several stories for us, but their introduction to the show was wildly unpredictable.

How did you and Mac end up writing the epic ten-part story 'The War Games' together, which wrapped up Patrick Troughton's run on the series?

That was a hangover from my predecessors, who had not one but two stories collapse on them. That story was really started before Derrick left, when he was still nominally script editor, and suddenly he was told, 'We need a ten-part serial!' I think a six- and a four-parter had been written, but they'd finally decided they were never going to work, and they had a ten-episode gap in the schedule to fill. I knew I couldn't cope with it on my own in that time, so I brought in Mac and we did it together. It was written at a great rate, an episode every two or three days, but I think it's got its moments. I'm always the first to say it's far too long, because you should never do a ten-parter. Rule one about doing a ten-part story is, 'Never do a ten-part story.' But we *had* to do it, and we made it work as best we could. I think it begins and ends well, but drags a bit in the middle here and there.

'The War Games' famously introduced the Time Lords, the powerful alien race of which the Doctor himself is a somewhat maverick member. Where did the elements of Time Lord mythology come from?

Derrick came up with that, and I have no idea where he got it from! We knew it was going to be Patrick's last story, so it was a writing-out story for the current Doctor. Derrick also came up with the basic idea that the Doctor met some problem so huge that he had to go back to his own people, even though he knew that would mean his capture, so he'd have to sacrifice himself. With that brief, Mac and I then came up with the concept of the war games, and I think it was Derrick who said, 'He comes from a people called the Time Lords,' so he deserves credit for that. What we knew about the Doctor from before was that in some sense he was a fugitive from his own people, but that was it. We didn't know anything about them, so Mac and I really created the Time Lords, and after that, they just tended to pop up and issue mysterious orders from time to time. The show didn't reveal much more about them until years later.

When Barry Letts came in as the new producer on *Doctor Who*, did he have his own agenda from the beginning?

Our agenda was to get a show on the screen on time, because the script situation had deteriorated very badly by then. For the first season, we were just desperately trying to get the show out and to not have thirty minutes of rankness on the screen on Saturday night! It was only later that we evolved the kind of thing that we wanted to do. In the first weeks, I think it was sheer desperation, just getting the show on the road. I was just talking to Barry a short time ago — we eat dinner together once a week at a restaurant. I think we've been doing that for about thirty years now. We are best friends and that's been lucky, because the producer-script editor relationship is very important.

When you and Barry were working out your first season together, what made you decide to launch Jon Pertwee's Doctor with a number of seven-part stories, instead of the usual four- or six-parters?

That again was an inheritance. *Who* was always in budgetary trouble, because SF by definition is expensive. You've got to build the sets and the weapons and costumes and everything, so in order to save money, Bryant and Sherwin came up with this idea of doing seven-parters. Barry and I hated them, and reversed it as soon as we could, but we couldn't reverse it for that first season. A seven-parter is cheaper, because you amortise your costs over a longer period. In other words, you have to pay for the sets and the costumes, but if you use them for seven episodes rather than four or six, it saves you a certain amount of money. It was done purely for that reason. Also for purely financial reasons, the Doctor was exiled to Earth, so they could go about shooting in the streets of London or wherever, and not have to go somewhere that looked like an alien planet. Barry and I didn't like either of those ideas, and as soon as we could, we changed them back. It's like turning an ocean liner; you can't do it on a six-pence, but we gradually got out of it during the next couple of seasons.

For me, the standard *Doctor Who* story is, the Tardis lands somewhere, the Doctor says to his companion, 'This is a charming little planet, let's go and have a look around, you go this way and I'll go that way,' and they get into terrible trouble. That's the basic format, and by and large, we liked to stick to that.

When those first scripts were in the pipeline, you weren't necessarily writing for Jon Pertwee's Doctor, were you?

There were some scripts that perhaps had been written for Patrick, or written when people weren't sure who the new Doctor was going to be. But I think we knew fairly early on that Jon was going to do it, and I would try and guide the scripts in the direction of Jon's character.

How did Robert Holmes come to write the first Pertwee script, 'Spearhead from Space'?

We'd already done one show together, called 'The Krotons', which had a very inept monster that didn't really work, but that wasn't Bob's fault, that was the design department. I liked Bob and got on well with him. He was a good, funny writer and he became one of the stalwarts. Obviously if I hadn't got on with Bob on 'The Krotons', I wouldn't have asked him to do 'Spearhead from Space'. Bob was rather formidable, and people were somewhat frightened of him. He was a tall, gaunt, bony man, and I remember he was interviewed in the papers when he was working on *Who*, and somebody said he looked like Sherlock Holmes playing Dracula! He joined the army at sixteen, lying about his age, and became the youngest commissioned officer in the British army, and had a very good war record. When he came out, he was a journalist for a while, then he became a policeman for a few years, and then he went into script writing, so he was quite a character.

What was Jon Pertwee like to write for as your leading man?

The thing about Jon was that his 'formidableness' was an act. It was a good act and it convinced most people, but all actors are children. They're not proper grown-ups, otherwise they wouldn't be actors, and they are riddled with insecurity, so they require constant praise and reassurance. Whenever Jon got to read a script which I'd worked on and knew was pretty solid, when we got to the rehearsal stage, you'd get notes from the director saying, 'Jon isn't happy with the script,' and I'd say, 'Jon is never happy with the script!' I'd spend ages with him talking it through, and making little changes here and there to let him feel that he was making a contribution. I'd also convince him that some things he didn't think would work *would* work; this was a good line, and he really could say it, so he just required nurse-maiding through it, which may not be what you were expecting to hear.

Would Jon come to you and Barry with ideas?

I think he came to us at least once with a script idea, or wanted to do a script, and we gently dissuaded him. I said to Barry, 'We can't have the inmates running the asylum; it's never going to work!' so I was against it on principle.

Why did you keep a relatively small stable of writers working with you during your tenure on the series?

When you get good people, you tend to stick with them. That's one of the things that makes it hard for newcomers, because people have their teams, the people that they like and trust. I think you'll find that with *Star Trek* or almost any show. You also see it with directors, who will tend to work with a 'rep company' of actors; people they'll cast again and again. We certainly had a rep company of writers, who we knew would come up with good scripts and who we could trust. So we would tend to go back to them, although occasionally newcomers like Bob and Dave would manage to get in by some kind of fluke. It's a question of time. If you're rushed off your feet all season, and if you get in a new writer, you have to give him a lot more time than you would an experienced one. And so you're reluctant to do that, unfortunately. In the early days, I gave Bob and Dave a great deal of time, and made a lot of changes, or got them to make a lot of changes. They hated me for it, but they did get their scripts on the screen.

As a script editor, was the ideal situation to basically parcel out a bunch of assignments and have your writers working on them simultaneously?

Well, semi-simultaneously, but they would be delivered in order. In the middle of the season, you'll be working on the show that's going through rehearsal and occasionally being summoned for some crisis; the show behind that will be in script form and you're practically doing the second draft; there's a storyline coming in for the third script so you have to work on that; and then the one behind that is maybe in the idea stage. So they're all at different stages simultaneously.

For Jon Pertwee's second season, you and Barry introduced a regular nemesis for the Doctor, in the form of the Master, a renegade Time Lord played by Roger Delgado. Was it a problem, essentially having the same villain each week?

Yes, we had Roger in every story in his first season, but there was a law of diminishing returns. If we kept having these mysterious and murky goings on and then, who is behind it all, "Good heavens, it's the Master!" then by the fourth or fifth story, you start saying, "Of course, it's the Master, who else?" and that's when you start getting a bit predictable. The way we eventually found the Master worked best was to keep him up our sleeves, so to speak. We'd do two or three shows without him, and then bring him in suddenly. It's rather like the Daleks. When they originally became the smash hit of the show back in the 1960s, every other story became a Dalek story. But if you play those cards too often, you devalue them.

Was it an unwritten rule on the series that, at some point, every script editor would get stuck having to do a Dalek story?

No, that's nonsense. We did that once with Louis Marks's 'Day of the Daleks'[*]. Louis had a story in progress, which was about guerrillas from the future coming back to change their past, and at that stage, they were oppressed by some evil alien race, but we didn't quite know who. We both felt that it lacked something, that it wasn't quite working, and also, it was going to be the first story of the season, and we always felt that the first story needed some kind of gimmick. We hadn't done a Dalek story for some considerable time, so one of us, and I honestly can't remember who got the bright idea, said, 'Let's make it a Dalek story.' That was fairly easily done, because as I said, in the future, Earth had been invaded by some evil alien race, and we just made it the Daleks. I don't think people dreaded doing a Dalek story, but the thing is, they mostly weren't allowed to, because the rights were held by [their creator] Terry Nation. So for a long time, he was the only one who would do them. You would have to get the rights from Terry, because when a writer creates a monster, he owns the copyright to it, and you can't use it without his permission.

The trouble was, we didn't remember to do that with 'Day of the Daleks'! We just put the Daleks into the story, and then we got a call from Terry's agent saying, 'I hear you're using Daleks, and you can't do that.' By that time, we were well into production, so we arranged a meeting to talk about it. Terry was charming about it all and said, 'Of course you should have asked me,' and we said we were sorry, we didn't

---

TERRY NATION

Perhaps no one was more surprised than Terry Nation (then best known as a comedy writer) when the menacing Daleks suddenly became a major part of British popular culture in 1963. *Doctor Who* was still in its infancy when Nation's metal monsters quickly caught the public's attention, giving the series a much-needed jolt of publicity. The Daleks exterminated their way through over a dozen *Doctor Who* stories during the next three decades, as countless items of Dalek-related merchandise sold around the world. *Survivors* (1975-77) grew out of Nation's fascination with the idea of mankind starting over without modern technology. The series begins with a deadly virus wiping out ninety-five per cent of the world's population, forcing small groups of survivors to band together in mutual co-operation. Today, the show seems even more timely than it did in 1975. *Blake's 7* first began taking shape when Nation pitched an idea for 'The Dirty Dozen in Space' to the BBC. When they responded by immediately commissioning thirteen episodes, the writer found himself with a brand new series to develop, and fast. In the end, *Blake's 7* ran for four seasons (1978-81), and the final episode's climactic shootout is still one of the most unforgettable endings of any genre series, ever. Terry Nation died in 1997.

---

[*] *Which opened season nine, Jon Pertwee's third year as the Doctor.*

think. Then he said, 'I'd like to have a look at the scripts, to make sure they don't do anything I am not happy about.' And *then* he said, 'If you're thinking about doing another Dalek story next season, I will be happy to write it for you...' and we said, 'What a good idea, Terry!' So on that basis, we were able to get away with it[*]. Terry was a very charming and amiable chap, and he was very fertile with ideas. He came up with *Blake's 7* and *Survivors*; he created several good series.

Robert Holmes, one of your 'regular' writers on *Doctor Who*, ended up replacing you as the show's script editor. How did that come about?

I left *Who* in 1974 when Jon and Barry left, and went back to freelancing and mostly writing those innumerable *Doctor Who* novelisations. When we announced that we were all going, I think Barry knew who was going to replace him, but he said, 'There's still the question of a new script editor, or do you want to stay on?', but I didn't. Having worked with Barry and Jon Pertwee for five or six years, I would have felt like a relic, and I thought they'd better have a new team. So I said, 'What about Bob?' and he was really the first and only candidate. We took him out to lunch, and he actually said, 'I hear you're leaving; what about my becoming the script editor?' We said, 'Well, it's a funny thing, that's what we were about to ask you!' so it just happened like that.

After you left *Doctor Who* as script editor, how keen were you to come back as a writer?

I was very fond of the show, and it was a relief not to have full responsibility for all the scripts, as it were. Over the years, every now and again, they would come back and ask me to write one. It was mostly, I'd like to think, when they got in trouble and needed somebody reliable and quick in a crisis. So I did a handful of stories after that, culminating in 'The Five Doctors'. I always enjoyed doing it.

Do you consider 'The Five Doctors', the twentieth anniversary special which had a rather fraught pre-production process, a good example of being quick in a crisis?

That's the sort of thing I'm good at, if I say so myself. That kind of thing doesn't throw me, I can handle it. There were many last-minute changes, but these were mostly for technical and practical reasons. They weren't just somebody's whim, which I would get stroppy about. It was simply that they couldn't get so-and-so, or they couldn't afford this or that. They were technical reasons, and as an ex-script editor, I understood them, so it wasn't a problem for me.

At what point did you begin writing the *Doctor Who* novelisations?

Before I left, the books were beginning to take off. I wrote the first few in the evenings and weekends while I was still script editing. In the early days, there was only a handful

---

[*] *Nation went on to write 'Planet of the Daleks' and 'Death to the Daleks' during Jon Pertwee's era, and 'Genesis of the Daleks' and 'Destiny of the Daleks' for his successor, Tom Baker.*

of us doing them, but the money wasn't particularly good, and script writers don't like writing books, because it's too much like hard work. It's also too solitary. So gradually, the other people dropped out, and I ended up doing most of them. And then of course — and this is another bit of luck — they started selling the TV series to America. They got enough shows together in colour, mostly the Tom Baker stories, so the books started selling in England *and* in America, and it all became very lucrative for a while. As they became bestsellers, more of the original scriptwriters insisted on doing their own, so it was like the process was reversed. First there was a handful of people, then it was all me, and then other people started doing them again, which is fair enough.

What was the process involved in adapting a *Who* script into book form?

It's a technical process, in that a script gives you what people say and what they do. It doesn't give you what they think and what they feel, and what the atmosphere is, because those things are created by costume, design, makeup and direction, so you have to do all those things when you're writing the prose. It's not easy. I always get very stroppy when people think it's a piece of cake, because it's not. It's a technical skill to do a good adaptation, so by the time you've done thirty or forty or fifty, you're getting pretty used to it.

In 1973, you and Barry Letts created *Moonbase 3*, a gritty series about a multi-national colony on the moon in 2003. How did that come about?

We were offered the opportunity, because we'd done so well on *Who*. I think *Star Trek* was beginning to air in England, and the BBC wanted their own, British SF series, so we were given this unprecedented opportunity to create our own SF show — and blew it big time. We decided to go for grim realism, which was not what the public wanted. They were good shows, but they were never popular, and we only did six. We should have done what Terry Nation did with *Blake's 7* later on. He looked at *Star Trek*, and turned it around. On *Trek*, the *Enterprise* is a Starfleet ship, representing authority, and they run into the bad guys. In *Blake's 7*, the authority is the bad guys, and the guys on the starship are the rebels. It is a terrific reversal, and it worked very well.

Do you think part of the problem with *Moonbase 3* was that it was produced before the *Star Wars* SF boom of the late 70s?

We were doing it in the style of earnest BBC drama, and it just wasn't entertaining enough. It wasn't what people want from SF, so it sank without a trace. It had a minor revival, though. There's a *Doctor Who* archivist who goes around looking for old shows and he phoned me up one day, years afterward, saying, 'Wonderful news!' I was thinking *Who* was coming back or something like that, but he said, 'We found a complete set of *Moonbase 3* in the BBC archives!' I said, 'Oh God, you haven't!' and there was this rather hurt silence from the other end. They later came out on video, and I think they did quite well in a cult way.

Moonbase 3 wasn't the last time you worked with Barry Letts, though. Your friendship led to you bringing in Barry as a director when you became producer of the BBC classics serials some years later, didn't it?

There again, it's what you know *and* who you know. Barry basically wanted to direct not produce, because directing is more of a fun job while producing is more hard work, but he was always being brought in as a producer. He was eventually made producer of the classics serials, with a fairly old BBC script editor who was on the verge of retirement. When this guy did retire, Barry and I were still meeting socially, having lunch once a week, and he said, 'Would you like to take over as script editor?' That was not only because we were friends, but also because we'd worked well together on *Who*. When Barry was going to leave the classics serials, because he got fed up with producing and wanted to go back to directing, he said to me, 'Look, you're obviously the next person in line for the producing job. Do you want me to recommend you, because I'm talking about my successor now with Jonathan Powell, the head of department?' I said, 'My God no, the last thing I want to do is be a producer and handle all that sort of authority and budgets!' but, for some reason or other, Jonathan Powell took me out to lunch and offered me the job. And for some reason or other, I found myself accepting it, so that's how it came about. There are always unexpected things, but it goes back to Mark Twain's line, which is actually very profound, although it sounds flip: 'The harder I work, the luckier I get.' You've got to be alert for opportunities, and you've got to be able to take advantage of them when they come.

THE ULTIMATE ADVENTURE

One of the more unusual additions to the Time Lord mythology was *Doctor Who: The Ultimate Adventure*, a light-hearted theatrical romp (with songs!) that reunited Dicks with the third doctor, Jon Pertwee, in 1989. 'Obviously if we had the money of *Starlight Express*,' reflects the writer, 'we could have done it even more successfully, but within the budget we had, I think they did quite a good job. There were some very good laser FX for instance, that were quite spectacular, and I was very pleased with them.' When Pertwee later decided to leave the production, Colin Baker stepped in, reprising his role as the acerbic sixth Doctor. 'When we were changing it over, I had some meetings with him, and we discussed "Colin Bakerising" the play. The action was basically the same, but the style of humour was slightly different. My overall impression is the production did moderately well but wasn't really a smash. I think the reason is because it was about ten to fifteen years too late! It should have been done back when Jon was playing the Doctor on television, and it was a cult show that everybody watched on Saturday evenings.'

After you'd produced the classic serials, were you keen to get out of television for a while?

I wasn't keen to, it's just the way that things went. If something had come up that was interesting, I probably would have taken it, but at that time, nothing did, so I quite happily went back to writing books with the occasional bit of television. I've been doing books for ages now, and that's a more tranquil kind of life, really.

What made you decide to get involved with some of the fan-made *Doctor Who* spin-off videos, such as *Shakedown* and the *Mindgame* trilogy?

By the 1990s, some of the people who grew up reading my *Doctor Who* books had got into the business on some level or another. I was quite unaware of it, but there's a straight-to-video market, in which you make a video, and while you'd like it to be shown on television, you can get your money back through video sales in the stores, providing the budget is modest. Some people who were doing these things contacted me and asked me to write a script, so I did a couple. It obviously helped them a little bit, because they're less experienced and their budgets are very low, and I was able to work with them and keep it down to a reasonable level. Because I'd been both a producer and a script editor by that time, I understood television pretty well, so I didn't turn in anything they wouldn't be able to afford to do. I think the first, *Shakedown*[*], is pretty good. Considering the time and money they had, it's *amazingly* good, and they did make a modest profit on it, so more power to them.

How did you break into the children's book market?

Again, that was market forces, and who you know. Brenda Gardner had been one of my editors on the *Doctor Who* books, and she started her own publishing firm, called Piccadilly Press, and asked me to work for them, so there was a fairly steady stream of work. I have a great tendency to go with the flow. I just do whatever turns up, and what turned up was that!

That's now become a major part of your work, hasn't it?

That's right, plus there are the original *Doctor Who* novels, which were started by Virgin, but are now published by BBC Books. I'm writing one of those at the moment, and I've got another book to do for Brenda after that, which pretty much sees out this year. That's about as much as you can hope for in this business. After that, we'll see.

Have you pretty much moved away from TV at this point in your career?

I don't write much of the kind of television that's on right now. As I said, I started on *Crossroads*, and professionally, it would have been a lot more lucrative if I'd stayed in soap operas, because our schedules in England are now knee-deep in them; there's

---

[*] *A tense, claustrophobic drama featuring one of* Doctor Who*'s most popular alien adversaries, the Sontarans.*

almost nothing else on. Everything is dumbing-down. It's following the American pattern of things getting simpler, and more straightforward, and understandable to anybody, and I think the BBC's standards have slipped very badly. What we've got now are these 'reality' shows like *Big Brother*, which I hate, and I hate soap operas, so I'm really the odd man out these days. The only things that get anywhere today are soap operas and reality shows, and it's a great shame.

Are you happier being a successful author?

Sometimes you miss the relationships with other people, and the fun and excitement of television. It's a more stimulating life; television is collaborative, you're always working with other people and taking them into account, and either getting on with them or not getting on, but it's a team effort. With writing, although you have a one-to-one relationship with your editor, it's far more solitary. That suits me, because I'm a straight-down-the-line split between extrovert and introvert, so my introverted side gets on quite well with that. The most recent television-related thing I did was with *Who*. They're putting out a second edition of 'The Five Doctors' DVD, and they got [Doctor number five] Peter Davison and me in together to do a commentary. I don't have a DVD player, because I haven't caught up with the technology yet, but they had Peter and I talking it through, and I thought that was great. I always enjoy talking about *Who*, because it's been such a big part of my life. ▌

PAUL DONOVAN

t's not often that the producer of a successful genre series decides to quit while he's ahead. Tell that to Paul Donovan, who plans to end *Lexx* at the end of season four, just when it's beginning to pick up some critical attention. Canadian-born Donovan went to film school in England, and began his career writing and directing what he admits were 'two-bit Canadian films', before winning Best Director at the Geminis (the Canadian equivalent of the Oscars) for his TV movie *Life with Billy*. But then came *Lexx*, best described as the bastard child of *Star Trek*, or *Farscape*'s evil twin. It's lewd and crude and subversive and strange, but most of all, it's fun. That's more than you can say about many genre shows (names withheld to protect the pretentious) that approach their subject matter with a solemnity usually reserved for reading Tolstoy. For the uninitiated, *Lexx* is the story of Stanley Tweedle, an inept security guard, who unwittingly becomes captain of a planet-destroying sentient spaceship, the *Lexx*. Along the way, he teams up with Xev, a sexy combination of love slave and cluster lizard; Kai, a centuries-old, reanimated assassin; and 790, a lovesick robot head (don't ask!). Aboard the *Lexx*, this bizarre foursome travel around the two universes, leaving a trail of vaporised planets behind them. This interview was conducted during the final weeks of production on season four. While Donovan was still reluctant to say how the series would end, his only hint was, '*Lexx* does Earth like *Debbie Does Dallas*!' A scary thought indeed...

Were you originally more interested in becoming a writer, or a director?

That's a complicated question. The way our system works in Canada, you don't become a director unless you're a producer, so you have to be a producer to become a director. It's not a mature system as I look at it, but I think my ego is too big to direct other people's stuff!

Growing up in Canada, I didn't have any particular knowledge or awareness of the film business. It wasn't part of my cultural programming to work in the film business, and there were no role models around. I finished university with no plan, so I decided to go to film school in the UK a short time after that, because it sounded fun. That was the first time it dawned on me that there might be something that I could seriously pursue. So I really committed to staying in the business, probably from the first day I set foot in film school, and then stuck with it, sometimes in a very low-budget way.

Were you more interested in film or television?

I was only interested in film. Television just seemed like a low occupation; I still consider it a low occupation! The problem I had with television was that everything was very generic. Every show had to appeal to the grannies and the eight year-olds at the same time, so there was very little speciality television, or very little interesting television. There was some good television, but it had to be generic by definition, whereas in movies, you had things like *Dr. Strangelove* or *Dark Star*; lots of small, interesting movies that seemed to offer better opportunities for a creative flight.

Did you have any particular influences either as a writer or director?

During the time I went to university, I started seeing movies that were completely different from what I was aware of prior to that, when I would only get to see the mass-market things. I remember seeing *Fires on the Plain*, which was a Japanese World War Two movie, and I realised that there were other things out there, so that was very exciting. I probably saw *Dr. Strangelove* about that time, and once I went to film school, there was a constant stream of interesting films being presented to us.

Have you found that your sensibilities are a bit off-centre from the mainstream?

That's sort of true. I can't do a sitcom because I don't like them, and I think you have to like them to do them successfully. There are some things that I like, that seem to work on a mainstream basis, like *RoboCop*, which was a good film which I would have been proud to do, or *Alien*. They're very mainstream, but they appealed to me at the same time. So professionally I've been trying to find projects that appeal to me, because a lot of things don't, while at the same time be able to put bread on the table.

So how did *Lexx* first come up?

I've had a sort of half-interest in SF for a while. I watched *Star Trek* when I was a kid,

PAUL DONOVAN

Date/Place of Birth:
1954, Nova Scotia, Canada

Home Base:
Halifax, Nova Scotia, Canada

Education:
Dalhousie University; London International Film School

First TV Work:
Life with Billy (TV movie)

TV Career Highlights:
Life with Billy, Lexx

and it was exciting, because it had a creative format. I like things that have fantasy worlds, as long as they're well developed. I've never been a huge SF fan, but I thought there was an opportunity in that genre. I know this is all going to sound a bit Machiavellian, but I was actually interested in doing a World War One film, but couldn't figure out any way to get the money. It would have been wildly expensive to do (and I still haven't done it), but I thought, okay, I can do it with computer animation, which was still more or less in its infancy five or six years ago. At the time, I'd done a bunch of two-bit Canadian films, which were very frustrating, and I didn't want to continue doing those. And television seemed to be exploding. More and more smaller, second tier TV networks were coming along, and at the same time, there was easy money available. So I thought, why not make a television show, in a genre that I'm kind of attracted to, using technology I'm interested in learning, feeding into a market that is all the second-tier channels around the world? The theory was that the smaller channels couldn't afford their own original programming individually, but if you string a bunch of them together, you can make something competitive.

What was the original concept behind *Lexx*?

There were things I had in mind very early on. I dusted off one concept I'd had for years, which was the evil twin of *Star Trek*. When I was a kid, I also liked *Lost in Space*, but the only thing I liked about it was Dr Smith, so it's sort of Dr Smith and characters from *Dark Star*, which is a movie that had an influence on me without a doubt. It's very amateurish, but had bold new concepts where suddenly you had these wonderful characters that just weren't likeable, and I thought that was really exciting.

Were you setting out to create characters that weren't necessarily heroic?

They were not so much in the standard mould. I have a problem, which a number of people who write our show also have. If I watch an old 1960s Vincent Price movie where he plays a bad guy, there's a hero trying to save the city or the castle, but I always start rooting for Vincent Price. You can't help it, because he's more interesting than the boring lead. So I often had a perverse reaction to the square-jawed good guy.

Who was the first character you developed?

I started with Stanley Tweedle the security guard. The idea of a security guard who's essentially a coward being in charge of the most destructive force in the two universes — that's fertile ground for comedy and drama.

You didn't really give Stanley a lot of positive characteristics, did you?

He's always had a moral compass; he just doesn't follow it all the time! There was a big study the British army did after World War One because their troops often behaved in a cowardly way in battle. They couldn't understand why, particularly when Australian troops behaved much more heroically. In World War One they cranked up their firing squads to shoot deserters and they really worked on patriotism, but when the enemy was pouring into the trenches, that seemed to fall by the wayside. What they found about the Australians, for whom it didn't fall by the wayside, was that they didn't want to let their buddies down. The units were very close and played sports together and partied together, and to me, that's a little bit how Stanley Tweedle is. He doesn't see himself as a hero, but when push comes to shove, when it really comes to the bitter end, when he has the choice between letting his mates die or having to reluctantly act heroically, he will. At every point up to that moment, he will claim that he will *not* act heroically and don't expect him to, but in the end, he does. So his rhetoric and his reality have always been slightly different. At all other times, he acts out of self-interest, which just makes him a normal person.

Other than Kai, these characters don't have much history, do they?

Zev[*] is a fantasy girl, and that's basically it. When I watched shows like *Star Trek*, like Stanley Tweedle, I'd rather watch a show with cute girls, particularly fantasy cute girls as opposed to the people next door, who I can see any time. But if she's going to be cute, let's make her *totally* cute. Let's make it, by definition as part of the story, that she's a love slave with an accelerated libido and then just throw it on further and further. Her cuteness is a function of the story rather than just coincidental.

By starting out with Zev as fat and unattractive, did that insulate you against complaints of sexism, because when she becomes the cute love slave it's basically still the same person, isn't it?

We're not that inclined to defend that position because I just think, 'What would I like to watch on television?' I'm more inclined to put the remote control down when I see a cute girl on screen. I looked at a number of television shows at that time, and I was thinking, what are they doing? Didn't they learn anything from Hugh Hefner? I find it humorous that other filmmakers deny that they do this on purpose, but yes, every time we do a shower scene, there's a naked girl in it. That's what we do. It's gratuitous; all our shower scenes are gratuitous, but I don't have a problem with that. We're pandering! It's the same with Kai. He is a very cute guy, and he is a female fantasy and very much constructed as that. We chose Michael McManus to play Kai in part because I've worked with him before, but he's also suffered perversely in Canada. He'd be cast as a lawyer and the people in charge would say, 'No, he's too good looking to be a lawyer, he's not believable,' and I'm thinking, 'Are these people retarded?' They don't care, because their money doesn't come from ratings.

So was Michael McManus in your head as you were creating the character of Kai?

To a certain extent. He was a model, and I knew him and wanted to try it out, but until we had tested him doing the part, I wasn't one hundred per cent sure if he could

---

[*] *The character played by Eva Haberman was named Zev, but when the role was re-cast with Xenia Seeberg, she was renamed Xev. Everybody got that now?*

do it. He hadn't done anything like that before.

Kai's pretty much the only character with a fully developed back-story, isn't he?

He has a back-story, which kind of helps the mythology. The back-story is a big part of the character, but there's also a lot of mystery to him. I think what the male audience and the female audience look for in their dream characters are very different. It wasn't necessary for Xev, but it is necessary for Kai.

Why did you add 790 into the mix?

Simply because our three main characters are human and 790 is not. And having a character that behaves like Dr Smith is important too. I think 790 is a bit of a Dr Smith, because he's always causing trouble; for the basic ingredients of drama, you need different characters to lead the others in different directions. 790 is also the jester. You could argue he's like C-3PO or R2-D2, or perhaps the robot in *Lost in Space*, but the twisted, evil version of them.

Lexx actually began as a series of TV movies, but did you always see it as an ongoing series?

Our plan was always to make it a series. In the television business, the series is the pot of gold at the end of the rainbow, and that's basically it. I was a part owner of a production company, and getting a series going was critical to developing the company, so the four Movie of the Weeks were just a pilot for the series. The problem was, we put them on Showtime, a cable channel who weren't that interested in the series business, and I don't think they liked the four movies that much either. I think they considered our shows a failure. They didn't see what some people saw in them, and in a way, they weren't wrong. A lot of things went wrong in the movies, and we were just developing the concept, so the thing I was pitching to them was, 'Okay, we didn't get everything right, but that's what the prototype pilot is for; now let's get it right in the series.' They said, 'Not interested.' That could very well have been the end of that, but eventually we were able to finance it out of Germany, Canada and the UK, and after a while, it sold in the US, and now it's doing pretty much the best in the US.

But I think that's because television shows take several years to catch on. They don't ever seem to start off successfully. It goes back to this concept I have that every person lives in a world where they know a hundred people well — their aunts and uncles and cousins and neighbours and the people they work with — but you also 'know' Keanu Reeves and Ally McBeal. They're all part of your lives, but it takes time to get to know those people. Once you settle in with them, you visit them regularly, but it's a slow process. I also believe that one of the errors that's sometimes made in casting is when you take someone like Keanu Reeves and he plays a sensitive gay man, and the audience hates that, because they never pegged him as a sensitive gay man. They wanted him to be Keanu Reeves, the tough guy/rebel, so they stay away from that character because it's off-putting, and they wait for him to go back to being the tough guy. They don't want John Candy to be a leading man; they want him to be the funny guy who does everything wrong. Once the actor is on the screen for long enough, and if they have a charisma, that's it, they're downloaded into the brains of millions of people, and the actor's future is glued to the psyche of the planet.

How difficult was it to find the international co-partners to fund the series?

It was a nightmare. In the US, it's simpler, because you go to the networks or the key production companies (which are the studios or their offshoots) who decide to do it, and then they either pay for it or they don't. There's no middle ground. Whereas in the world that I live in, you get a Canadian network to agree to do it — well, now you've got ten per cent of the money! Two years later, you might have found seventy-five per cent of the money, so it's hard.

How did you end up getting German and British partners for this project?

If you make a Canadian/German co-production, mostly all you can hope to get in the UK is a buy from a UK network, and there are various pressures on them to buy British shows. But once you've made the show British as well, it also becomes Danish, French, whatever, because all the European Union countries are connected, and that makes it easier to sell in the various European countries. So there are pockets of money that you can get into by making it an official co-production. Some of it is tax benefits or whatever, but it gets ridiculously complicated, and the argument against that is that it takes away from the creative area. But if it's the only way you can finance the show, then that's what you have to do. The one thing we don't want to do is have to rely on real estate magnates who decide they want to become film producers.

From the outset, *Lexx* was envisaged as a very CGI-heavy series. Was it difficult to find companies that could handle the complicated visual FX at a reasonable price?

I didn't know much, but we had a slight advantage, because a lot of the key programs used for creating computer-generated imagery come out of Canada. So there were people around who were fairly familiar with them and were ahead of the curve, and I had access to them, but that's about it. We really didn't know what we were doing, so we were just figuring it out as we went along. There was no such thing as a television show that had 300 to 400 FX shots per hour! There was no example to follow, no methodology, so we pretty much developed that on our own. The look of the show has dramatically changed for the better. From the very beginning, we decided we were doing a CG-based show with live action characters, so we weren't going to go on location at all. We had no trucks or location lighting equipment, so we abandoned those things and pushed that entire budget into CG. If you have a location-based show, you drive around with all those trucks, and you don't have any money left over. So one or two FX shots on a show like that become a problem, because you don't have an FX director and co-ordinators and storyboard artists and all of those things. We have all that stuff, but we don't have truck drivers.

How extensive was the casting process for the *Lexx* TV movies?

Once again, coming from a small country, the pool of actors in Canada is probably one-twenty-fifth, or maybe one-fiftieth of the US so it's harder to cast. But if you can add in England, France, Germany, Sweden and Italy, it gets easier, and in a SF show, an accent is not going to be a problem. To me, it rings true if you encounter a space-ship, and one person has an Italian accent and another person has a British accent, but if they all have Italian accents, it begins to get odd. We've had a few problems with that ourselves. Fortunately, Canadians are fake Americans, and the accent that a Canadian actor will have is acceptable to both Americans and an international audience because they're used to it.

Who did you cast first?

Brian Downey as Stanley. I'd worked with Brian previously on a couple of things, and I knew he had the charisma to carry a series. He was a guy who was doing travelling theatre on a small-scale level, mostly in Newfoundland, and a few bit parts in television, but he wasn't cast in any big shows. I'd seen him in one weird little movie made in Newfoundland, and within three seconds of seeing him, I thought, 'He's got the juice!' Showtime's approval was required, and that was a rigorous process, because I couldn't cast *anybody* without it — although we'd shown them tapes of Brian, so they were in from the beginning. I really didn't want to cast anyone without their approval anyway, because they should reasonably be a check. If Showtime didn't like someone, then I'd have to wonder why, and as they had no particular prejudices in terms of casting, they could filter out any biases that I might have. Michael was one of many people I auditioned for Kai, and I favoured him, but Showtime made the ultimate choice and they were happy with him.

What about Eva Haberman, who played Zev?

We cast her out of Germany. We auditioned there, and she showed up in the audition. She appeared in the movies, and we would have used her in the series, but we didn't get the money in time. When we phoned Eva and said, 'Okay, we've got the series,' she'd already accepted another part, so we had to re-cast, and were very happy to find Xenia [Seeberg].

How did Jeffrey Hirschfield, one of your writer/producers on the show, end up doing the voice for 790?

He just does it well. I don't think it was the original plan, but we used to talk through our ideas for the characters, and Jeff would do the voice. We finally said, 'Look, nobody is going to do it any better. No one is as twisted and evil as you are, so you should do it!' So he did, and that acidic wit really comes through.

Did you, Jeff and Lex Gigeroff basically write the movies together as a group?

Yes, and it's still mostly myself, Jeff and Lex doing the series now. What tends to happen is I'm king of plot, and then together with Jeff or with Lex, I'll work up an outline that gets approved by the network. Jeff will then do a first draft, and I'll often rewrite that, and we may rewrite that again. But most of the outlines start on my desk, after lots of beer and discussions. We'll often throw around ideas together. For example, one of the shows we were recently talking about doing was called 'Viva Lexx Vegas'. I don't think we're going to do that one anymore, but images start popping up and you say, 'Wouldn't it be nice if we could do this or that?' We start putting together four or five ideas, and I'll take those ideas and work them up into a plot. There's quite a lot of back and forth with various people over a four- or five-page outline, with them expressing opinions and then going off to the Sci-Fi Channel [which now broadcasts the show in the US], and them inputting and criticising. Sometimes we throw outlines out; we'll say, 'We'd love to do this, but it's not going to happen, because it would take too many days, or there are too many guest stars or whatever.' It is a TV series, and we're hampered by the normal restrictions of television, which is you've got to shoot it in seven days, plus there's the peculiar restrictions that we have. We have broken one of those restrictions now actually; I said earlier that we couldn't go on location, but in the third season, we created the concept of having a second unit that goes out on location and just shoots the background, that we then plant the actors in. Sometimes we just go off with three or four people: two actors, a cameraman and a hair or make-up person and pick up a couple of people locally, and we can put the actors in fantastic locations for very little cost. This year for instance, we've been to England, Washington DC, Florida, Texas, Arizona, Newfoundland, various locations around Nova Scotia that are meant to be Idaho, and Iceland! We're also going to Vietnam, or somewhere in Northeast Asia anyway, maybe Thailand, and then to Japan.

Looking back at the first four *Lexx* movies, how do you feel they worked?

I thought they were a bit of a mess. We blew our FX budget by the end of the first show and we still had three more to go, so we were in a scramble and really had to short-change a lot of FX for the subsequent shows, so some things didn't make sense. Some of the FX were cheap looking, and I also felt at the end of it that we should only have done one two-hour. The rest of them should have been one-hour shows, because they just didn't hold together for two hours.

How did you then go about selling an ongoing series?

Our foreign sales were spectacular, so, weirdly, Showtime triggered the whole thing. It wouldn't have happened but for their original involvement. Once they got involved and we did the four Movie of the Weeks, we did very well selling the product, and that allowed us to make the series. But by then Showtime was no longer interested. After a lot of visits and cajoling and travelling and sales conventions, we were finally able to put together enough money to do twenty episodes. Critical to that was making it a German co-production, because there's always one place that has crazy money, and at that time, it was Germany. There was some weird tax scheme where people would put money in films and they thought they could make money on their taxes, and we were able to benefit from that. The next year, it was England that had financial incentives for productions there, so we would run around with the crowd, including half of Hollywood, trying to cash in on those things.

Was it difficult for the three of you, writing virtually every episode for the second season*?

I think it shows after a while. Once you get two-thirds of the way into the season, they start to get flabby. What we did this season, where we're doing twenty-four episodes, is we have a two and a half month hiatus, a 'school vacation' between shows eighteen and nineteen, allowing us to catch our breath. We did talk about bringing in other writers, but we couldn't find anyone who worked out for us, and then suddenly we were over budget, and there was no money left to find other people, so you just make do.

By the time you started writing season two, was there a long-term story arc planned for the series?

We didn't know exactly how we were going to get there, but on a very basic level, I'd always hoped that we would do sixty-five hours, and the last season would be on the Earth, and then we'd have an end related to the Earth. I was hoping all those things would come to pass, and most of them have, but we've been modifying our plans as we went along too, so it's not exactly as we originally planned.

How did the casting of Xenia Seeberg change the dynamics of the show?

We couldn't believe it when we saw her first tape, because the shocking thing was that the German casting person who presented it to us had showed us a lot of people by that stage, and we were really depressed about it. To be quite frank, we were saying, 'You could go into any bar in Berlin and there are fifteen girls way cuter than the ones you're showing us, and our character is supposed to be a love slave fantasy!' It seemed like for 'serious' actors, people who went to acting school, the acting school seemed to filter out modelly babe-looking types as being not serious. Finally, after a lot of moaning from us, they said, 'Well, there is one person; you're not going to want her, but we'll show you the tape.' They showed us this tape that Xenia had done, which was a really cool movie called *Hilda Humphrey*, and we said, 'That's it!' They couldn't

---

* Lexx *purists consider the four TV movies to be 'season one'.*

believe that we wanted her, and they said, 'But look at her, she's so extreme. She's got large breasts and a thin waist and big eyes; she's like a caricature of a woman!' And we said, 'Is that a problem? That's what we've been asking for, someone who's larger than life.' Xenia has a larger than life quality; she's like a manga character come to life.

So, she had all those attributes that we could see, but a series is like a marriage; we had to know that we could work with her as a person. Many series are horrible personal experiences for all involved, because of conflicts between the producer or the actors or the director, so we would have sacrificed working with her if she had turned out to be an asshole. Life is too short. So she was flying back from Kansas City to Düsseldorf, and I flew down to New York to meet with her and spend a little time together. We had to change terminals, and deal with a bunch of practical things, like luggage, and she dealt with them on a very humble basis, and I thought, we can work with her. She's a real person.

Are you able to look back at season two and determine which scripts worked, and which didn't work?

That's easy. I like the shows that either pushed the envelope, like 'Brigadoom', which we did as a musical, or '791', where we had a heterosexual robot head on a gay body and an *Alien* kind of plot. Those things appeal to me a lot, whereas we did shows like 'White Trash' that just didn't work. There are some shows later in the season like 'Woz' and 'Patches in the Sky' where I felt we were producing too many scripts too quickly and were becoming dry. And then there were shows like 'Norb' which was a very straight-ahead thriller, and those kind of worked. In a way, they were easy to do, but they're not as satisfying as doing something crazy like 'Brigadoom'. We did 'Lafftrak', the show with the planet made up of TV shows, which is not a very successful episode and didn't all come together because of a number of problems, but the concept was interesting. So that's more satisfying than a show like 'Norb' that worked, but the concept wasn't as interesting. And then you had 'Brigadoom' and '791', which worked *and* were interesting concepts.

Can you start out with a great script, but various outside factors conspire against it?

We'll often start out with a good script but if we get a bad first cut, which is often the fault of the director, or there's mis-casting involved, we'll have to change it in the edit. Once in a while, there's a show that's a mess and in the end, it's the composer who makes it work, or the guest star who we didn't have that much faith in made it great. 'Lyekka' was like that. It was a complete mess, but in the end, it was a really good show, because two of the guest stars were fantastic. The composer did a really good job too, and we sort of patched it together in the editing room, but when I saw the first cut of it, I was thoroughly depressed.

What made you construct season three as the thirteen-part serialised story, 'Fire and Ice'?

We felt it might work better creatively, and visually in terms of computer animation, and that we could do a fine job if we really built the two worlds where the story's set and amortised the cost of doing that over the entire season. Whereas with some of the shows in the second season, we'd try and create all-new visual elements for just one show, and then throw them away, so we did them poorly. Also, our series has always been on the edge of survival, barely getting from one season to the next, so we thought maybe it would break out better if we tried the serial concept, because a lot of shows have done that and been very popular.

It also allowed you the opportunity to bring back a lot of characters from the show's history, didn't it?

Yes, and we continue to do that. Part of that is strictly pragmatic. We shoot in a ridiculously stupid place, which is Halifax, Nova Scotia, where we have an acting community of about 112 people, and there are twelve that we like, so we re-use the twelve people as much as we can. I also think people like to see the same faces again on television, and since we always kill our characters off, they can't come back and

MUSICAL EPISODES

Anyone who thinks SF and musicals are a viable combination has probably never heard William Shatner's unique recording of 'Lucy in the Sky with Diamonds'. Still, there have been a few successful forays into musicals on genre shows. *Xena: Warrior Princess* produced the lavishly staged musical episode 'The Bitter Suite', hiring lyricists to write original material, and a choreographer to stage the major set pieces. 'I understand the process was arduous, intensive and difficult,' notes Melissa Good, who wrote the never-produced musical 'Last Chance' for *Xena's* final season. 'All the songs and lyrics were custom-designed, rather than using existing music, which is what they did after that.' *Lexx's* musical episode, 'Brigadoom', came from an idea that Paul Donovan had after listening to traditional German children's songs. 'I could hear a relationship between them and the melodies of the great American musicals,' he explains. 'So we took a series of German children's songs and took the melodies from them very consciously, not changed or developed, to create the melodies for our musical.' And with Joss Whedon getting in on the act, writing all the songs himself for 'Once More with Feeling', a musical episode of *Buffy*, it appears that SF, fantasy and song do work well together after all.

revisit us as the same person very easily. So we just created a rationalisation that in the universe, because there are only so many models of human beings, there can be exact duplicates of different planets with the same character. In those thirteen episodes, since we were in the afterlife the whole time, we could have the same people coming back, and then since they all wound up on Earth in season four, we could have the same people again!

Do you feel season three worked as a whole?

Once again, we fell down in the late middle with the scripts, but I was still reasonably pleased with it. I believe we created a set of worlds that had some coherency and were kind of interesting. And then there was the fun part, the big revelation at the end that this was actually Heaven and Hell, but you couldn't know that from the beginning.

When you finished season three, were things going better for *Lexx*?

A lot of people argued that this show would never work in the US. I think that was the view of Showtime who said, 'It's too weird.' They said there were lots of people in England who watch weird stuff, but Americans don't want stuff like that. I said, 'Well, explain *RoboCop* or *The Simpsons* or *The Beverly Hillbillies*.' They said, 'Well maybe, but you can't get a network to see it as anything other than a show that is too weird for a US audience.' I certainly don't agree with that view. I think there are plenty of people in the US who want to watch more than sitcoms. So getting on in the US was critical in terms of *Lexx*'s survival, and also it is very satisfying that it's proven to be the case that people there do seem to want to watch the show.

Does the Sci-Fi Channel pretty much leave you alone on a creative level?

When the Sci-Fi Channel first bought it, they didn't think it was going to work. There was very little enthusiasm, and it took a long time and essentially a change of management to get over that. When the new management came in, [vice president] Bonnie Hammer looked at it and said, 'At that price! Sure, we'll give it a shot.' From time to time, they'll buy something that is so cheap, how could they not buy it? So we fell into that category, and then it worked, so they said, 'Do more, don't change the concept.' They never wanted to rework it into something that it wasn't. This season, which they've had considerable participation in, they haven't been changing it.

Do you have to do a different edit of the show for the US market?

Basically, every episode is slightly different. You can safely assume if there's a shower scene, there's more in the European version or on the DVD than on the American TV version. Once again, the Sci-Fi Channel didn't have any problem with any of the content we're doing. What they said was, 'Look, if you show a naked woman in the shower, we cross Standards and Practices regulations, and there are advertisers who will face pressure from various consumer groups to withdraw their adverts, so we can't do it; we'd love to but we can't.' For instance, we did one show this season called 'Fluff Daddy'. I don't know if you know what a 'fluffer' is, but we're pushing things with that show, and we had to make quite a few edits. A fluffer is a person who works in the porno business and gets the male star 'ready for their close-up', if you know what I'm saying. In 'Fluff Daddy' Stanley gets a job as a fluffer, so there were quite a few scenes we had to trim...

Did you know from the beginning of season four that this was going to wrap up the story, and be the end of the show?

That's absolutely the plan. I'm personally committed to not doing any more; that's the psychological position I've put myself in. If the show suddenly takes off in the ratings, I'll get some pressure, but I'd rather the show ended. None of the actors' contracts extend beyond this season, and I would argue with the network, that if they wanted to do more, we should do a spin-off and create a new series.

Is that something you're interested in doing?

I'm prepared to assist on it, but there are other things I want to do. But another idea that was floated by the network was they asked, 'Are you interested in doing some whiz-bang Movie of the Week type of thing, like a prequel or something?' I thought that could be an interesting concept.

Do you want to abandon the *Lexx* universe, or just this particular story?

No, I'm interested in abandoning the *Lexx* universe. There are other stories that I'm dying to work on and I'd like to get started.

How happy are you with season four?

There are still some weak episodes. We managed to fix some things, and our quality of FX is the highest ever; our whole visual look is the best ever. We've developed a new approach to how we shoot; we shoot on a mixture of 24P, which is a new type of high definition film that was developed, and standard 35-millimetre. We shoot with 24P in the studio and 35-millimetre for exteriors, because 24 is a little hard to control in the exteriors, and there I really don't like the look — we've done it twice and now we've pulled back on it. But the 24P in the studio, under controlled conditions, particularly *vis-à-vis* the FX, is fantastic. Even 35-millimetre film bounces around in a camera, so it can be a problem adding CGI.

At this point, is there a feeling of relief as the end draws near?

Absolutely. I've lived this show for probably going on six years, so it's time to move on. I can't reveal much about the end of the season at this point. The basic thing I can say without any trouble, is that in a typical television series, when they finish shooting the last season, they don't know if they're doing any more, so they just end with a whimper. It's rare that a television series is able to wrap itself up neat and tidily. Our view is, it's the end, we are wrapping up the story, and we're wrapping it up in a story that will make sense all the way back to the first episode.

Have you pretty much had your fill of the SF genre at this point?

I don't know. The problem is, I've ended up very skilled at putting thousands of FX into a television show — and that's seen as an SF thing. So I could work in SF and use this very specialised skill, that other people would have to spend the same six years as me figuring out how to do. I enjoy creating very intense visual imagery, and on a television basis, we often look at something and say, 'Boy, if we could spend two weeks on this one-minute scene, it would look so different, but we can only spend two days on it.' I'd like to spend that two weeks once in a while.

Has this show opened any doors for you as a writer or producer?

I think so, but I don't know yet. I'm sure it will open doors on the CG side. I could probably answer that question a lot better a year from now, because I've had no time

EARTH-BOUND SATIRE

Lexx has never been afraid of using satire as a component of its stories, but with much of season four being set on Earth, Paul Donovan and his writing team were able to find targets a lot closer to home. Politics were an easy mark, thanks to an ineffectual and philandering American president, whose actions are dictated by Prince (played by Nigel Bennett), in charge of Washington's Bureau of Alcohol, Tobacco and Firearms. There's even an assassination scene set in Dallas, albeit with a very different resolution. The writers' barbs were also directed towards broader targets, such as women's prison movies ('P4X', which guest starred *Red Dwarf's* Craig Charles and Hattie Hayridge), the horror genre ('Walpurgis Night,' 'Vlad') and even porno movies ('Fluff Daddy,' featuring the production of a porn epic called *Deep Space 69*!) 'We're not being very politically correct,' claims Donovan, with a fair amount of understatement. One of Donovan's favorite targets is the current glut of so-called 'reality shows', lampooned in the aptly-named 'Xevivor'. 'We started with *Survivor* as a concept,' Donovan recalls, 'and then moved into *The Blair Witch Project*, and finally back into *Lexx* by the end of it.'

or ability to do anything else but focus on this show. When it ends, and I try to start up a new one, I can answer that question. Right now, my ambition is for us to go to number one on the Sci-Fi Channel.

What sort of projects are you interested in doing after this?

Using this technology, I have a Renaissance story that I'd like to do, based on real events. I feel completely confident now on how to create the Renaissance period very realistically using computer technology and live action. To be frank, there are a couple of complicated factors involved in setting up a show like that. One of the things we're always butting against is that a lot of people consider *Lexx* to be the worst show on TV, because it's juvenile and stupid and offensive and sleazy and amoral. But in my research of the Renaissance, I was reading a book written in the mid-1500s, and I realised, 'Hey, this author could have written for us; we could have hired him!' He lived in that time and thought the same way, so I realised that these things come and go over time. To a certain extent, we live in an age of liberal thinking, that started around 1920 and maybe peaked when you first started hearing the word 'AIDS' on television, and we now seem to be going into a less liberal world. But I realised that our world isn't nearly as liberal as Florence in 1490. So the same accusations that were made back then are now being made against our show. There are a number of incredibly important events that happened around that time, the key one being the arrival of syphilis in Europe. It changed history completely, because it created Protestantism and the Puritans, but to look at the world before that time, it was different and so interesting.

Are you more interested in working solo from now on, or do you prefer slinging ideas around with a group of people?

Both. I've come to accept that television is absolutely a collaborative art, if you want to use the word 'art'. One person can't make television by himself.

With one series coming to an end, and other projects on the horizon, is this an exciting time for you?

Well, maybe. I don't know what the future holds, but I feel I've climbed the mountain and I didn't give in and do what I was supposed to do. If ninety-five per cent of the world doesn't like our show, so be it, but if just one per cent really like it, I feel intensely satisfied by that. At the same time, there's a lot of self-importance in the world of SF, but we can't take ourselves too seriously. We feel good about what we've done but it's littered with the carcasses of bad ideas and mistakes and failed attempts. What we feel good about is that, despite all the things we did wrong, there's still something there at the core that is very satisfying. ▮

CHARLES EGLEE ON DARK ANGEL

How does a writer with no knowledge or experience of SF go about creating one of the hottest new genre shows of recent years? For a start, it probably doesn't hurt to hook up with a visionary Hollywood film-maker whose résumé includes such hits as *The Terminator*, *Aliens* and *The Abyss*. That's probably why Charles ('Chic') Eglee had no hesitation about teaming up with James Cameron to create *Dark Angel*, a series about a genetically-enhanced heroine (Max, played by Jessica Alba) evading her government captors in a post-apocalyptic Seattle. Eglee, whose credits include *Moonlighting*, *St. Elsewhere* and *Murder One*, had worked with Cameron many years earlier when they collaborated on the director's début: *Piranha II: Flying Killers*. Two decades later, Eglee's work had been nominated for just about every major writing award there is, and Cameron's films had earned billions of dollars at the box office. Needless to say, Twentieth Century Fox was only too happy to talk about putting their new show on the air. A year or so later, with *Dark Angel* in its second season, Eglee moved on to new projects, entrusting the series to his former second in command, René Echevarria. This interview was conducted just before he finished production on season one.

What was the starting point for you and Jim Cameron when you began developing *Dark Angel*?

We had a bunch of different ideas. Number one, we knew we were going to be doing something for Fox, so we wanted to tailor our ideas for something that made sense with Fox's branding. And then I was really adamant that if I was to form a new company with Jim and produce a programme with Jim's name on it, we needed to go out with something that lived up to the promise that we were making to an audience. If Jim Cameron is involved, it should deliver on those expectations; truth in advertising if you will. Then we just started talking about ideas. There were three or four of them, but this was the one that we both kept coming back to.

Will some of those other ideas resurface at some point?

You never know. You love an idea when you're thinking of it, but sometimes it's not the same when you come back to it a couple of years later. This is the one we ran with because we were really interested in the character and the world, and I liked this urban youth ensemble and the environs of the whole thing. Jim is great at spinning ideas, so he came up with the electromagnetic pulse [the technological 'apocalypse' which has reduced America to the 'third world' totalitarian state introduced in the pilot], and Max being genetically engineered, so our collective sensibilities just pooled together.

You've gone on record as saying you're not a SF writer, but is that necessarily a bad thing?

That was Jim's point to me. I was a little cowed by it at first, just because SF people tend to own it and really be into it. They're adepts; they read it and they know all the rules and it's this whole culture... and I'm just outside of it. I've never been interested, so I felt, 'Gee, it's SF, I didn't go to *Star Trek* conventions as a kid. I can't do this!' But Jim said, 'No, no, you don't understand. This is actually a *good* thing, because you're not coming to it with a whole set of expectations and rules, so it really allows you to prosecute this as a writer!'

Did you extend that to the other writers you hired to work with you on the series?

Well, it's helpful to have a few people around that have some facility or knowledge about SF, and we do have a couple of people on our writing staff who know all that stuff. So if I come up with an idea and think it's really cool, they can say, 'No, that was done twenty years ago by so and so.' It's nice to have somebody in the room that knows the whole culture of it.

How long did it actually take to bring *Dark Angel* to the screen?

About a year. Some of it was finding Jessica Alba and then getting her in training to get in shape for the role. It was actually a wonderful luxury for me as a writer that we found our actress before the script was done, so I was able to write the script with a particular actress in mind. That's something that doesn't happen too often.

So your next step after casting was to write the pilot script?

CHARLES EGLEE

Place of Birth:
Connecticut, USA

Home Base:
Los Angeles, California, USA

Education:
Yale University

First TV Work:
Moonlighting

TV Career Highlights:
Moonlighting, St. Elsewhere, L.A. Law, Byrds of Paradise, Murder One, Total Security, Dark Angel

That's right. But before that, Jim had had an idea about what the story was, and I sat down and wrote the scene in the hospital [where Max visits the recently crippled Logan Kale]. The reason it was a monologue was that we wanted to have a scene that could show off our actress. It was a scene that defined the character in some ways, because that scene is about 'Fuck you, I don't care about you,' and it's kind of a confessional about how much she *does* care about this guy. So we wrote that scene, and used it during casting. We found Jess, and then went off to write the full pilot script. So Max's phraseology, and her attitude and poutiness, and all of that was really in my mind as I was writing the script, because I knew who the actress was. Normally when you're writing a TV pilot, you write the script and you go out and cast it and plug your actors into it. This was a much more organic process.

With Max in place, you then had to find the right actor to play Logan Kale, the crusading cyber-journalist. Was it a concern right from the start that these two characters would develop chemistry between them?

There always is. I've certainly been on TV series where the guy and girl end up kissing around episode six or seven, and everybody is sitting there in dailies going, 'Ewww!' It really ends up being the heartbeat of the show, so it was essential that this character worked, particularly because we were giving him a whole set of limitations by putting him in a wheelchair. When Michael Weatherly came in the room, there was definite chemistry between him and Jessica. It was so apparent; you had to be blind not to see it.[*]

Was Lydecker, Max's would-be captor, difficult to cast?

Villains are always tough, particularly in the pilot where he's written like 'Shoot the children, kill them, get them!' There was a somewhat two-dimensional quality to that role, and that's the thing that made getting John Savage to fill out the character so appealing. First of all, he's such a good actor, but he also took that material, which as written was pretty spare, and brought an emotionality to it that I think surprised both Jim and I. You can have a villain in a movie that's a bit two-dimensional because it's only a couple of hours, but in television, week after week, that gets pretty boring. John brought a whole lot to it, and got us thinking about what this guy's inner life is like.

Did you deliberately set out to create a multi-racial cast of supporting characters?

I just wanted to tell the truth. The show is obviously informed by one of my great passions, which is hip hop and hip hop culture, and it's just extrapolating from the world we know now, twenty years out; the world is going to be very diverse, but not in a self-conscious way, just in a natural, organic way. Look, if you pick up an issue of *The Source* magazine, that's what our show looks like, just the way people are living their lives now.

---

[*] *The chemistry was not lost on Alba and Weatherly, who have since announced their engagement.*

But to some extent, the show is grounded in reality, isn't it?

We wanted to avoid the whole thing where you say 'SF', and the art department immediately runs off and starts getting out the big aluminium balls with laser beams shooting out of them. It's just so cheesy. Also, on a television budget, it's not like you can do *2001* where you've got a lot of time to do R & D [research and development] and a budget to really make it happen. It just ends up looking kind of horrible on television, which is why I never watched SF; it always seemed and smelled fake. The thing about the electromagnetic pulse — our show is actually kind of informed by that documentary about Cuban musicians, *Buena Vista Social Club*, because I'd just seen that, and I thought, how cool is this? A revolution happens in 1959 in Cuba, and everything just stops. Years later, and everything looks exactly like it looked in 1959, the technology is just frozen. So our electromagnetic pulse, while giving us a compelling back-story, also allowed us to play the technological present with a narrative future; so we could take what everything looks like now, extrapolate it out twenty years and it's pretty much the same because the economy stopped. I think that's what gives the show a reality. What we always have to do in every episode is pinch ourselves and remind our audience that this is twenty years in the future and we're transported temporally, so we just have to be aware of that on a week-to-week basis.

Is Seattle meant to be a microcosm of America at that time in the future?

Because Seattle is the dot.com *au courant* place, where Microsoft's based, it's the Valhalla of the technological present. The idea that we're using that as the post-technology future was just a fun idea. There's also the Seattle Space Needle of course, being the symbol of buoyant American optimism, the space age and going to the moon, which we then see as this wreck. Originally, we just wanted a meditative, high place for Max to be. It was going to be the Golden Gate Bridge, because the show was originally going to be set in San Francisco. We didn't want it to be LA or New York, because both of those cities have been portrayed as post-apocalyptic cities, but then we hit on Seattle, which seemed like the right place. And then of course, you think of Seattle and you think of the Space Needle, so we sort of found our way to that symbol.

This is a pretty dark world, isn't it?

Yes and no. We've created this world for a specific reason. In order for a hero to emerge, we wanted to come up with an environment where the normal social infrastructure has fallen away. If you had Max walking around in 1999, kicking ass and taking out bad guys, everybody would be asking, 'What the fuck is up with this girl? Why doesn't somebody just call the police?' But if all that social infrastructure has collapsed, it allows for a real hero to emerge. We were thinking of a place like Mexico or Russia, where everything has been corrupted. And we were really taking a page from the Wild West, or even 1930s America, when City Hall is corrupt and the cops are on the take and everything is being run by gangsters; it allows for one good man to come forward and do the right thing. We did that so Max, and Logan, could be truly hero-ic. It's the litmus test you always have to run. When I was working on *Moonlighting*, we would ask ourselves, 'Why is this a detective matter, and not a police matter?' Even though that show wasn't necessarily about verisimilitude, we still tried to make those cases something that would be in the locus of a private detective. When I was doing *Murder One*, we were very careful to have the lawyers behave as lawyers; they're not private investigators, and they're certainly not cops, so they have to behave in a way that is lawyerly, that would be within the wheelhouse of their responsibility, and their job. So in order to have Max as this reluctant hero being drafted into service, we need-ed to make the world broken.

When you do a show like this, don't you have to create the 'rules' about Max and her abilities right from the beginning?

The thing about Max is she's a bit of a surrogate for our audience. I would say we have a primarily teenage audience, so here you've got a character who's a surrogate for them. She's youthful and strong and beautiful, and seemingly immortal, but feels dis-connected from the society she's in, and can't seem to access any of her powers. Instead, everything she has that marks her out as superior is something that disen-franchises her, and makes her feel even more alienated. She's a bit of a Frankenstein's monster, only in this case, her stitches are microscopic. Also, we've given her a weak-ness, her seizures. She has to take a drug, Tryptophan, to combat them.

Is that the reason for 'Flushed', the episode where Max's dependency on Tryptophan comes to a head?

We wanted to demonstrate her vulnerability early on, and there were some misgiv-ings on the part of the network about that episode. I felt it was important to show that this was a flawed hero, because if she's invincible and invulnerable, then the audience says, 'Oh, well I can't relate to her. She's not like me, she's a super-person!' So it was key to demonstrate that there were things wrong with her, that she really could get hurt and could even die. The network would have preferred it if we'd held off showing her weak and powerless and very mortal until later on in the series, and they may have been right about that. I think it's kind of interesting that she need-ed the help of her friends, these people who care about her. And it's a very new turn for Max, being a part of any kind of society, even if it's *ad hoc*, the idea that some-body cared enough about her to go and help her, it was an important element of her character growth.

Was it difficult to find a way of using Lydecker on a regular basis?

The thing that's interesting about a villain in television, which is different than a movie villain, who only has to be sustained for two hours, is that on the one hand, you have to keep them menacing and threatening and make them a true antagonist.

But on the other hand, you've got to make them interesting and three-dimensional enough so that people want to pay attention to them. As you're seeing with Lydecker, you can't just have him saying, 'Drat, she got away again!' every week, because you then do harm to him as a bad guy, because there's no threat there. So you have to give him a win, or if he fails it's not because of him, it's because of something else, and we have to get to know that guy. 'Prodigy' was an interesting episode in that regard — let's sit down and hear what's in this guy's head. There's that whole scene where they're sitting together and Max is quizzing him on his use of the word 'hope'. Lydecker says that language is riddled with all kinds of anachronisms, and he would speak digitally if he could because it's more precise. That's an interesting thing to hear from your bad guy. And then there was one show where you get to see Lydecker at an Alcoholics Anonymous meeting. Here's a guy we've made an alcoholic, but he goes to AA meetings to humiliate everyone there for being weak; it's such an interesting turn. You're demonstrating his evil in a different way, not necessarily *vis-à-vis* Max and the main story, but you're showing the emotional and psychological disconnect on this guy in another setting.

At what point in the first season did you feel you had a handle on the characters?

I felt pretty strongly about everybody from the pilot really. I had worked with J. C. McKenzie before on *Murder One*, and I had a very strong sense of who that character of Reagan Ronald was. With Original Cindy, I don't know why, but I must have been a black lesbian in another incarnation, because that character tends to fall out of my head onto the page very easily. I have a really strong sense of who Max is of course, and it's been interesting to watch Logan emerge. I suppose that's been a little surprising to me, because he was a bit of a cipher in the beginning, and Michael just so owns that character now, with that wonderfully wry, very smart sensibility of his. Lydecker has been the hardest one to find, for the reasons we discussed, about trying to find the dimensionality in a villain.

Going back to the issue of sexual tension between your lead characters, how did you try and deal with the 'will they-won't they' problem?

That's why I had suggested to Jim that we put Logan in a wheelchair. First of all, you've got an audience that is looking at two incredibly attractive, gifted people, that are clearly drawn to each other, so they're going to be rooting for that to happen. Also, there's the pressure from the network, because every network is like this, the whoreishness of wanting to cash in on what they see as a way to hook the audience, that romantic commodity in any TV show. They start banging that drum very early on, but you're right, the minute your characters get together, everybody is hooked for two minutes, but then what do you do afterwards? We lived through that on *Moonlighting*, and paid the ultimate price for it! So, in order to keep these two attractive people, who are clearly drawn to each other, apart, you frequently end up having to invent all kinds of neurotic behaviour. Now that works well in romantic comedy, but again, it's inevitably marching towards some kind of union. For *Dark Angel*, I thought of the idea of having Logan end up in a wheelchair, with his feelings of shame and embarrassment about that — here's a guy in the prime of his life, who's denied his manhood. Then you've got Max, who feels terribly guilty that maybe she could have prevented this from happening. We were taking our characters and dumping them in a really interesting hole, and then watching them crawl out. For a writer, it was a perfect place to put our characters.

Did you have to make any major changes in the series at the behest of the network?

I wouldn't say that we've changed anything to accommodate them. The job is really getting them to try and understand what we're doing, and it's hard. The job of any network executive is to manage their fear, because they're not creating something, and yet the whole thing is riding on whatever these crazy guys that are locked up in a room are doing, so — and this happens at every network — they're understandably nervous and anxious.

Do you ever invoke the Cameron name?

That's not something that any of us like to do. Jim doesn't like to do it, and I don't like to do it; let's have an argument on the merits of the material and not get into power plays. I like to keep it a purely conceptual, creative discussion.

Does Jim take a hands-on role in the series?

Jim has a day job, but he was very involved in the breaking of the story. Jim is so great at conceptualising worlds and coming up with those rules that you alluded to earlier. I guarantee, if you stuck me in a room with a stack of paper, I probably wouldn't have come out with an electromagnetic pulse and somebody who was genetically engineered from Project Manticore. As the show unfolds, the stories are really implied in the characters that we created in that pilot. The thing about Jim is he's so great with the background, the mythology, because he is one of those sci-fi guys, and it's fun to sit down with him every now and then and pick his brain about this world; who's in it and what they're up to. He's so great at spinning mythology, and that's where I see his role in this series over time. As we develop, or use up the mythology we have, and that leads us to other levels of this world, I think that's where he will continue to make an enormous contribution.

What does that mean for the continuing development of *Dark Angel*?

I think what it means is that each hour has to be compelling in and of itself, and has to be interesting and dramatic and hard-hitting, and it can be informed by mythology, but we're not really in the cliff-hanger business. There's one episode later in the season that's an atypical *Dark Angel*, because it's frothier and funnier ['Art Attack']. It's nice to mix up that palette a little bit. We've got a couple of gritty, hard-hitting episodes and then we run a funny one, and then we do another show that may kick off another level of mythology, but each one of them is a self-contained story. It's not a 'to be continued' kind of thing.

Has this show given you a fair amount of on-the-job training in the SF genre?

Yes, but again, when we sit down to break stories and things like that, we're really telling stories about people. I asked René [Echevarria] about this when he was working on *Star Trek*, and he said, 'You know, you'd always sit down to break stories, and it never seemed like you were talking about SF, it was always like, what's emotionally at stake for this character?' Also, *Dark Angel* really isn't a show about robots and stuff.

So how would you pitch this series to someone who hasn't seen it?

That's a tough question to answer, because I don't watch a lot of TV, and I tend to watch pretty much what I'm working on. People have asked me to compare our show to *Buffy* or something like that, and I wouldn't know how to do that. What I think is interesting about the show is the layered-ness of it. It's got a lot of different things

RENÉ ECHEVARRIA

One of several writers who got their start working on *Star Trek: The Next Generation*, René Echevarria has become one of the more successful writer/producers working in genre television today. During the third season of *TNG*, he wrote the critically acclaimed episode 'The Offspring', which led to a number of subsequent freelance assignments before he was invited to join the show's staff in season five. Some of his more popular episodes included 'I, Borg', 'Face of the Enemy' and 'Lower Decks'. When *TNG* finally ended, Echevarria moved over to the staff of *Deep Space Nine*, where he became one of their most prolific writer/producers, with more than two dozen episodes to his credit. After *DS9*, Echevarria worked on scripts for the Las Vegas attraction *Star Trek: The Experience* before moving on to *Now and Again*, a show about a man brought back to life in a super-powered body, and made to perform covert work for the government without being able to tell his family he's still alive. When the series was cancelled after one season, Echevarria joined the staff of *Dark Angel*, ultimately taking over from the departing Charles Eglee as show runner and head writer at the end of post-apocalyptic drama's first year.

going on, it's not a specific franchise, it's really a world. It's also a relationship show about a man and a woman; it's an urban youth ensemble with a certain kind of irreverent, naughty hip hop/sexual sensibility. It's a view of the future that's more complicated than pure dystopia. There's that line, 'I don't know why they call it a depression, because nobody is that depressed.' I think people look at the show and feel optimistic, not depressed by it.

It's interesting how it straddles demographics. Older people remember the depression, and they tune in to it because it reminds them of their youth. Even though everybody was poor, it was their youth, so there's that romantic aspect to it. I also think it appeals to young people, because a lot of them are also under-employed, looking for a job and sharing an apartment with three other people trying to make the rent. So I think they can look at the show's world and relate to it. Just the idea that there's been a financial setback, but America is still there. There's a beating heart: people are still getting up in the morning, and going to work, falling in love, having sex, drinking and partying and fighting bad guys; I think all of that draws people in. Before it started airing, particularly when I was doing press, people would say, 'So tell me about your show, what's it about?' and I'd say, 'Well...' and it would get so complicated, because there's not an easy log line to it. I think that's the good thing about it, that there's a lot of stuff there. We're not hitting the same note every week. ∎

D. C. FONTANA

Dorothy Fontana has been working in television for four decades now, with a writing career that spans just about every genre. Starting out with scripts for Western series such as *The Tall Man* and *Frontier Circus*, she's written episodes for cop shows, medical dramas, even *The Waltons*. But the series that she'll always be most associated with is *Star Trek*. Fontana was there from day one, first as Gene Roddenberry's production secretary, and eventually becoming one of the show's most prolific writers. She later became a producer on the short-lived *Star Trek* animated series, writing the critically acclaimed episode 'Yesteryear', before moving on to other frontiers. But her relationship with *Trek* was far from over. In the late 1980s, Roddenberry contacted Fontana about working on the new *Star Trek: The Next Generation*. This time however, the experience was less rewarding, and Fontana left the show when her contract was up. She later wrote an episode of *Deep Space Nine*, and is now working on a *TNG* interactive game, so it seems unlikely that she'll ever leave *Trek* completely behind her. Today, Fontana divides her time between television, books, teaching and a score of other projects, both SF and non-genre. And she's not about to slow down any time soon...

What made you decide to move out to the West Coast to seek fame and fortune?

I worked in New York briefly as a junior secretary to the head of Columbia Television, which was called Screen Gems at the time. I liked it and I liked the scripts; before that, I had always thought of myself as becoming a novelist. I'd always watched television and movies, but hadn't thought of writing for them. When I got involved briefly in New York, I said, 'Oh yeah, I really like this; I can do this!' so I moved to California where all the production was.

How did you finally get started as a TV writer?

I was working as a production secretary on the series *The Tall Man* for producer Samuel A. Peeples*. He knew I wanted to write, and he looked at material I'd submitted, and finally bought a story for *The Tall Man*, and then I wrote another story, which he also bought. And then I said, 'Let me try a script,' and he said, 'Okay, if I approve

---

* Who would soon be writing for Star Trek himself.

the story, we'll let you go on to the script,' so in other words, I was there. I also worked on another show called *Frontier Circus*, and it was the same situation: I only sold a story. But then later on, I did a major rewrite and got a credit for *Shotgun Slade*, which was a syndicated show. I've never seen it, because it wasn't showing at the time in Los Angeles. It was one of those lesser-known Westerns that never got circulated much, so that was one of my episodes I never did get to see. There are one or two others that came along later that, for whatever circumstances, I never got to see either.

How did one go about learning to be a TV writer in the early 1960s?

Basically, I had an advantage in being already inside the studio and working on the shows, because I obviously knew those series and their producers, who would read my material. After the first couple of sales, I did have an agent, and if I was interested in a show, I'd try and get an appointment and pitch, which is basically what you had to do; you went in and verbally pitched.

When Westerns were going out of style, there was a transition in the business from Westerns to more contemporary stories, and from half-hours to hours. There was an education process in my own way of writing, and learning how to deal with longer and different kinds of material, so I wrote a spec script for [medical drama] *Ben Casey*. Also, it was a matter of people saying, 'I don't know if a woman can write my show!' I'd say, 'Well, I just wrote six Westerns, what are you talking about?' That's when I started hiding behind my initials, so that they wouldn't know in advance that I was a woman. I sold a *Ben Casey* that way, using my initials. My agent put the script in and they liked it, and it was bought. Pretty much from then on, I used D. C. Fontana, although after I'd written more scripts, a lot of people knew I was a woman and didn't care.

Was it difficult to break in if you were a woman?

Yes, especially if you were writing action-adventure. There were not all that many women; I can think of Pat Fielder and Margaret Armen, who both also wrote for *The Tall Man*, but not many in television. There were several writers, like Leigh Brackett for instance, who were writing motion pictures [Brackett later wrote *The*

D. C. FONTANA

Place of Birth:
New Jersey, USA

Home Base:
Los Angeles, California, USA

First TV Work:
The Tall Man

TV Career Highlights:
Frontier Circus, Star Trek, Then Came Bronson, Star Trek the Animated Series, The Six Million Dollar Man, Star Trek: The Next Generation, Babylon 5, Hypernauts

Empire Strikes Back], but there was never that great a group of women writing action-adventure, so we were a small, close club. When you look at the percentage of women writers as compared to male writers in the overall membership of the Writers Guild of America — we're still no more than twenty-five per cent, and that hasn't changed over the years. I'm including women who write different kinds of material, whether it's character-driven, women-driven stories, whether they write comedies or daytime soaps — a majority of writers in that area tend to be women — or whether they write action-adventure, mysteries, whatever. There are also women working in animation as well. But the percentage of women writers to men is still about the same today.

During the mid-60s, were you writing freelance scripts while holding down a full-time job?

That didn't change until 1966. Toward the end of that year, I became a story editor on *Star Trek*. Actually, it was a little earlier than that, when I quit production and my secretary job for Gene Roddenberry and said, 'I want to freelance. I want to write.' Then Gene came along and said, 'I need a story editor, and you know the show.' He knew I wanted to write, and he'd read a couple of things I had written that weren't related to *Star Trek*, so when he was first assigning scripts, he said, 'Do you want to do one?' I said 'Yes, of course,' and that was 'Charlie X'.

Wasn't that script on its way to being scrapped before Gene gave it to you?

Not true. It was in the original bible, and I said, 'I would like to do this.' I developed the story, and gave Gene full credit for the story, although it was really just a couple of paragraphs, and then I wrote the teleplay.

Was your work on 'Charlie X' enough to show you had the stuff to be a full-time writer for Roddenberry?

I also wrote 'Tomorrow is Yesterday' while I was still a production secretary. I think it was in September when I said, 'I really want to try and freelance. Whether it's for this show or not, I want to get out there and stop being a production secretary.' He said fine, and another secretary came in, applied and got the job. So I left, and he handed me the rewrite for 'This Side of Paradise'.

How scary was it, jumping into the freelance market?

I wasn't coming out of school with very little background in some profession, and saying, 'Now I want to be a freelance writer.' I did have experience as a production secretary I could fall back on. Even in high school, I'd been a secretary, and then in college, I also worked part-time as a secretary. When I got out of college, I became a production secretary, so I had about six years in the business and very good references. If it didn't work out, I could still go back to being a very good production secretary. But of course I wanted to be a freelance writer.

Were you able to find the different voices of the various characters on _Star Trek_ fairly quickly?

You have to remember that I'd been with Gene since the day he started on it. I typed all of his drafts, so I was constantly reading what the _Star Trek_ characters were going to be saying. Now, how the actors delivered the lines then adds another layer of something you have to listen for. But once you've seen enough film, you go to dailies every day and you're reading the scripts as they change, and you go down to the stage and listen to the actors deliver their lines, you start to understand. 'Oh yes, Leonard Nimoy would deliver that line this way, but if it was a Kirk line, it would be delivered this way' — you start to hear their voices. When they're abstracts, when they're not made flesh by the actors, it's a different thing; it's just paper, and you have to imagine how those voices are going to sound. But once the actors put it on the stage, there's a real person there, delivering those lines, and you know their cadences and how they're likely to deliver a line. I think that's where the education comes in, and that's why it's sometimes difficult to write for a show that you're just coming in on and you haven't been with it forever. If it's been on the air, your job is to watch it and start to see how the actors sound in-character, delivering lines.

One of the very good things on _Babylon 5_ — where again, I came in early on the show and didn't know all the actors — was that Joe Straczynski would make copies of dailies, or a rough cut of an episode, and say, 'Here, I want you to look at this.' He'd then give you a stack of scripts so you could see how that voice was developing, at least on paper. That helped enormously, coming in to a new show. With a series like _Bonanza_, which I wrote two scripts and a story for, the show had been on forever, so you knew who these people were and how they sounded. Those are different situations, but if it's a new show, you either must do your homework, or the producer has to help you do your homework.

So you had a huge advantage on _Star Trek_ in the first season.

Yes, but we were also dealing with a lot of professionals who came in and did a great job; on the first and second seasons of _Star Trek_ anyway — I really wasn't involved with the third season.

There were some great writers on the series, such as Robert Bloch, Ted Sturgeon and Harlan Ellison, to name just a few. Were you interested in SF yourself?

Yes and no. Before 1964, I wasn't especially a fan of SF, except for a few things like _Forbidden Planet_ and _The Thing_, which were favourite movies of mine. I hadn't done much reading in the genre, but Gene put me to work on a project of reading a stack of books. It must have been thirty or forty anthologies by different writers and best-of-SF, analysing them and breaking them down into potential story buys. I still have this huge notebook, where I'd done all this and typed it all up, and I got to know some of the best of the best writing for SF of the period over several years. Of course Robert Bloch was a good friend of Sam Peeples, so I knew Robert personally and had a couple of his books. But through the magic of books I 'met' Theodore Sturgeon and Richard Matheson, and many other writers who we looked at and said, 'Are there any stories here we can buy?' There were a few, and we also went to those writers and said, 'Okay, we can't use that, but we'd like you to do a show,' or a couple of shows, as Sturgeon and Robert Bloch did. I got to know some of the better work in the genre at the time, and I haven't stopped reading SF since. At first I didn't especially care for it, but once you start reading the really good stuff, you get hooked.

Were you freelancing on other shows at the same time?

I was pretty exclusively working for *Star Trek* until the end of the second season, because I really only did the one script in-between being a production secretary and becoming story editor, and that script was the one that got me the job as story editor. So that didn't allow much time to do anything else. So from 1966 to early 1968 (and then I did a couple of things for the last season) I was pretty much on *Star Trek*. Then I started branching out and writing other material. I did *Lancer* and *The Road West* and a bunch of other Westerns — there was a flurry of Westerns at the time, and I wrote for a number of them, and then went on to other things as well.

Would writers come in and pitch ideas to Gene, or did he give them a premise to work with?

Generally speaking, writers would come in for a pitch session with an idea. Some of them worked and some of them didn't, but if Gene was interested, you'd try to make the story work for *Star Trek*. This included me as well, even though I was there already. If I said, 'I've got an idea,' he'd say, 'Well, let me hear it.' Gene Coon* was also excellent at saying, 'Okay, let's make this work as a story; you have to do this and this to make it a *Star Trek* story.' Once they liked the pitch, you would have an assignment, the contract would be written up, and you would write the story. You'd turn that in, and once it was approved (and you might have to revise the story before it was finally approved) then you would go on to the first draft script and essentially do the same thing. You would turn in your first draft script, you'd be given notes and comments, and you'd write your second draft script, and then you were pretty much done. You might have to do a light polish after that, but that's how the contracts worked then, and still work now. Those are the delivery steps and what you have to do.

Do you agree that producer Gene Coon was one of the unsung heroes of *Star Trek*, who never really got the credit he deserved?

---

* *Gene Coon (1924-73) created a number of the show's most enduring concepts, notably the Klingons.*

I think that's quite true. Unfortunately, he died young and didn't get to reap the rewards of people realising that he made an enormous contribution. Gene Coon was certainly one of the more inventive people on the show. He had a great sense of humour, and was always willing to try something, or let somebody else try something. He was the person who really championed David Gerrold's first script, 'The Trouble With Tribbles'. He said, 'Yeah, we need some humour on this show,' and told David he was willing to let him try to write a script. He bought the story, and then said, 'Let's let the kid try,' because David was still a college student at the time. Gene was a great contributor to the show. Great characters: the Gorn, based on the Fredric Brown story 'Arena', the Horta in 'Devil in the Dark'; there were so many others that he had a hand in, and of course he was a very fast writer. He could do a script in three days from start to finish! He was very creative, and was I think one of the mainstays on the show.

There have been accounts in the past that claimed David Gerrold was actually your discovery.

No, the story for 'Tribbles' originally came in with a couple of others (including 'Bem', which later became an episode for the animated series), and that came directly to Gene Coon through David's agent. Gene said to me, 'I have my opinions on these;

DAVID GERROLD

Now a successful author and screenwriter, David Gerrold was still in college when he approached the producers of *Star Trek* with the idea for a story about some endearing but extremely prolific alien creatures. 'The Trouble With Tribbles' became one of the show's most popular episodes, eventually spawning a sequel of sorts for the animated *Star Trek*, 'More Tribbles, More Troubles' and 'Trials and Tribble-ations', an episode of *Deep Space Nine* that seamlessly blended new scenes with footage from the original. Gerrold's other television work includes *Land of the Lost*, *Space Cases*, *Babylon 5* (for which he wrote the acclaimed first-season episode 'Believers') and *Sliders*. He also helped to create many of the original concepts and characters used in *Star Trek: The Next Generation*. In addition to his TV work, Gerrold is a Hugo and Nebula Award-winning novelist. His many books include *The Man Who Folded Himself*, *The War Against the Chtorr*, *Jumping Off the Planet*, *The Martian Child*, *The Voyage of the Star Wolf* and an autobiographical account of the making of 'The Trouble With Tribbles'. He's also written *Worlds of Wonder: How to Write Science Fiction and Fantasy*, in which he shares the skills and techniques he's built up over his lengthy writing career.

what do you think?' As I recall, my opinion on 'Bem' was, 'We can't do this, because it's more than we can do with what we have.' That's why we later did it as an animated episode, because I remembered the story and said to David, 'Now we can do 'Bem'.' What I did think — and there's a memo to this effect somewhere — was that the story of the Tribbles was charming and certainly worked for Star Trek, but that we should have a professional writer develop it, because at that time David was literally unsold and a college student. But Gene Coon said, 'I'm going to give him a crack at it,' and he did.

How did you feel about having to rewrite Gene Coon's draft of the now-legendary episode 'The City on the Edge of Forever', when he'd already had the unenviable task of rewriting its original author, Harlan Ellison?

It became an interesting progression of pushing and pulling at the script to satisfy Gene Roddenberry, so that was basically what we were trying to do. We all had our little take on it, and what was ultimately filmed was the final Roddenberry take, but the rest of us

FONTANA AND STAR TREK

Gene Roddenberry, ex-bomber pilot and LAPD officer, started writing for TV in the early 1950s. He had created one fairly successful series, The Lieutenant, when in 1963 he had an idea that was to change his life: 'How about doing a show that's like Wagon Train in space?' The idea became Star Trek, and D. C. Fontana was there from the beginning, first as Roddenberry's production secretary, then as one of the show's best writers. While still a secretary, she wrote 'Charlie X', a touching episode which demonstrated her knack for creating strong characters. By the time she'd finished writing 'Tomorrow is Yesterday', she'd already expressed her desire to freelance for the series, and Roddenberry gave her the rewrite assignment on 'This Side of Paradise'. She also did an uncredited rewrite on Harlan Ellison's 'The City on the Edge of Forever', adding the cordrazine that drove Dr McCoy mad, and building up the relationship between Kirk and Edith Keeler. In season two, Fontana worked on 'Catspaw', for which she was co-credited with Robert Bloch. 'Journey to Babel' featured Spock's parents, Amanda and Sarek, and created new alien races such as the Andorians. 'By Any Other Name' was developed from a story by Jerome Bixby, and she finished the season with 'The Ultimate Computer' (from a Lawrence Wolfe story) and 'Friday's Child'. For Star Trek's third and final season, Fontana contributed 'The Enterprise Incident' and the story for 'That Which Survives', before moving on. But her relationship with the Trek universe was far from over...

had our fingers in it; first Gene Coon, then myself and then Gene Roddenberry.

Was Harlan still unaware that you'd done a rewrite until you sent him the afterword for his book of the script*, two decades later?

He called me up and said, 'My God, I've been pillorying Steve Carabatsos[†] for years, and it was you and Gene Coon!' I said, 'Well, now that you know, are you going to kill me?' and he said no.

Do you feel there was a bit of revisionist history concerning Gene Roddenberry's universe in later years? For example, there's this idea that there is no conflict in the future, which certainly wasn't true of the original series.

The first series, '*Trek* classic', is different from the others. By the time that twenty years had gone by, and we got to 1987, Gene's view of his universe had changed. It started out in *Next Gen* that everybody loved everybody else, and there were no conflicts on the ship and so on, and that is hard to deal with dramatically, because if you don't have conflict, you don't have drama; you don't even have comedy. Gene's view of his own universe had changed in that time. Drama is conflict, that's the basic rule, and if you don't have it, you don't have anything that's really worth looking at, as far as entertainment goes.

Where does the dreaded *Next Generation* techno-babble factor into this?

I think it just happened, but I wasn't there when they were doing that. I was on the first thirteen episodes of *Star Trek: The Next Generation* and we didn't have a lot of techno-babble. If you look at them in sequence, you will see that. I think it came in later, and honest to God, I don't think it's worth much as dialogue. That's my opinion, and you'll notice I'm not a *Star Trek* writer any longer as far as those things go, but I don't think you need it. One of the classic examples, when I go back to the first show — and people have told this story before and so have I, because it's true — was when Theodore Sturgeon, bless his heart, had written an entire page of dialogue for... I think it was 'Amok Time', to turn the ship about so that we could go back to Vulcan. Ted was doing it out of technical expertise, because he had been a merchant marine sailor, and he knew what was involved. So he literally wrote an entire page of dialogue to turn the ship around. Gene looked at it, and he struck out the whole thing — I was standing there next to him when he did it — and wrote in one line: 'Reverse course!' That's all you need to do, so I don't necessarily agree with techno-babble, because most of the time you really, *really* do not need it.

Why did you decide to move on from *Star Trek* in season three?

I'd decided at the end of the second season that I wanted to branch away from *Star Trek* to do other assignments anyway. I did have a multiple deal to do *Star Trek* scripts,

---

* Harlan Ellison's The City on the Edge of Forever, *White Wolf Publishing, 1996.*
† *Who took over from writer/producer John D.F. Black.*

but was having some difficulties with the new regime in place. Gene Roddenberry had left as executive producer, and they weren't talking the same language I was talking, so I finally decided to go. There were two stories and a script, so I said, 'Here's the work,' my agent got me out of the contract and I went on to write other things, including a lot of Westerns at that point.

What was your agenda in producing the animated *Star Trek* series in the early 70s?

We just wanted to make it *Star Trek*. We didn't want to talk down to the audience, because we felt our audience was intelligent enough to come up to us, so we never wrote down to them. It was *Star Trek*, but of course they were shorter stories. We only had twenty-one minutes of story-telling time in the half-hour, but we did have an advantage in that we could do things we couldn't have done on the live action show, with the technology available at the time. In animation, you just draw what you want: environments, aliens, strange landscapes, whatever. So we were able to do stories like 'Bem' for instance, that we couldn't do on the original show. Margaret Armen did two I believe, and I did one of them, 'Lorelei Signal', which was set underwater. We couldn't have done that effectively on the original show at all. We also had a couple of new alien characters, Arex and M'Ress, that we couldn't have done as effectively on the original show. We were able to buy a Larry Niven story* starring the Kzinti, which was an eight-foot orange cat; that kind of thing. There were obviously pluses and minuses. The quality and range of animation on the budget we had was certainly not Disney, but we tried to make the characters look as much like the actual actors as possible, and we got as many of the original voices as we could. Because the budget was limited, we couldn't have Walter Koenig [Chekov] as a regular, but we did have him as a scriptwriter on the show, so we tried to involve as many original *Star Trek* people as possible.

What kind of adjustments did you have to make, if any, for the children's television market?

There are censorship standards and so forth, but we never really had a problem with that. Our *Star Trek* stories tended to be moral tales, stories with a message. As a result, NBC, who carried the show, was pretty happy with them. We didn't have any show or script cancelled because of censorship problems. I know the fans were dubious at first: 'Oh what could it be, it's just a Saturday morning cartoon, it won't be *Star Trek!*' But then we started telling them as much as possible (although the word was harder to get out at the time because we didn't have the Internet) that, 'Hey, we have all these *Star Trek* people involved; it's going to be *Star Trek*, only animated.'

That year, the World Science Fiction Convention was in Toronto, and it's usually held over Labor Day weekend, which is the last weekend in August. I was going to bring over some footage from Filmation [the show's production company], but all we had

---

* The episode 'The Slaver Weapon' was adapted from Niven's short story 'The Soft Weapon'.

that was ready to run was the opening credits. I said, 'Well, it's only a minute and a half of film, but let me have that,' and then I begged a place on the World Con schedule. Robert Bloch made a keynote speech on Friday evening, and said, 'We have a little special thing from *Star Trek* animated,' so the hall was filled. The minute they heard the music and saw a pretty darn good *Enterprise* come across the screen the way it used to, the audience was with us! All I had was the credits, but they liked it and said, 'We'll give it a try.'

Wasn't there a writers' strike at that point, which worked in your favour?

That's true. It was 1973, and I believe it was May that the Writers Guild strike went into effect. It lasted for three months, and no member of the Writers Guild could write for a show with live action actors, so nothing was being written. But they *could* write for animation, and write at least one script without having to become a member of that local [union]. So we got Gene Coon and David Gerrold, Steve Kandel, Margaret Armen and Sam Peeples. We got a group of people that knew *Star Trek*, and of course I did one. We had other writers who said, 'We love *Star Trek*, can we try?' They came in and wrote things, so in terms of a strike, it was legal for our writers to write for animation, and they got some money for it.

By the 1970s, did you find that you were starting to be identified as a SF writer?

I'd done *Streets of San Francisco* and a couple of action shows like *Assignment Vienna*, and other sorts of contemporary shows. In other words, I wasn't doing that much SF. But I did do some: a story for *Wonder Woman*, and two episodes of *The Six Million Dollar Man*, so I wasn't entirely out of it. Also, there weren't a lot of SF shows on, so you just do what's available — my brother and I once did a story for *Dukes of Hazzard*! (It didn't get made, but we actually did a whole script.) So there were shows that were totally off the beaten track as far as SF goes. I did get hired by [producer] Leonard Katzman on *Fantastic Journey*, and worked for him again in 1977 on *Logan's Run*, so that was two SF series in a row, but then I went back to writing other things, *Dallas* and *The Waltons* and stuff like that. It all depends on how much SF is out there; it goes in cycles. SF is very heavy right now, and in another year or so, it might die away again.

How did you get involved in the first season of *The Next Generation*?

Gene contacted me and invited me to dinner with him and his wife Majel, so we talked about it, and he asked if I was interested. I said, 'Yes, sure,' and was actually asked to write the pilot. That was the first assignment. I wasn't on staff at that point; that was later on.

Wasn't there some question at the time about the precise nature of your responsibilities on the show, concerning whether you were a writer or an associate producer?

A writer is a writer. You're either a freelance writer or a staff writer, which is the low-est of the low on the roster of positions. The next step up, as defined in the Writers Guild manual is 'writer with additional capacities', which means story editor, execu-tive story editor, consulting story editor, or anything with 'producer' attached to it — from associate to producer to co-producer to executive producer to supervising pro-ducer. Any of those things are 'writer with additional capacities', which means you don't just write, you're also involved in the production.

But there was a strange account in David Alexander's biography of Gene Roddenberry[*], saying that you told *TNG* producer Bob Lewin that, as an associate producer, Writers Guild rules meant that you weren't allowed to do some of the writer-related activities...

Oh, that is such total bullshit! There were no problems. All they had to do was call the Writers Guild. A writer with additional capacities, as I said, is anything with 'pro-ducer' or 'story editor' attached to it, which means you work with writers, you write scripts, you rewrite scripts, but you also watch dailies, you have input into rough cuts, you get involved in casting, and so on. And if you do that work, the Writers Guild has a category for it, and an accompanying pay scale...

When did you begin to realise that things had changed from the days when you'd worked on the original series?

I really don't want to go into that. Read Joel Engel's book [see box]: it lays everything out in chapter and verse, and it's the truth. David Alexander's book is a cover-up to make Gene look good. There's a lot of glossing over, but the simple fact is, there was a dis-agreement of opinion about assignment of duties and what he wanted me to do, which I could not legally and morally do, and I said, 'End of my contract, I'm out of here.'

Was that difficult to do?

Sometimes it's a situation you have to deal with. I think what's indicative of the entire situation is that there were a lot of original *Star Trek* people involved with *The Next Generation* when it went into production, and something like seventeen people had left by the end of the first year. Not just writers and producers, but below the line peo-ple. That tells you something.

Michael Piller, who was also interviewed for this book, claims that by the third season, *TNG* was considered the worst place to work in Hollywood, because Gene's vision was sacrosanct.

What do the British say: that's a fair cop? I think that's just about right. I wasn't there beyond the first thirteen episodes, but it was bad for everybody. But by the third sea-son, it was worse. Read Joel Engel's book again. The situation was bad for everybody.

---

* Star Trek Creator, Roč (US), Boxtree (UK), 1994.

What did you move on to after leaving *The Next Generation*?

There were other series I was writing for. I finished a *Star Trek* novel, *Vulcan's Glory*, but I was also writing on other shows; I can't remember them all anymore!

You were back in the freelance market again?

And basically have been ever since. But I do other things too. I teach at the American Film Institute, and I was also working on books and pitching projects, and doing episodes for other genres and other types of material.

How did you end up working on *Babylon 5*?

Joe Straczynski had called David Gerrold and I a year before the show went on the air. He had us over to his house, and ran some pieces of film that Foundation Imaging was working on for a CGI presentation to go with the script, which showed the *Babylon 5* space station, some of the ships and things like that. So he showed us the clips and said, 'This is the look we're going for,' and we knew a little bit already, because Joe had been talking about it for some time. He'd also given us both a T-shirt that said, '*Babylon 5*', and on the back, 'Accept no substitutes', because *DS9* was going

FONTANA'S NEXT GENERATION

In Joel Engel's 1994 biography, *Gene Roddenberry: The Myth and the Man Behind Star Trek* (Hyperion US, Virgin UK), the author goes into detail about some of the behind-the-scenes conflict on *The Next Generation*. By his account, Roddenberry had solicited Fontana's opinions on the new series, indicating that she would soon become an integral member of the team. While waiting for that position, Fontana became an unpaid consultant, offering her take on the material being developed. She'd even started work on ideas for the pilot episode 'Encounter at Farpoint' before finally being hired as an associate producer. That script went through a number of changes, as did 'The Naked Now', which ultimately went out under a pseudonym. She only stayed for thirteen episodes. According to Engel, 'In February 1988, a few months after leaving *Star Trek: The Next Generation*, Fontana filed a grievance with the Writers Guild. Alleging that she had performed the function of a story editor without receiving appropriate compensation, she settled more than a year later, before the arbitration hearing, and received an unspecified amount.' The terms of the settlement reportedly prevented Fontana from discussing the case, although reading Engel's book gives one an idea of the issues involved.

on the air, and *Babylon 5* went on later. When the show was bought, he called me in and said, 'I've got a story I'd like you to do,' and that was 'The War Prayer'. It was a short outline, and I had to develop all the scenes. So you do the story, develop all the scenes and then say, 'Is this what you want, Joe?' He'll say, 'Yes it is, okay, go,' and then you go into the first and second draft scripts. I put in the little Romeo and Juliet story*, which Joe was a little hesitant about at first, saying the story wasn't about those kids. I said, 'You're right, it's not about those kids. It's about Londo, but just let me write it,' because this was still in the story breakdown period. He said okay, and then he was happy with it, because it *wasn't* about the kids; it was about Londo and how his life had failed in that area. That all worked, but Joe was a little hesitant at first until I said, 'Trust me on this, and if it doesn't work, I'll rewrite it,' so we worked it out.

I did that one well enough that he asked if I wanted to do a second one, so I came in and he said, 'We've got another story we'd like you to do.' I said, 'Let me pitch you a couple of ideas first.' Among others, I pitched 'Legacies', and he and [producer] Larry DiTillio liked that one so much that they said, 'Okay, do that one,' so I did. I later found out from Larry — I didn't know this — that they had wanted me to do this other story, but they liked mine better, so they threw theirs out and took mine instead. In the second season, they had 'A Distant Star', which they wanted to develop, so again, I took one or two pages, developed the whole thing and wrote the script.

Were they respectful to your scripts in terms of rewriting?

Generally speaking, but once the script was down in terms of 'This is what we're going to shoot,' there were no changes allowed on the stage. If there were changes that came up for some reason, whether it was through an actor or director or a tech problem, they had to call Joe Straczynski and he would come down to the set and see what was going on and say, 'No, do it my way,' or, 'Okay, we can change this line, it's for a valid reason.' But generally, once the script was set, it was set in stone.

As a freelancer, were you sorry to see Joe writing all the episodes himself after season two?

You have to go with what the producers want, and if Joe wanted to do that, you have to respect his vision and what he wanted to do. I always do feel that bringing in outside writers gives you a perspective that you sometimes don't have when you're working closely on the show, because somebody from outside can come in and say, 'Gee, we can do a story about so-and-so doing this,' and you never thought about doing that story because you're so close to it. So I do think outside writers bring in a perspective sometimes that is difficult to see, but I do agree in part with the point of view of, 'We know the show best, so we can write it best.' I think there are advantages to both ways, and I really prefer to see a lot of writers on a show, all contributing to the 'inside' point of view. That's how I feel, but hey, that's *my* point of view.

* *Aria and Kiron, a young Centauri couple, have run away to escape arranged marriages to others. Placed in his care, Londo eventually decides to let them choose whom they marry.*

Did *B5* lead to the teen sci-fi series *Hypernauts*, which involved a lot of the same people?

In part yes, because I had met Christy Marx[*], and of course I'd known Ron Thornton[†] for forever and a day as well, so that's what led to that assignment, which I enjoyed very much. Christy was also involved with [animated series] *Captain Simian and the Space Monkeys*, so I met her on *Babylon 5*, re-met her on *Captain Simian* and then met her again on *Hypernauts*, so it's been a continuing relationship.

Is the project you were recently developing with Foundation Imaging a children's show?

No, it's not. It's with a distributor, and the production company would essentially be Foundation, so it's being marketed out there to see if they can get it on the air, and for that, you need a distributor. So it's with them as far as I know, but at this point I have no idea where it stands. I haven't heard anything for a month now. It's called *Mech Warrior*, and it's based on the *Mech Warrior* universe, which is a computer game, but there's also a twist to it, and I don't want to mention what that is. We just did four pages of presentation, and then Foundation Imaging was doing a visual presentation as well, and that's the package put out there as a pitch.

Has teaching at the American Film Institute been taking up a lot of your time, or is that a sideline?

I've done that for three years now, and I'm entering my fourth. It takes a minimum amount of my time, because it's only once a week, and because it's a project that's to the school's specifications — it's actually a fairly minimal product that the students have to turn out. They have to write a treatment for a motion picture, or mini-series for television, or a pilot episode. It may run twenty to thirty pages, but it's not like having them write two or three full scripts in the year, which is what the writing students have to do. I teach directing and producing fellows, and this is to go in their thesis project, which is basically a package that they can take out and try to market themselves with after they graduate the AFI.

What other projects are you currently working on?

I'm putting the final touches on an interactive *Star Trek* game from Activision, which is called *Star Trek: Bridge Commander*. I was working with a writing partner named Derek Chester, and it's a *Next Gen* game. It has eight episodes broken into several missions each, so it's a fairly complex game, and I think people will like it. Patrick Stewart lends his voice to it, as does Brent Spiner, and there are several guest voices that are associated with *Star Trek*. I think it might be an interesting game by the time they're done; there were changes made by the game designers that I had no control over.

---

[*] *The story editor on Hypernauts, who'd written the episode 'Grail' for B5.*
[†] *Foundation Imaging's FX wizard and an Emmy-winner for B5, who went on to create Hypernauts.*

Do interactive games require a different way of thinking in terms of the script?

Mostly it's writing script, and I've certainly done that a lot, but you have to come up with situations where you have alternate endings and other solutions, things like that. If the game player chooses the wrong action, then it's 'game over, man.' Or they lose the mission at least.

This past year, in addition to the game, I did several episodes for a childrens' animated show, based on the famous British children's books about Noddy. It's a new production of the *Noddy* story from an American company, but with the help of the people in England who were closely associated with the author, and those will be coming out in the next year. So I find other work elsewhere.

Are you still interested in writing books?

Very much so, although not necessarily in SF. I'm a member of Mystery Writers, and also a member of the Society of Children's Book Writers and Illustrators, so I have several projects that are non-SF that I'd like to get done.

Given a choice, would you still want to ease out of the SF genre?

Yes and no, because I still love it, and I have ideas there. It just depends on what I can get to first. One thing's out of the question though — retirement. Writers never retire! ∎

NEIL GAIMAN

Having established himself with *The Sandman* as an award-winning comic book writer, Neil Gaiman turned his attention to the medium of television in the early 1990s. The result was *Neverwhere*, a richly detailed fantasy series about a young man named Richard Mayhew, who discovers a strange and dangerous world that exists beneath London. He encounters a bizarre mix of characters, many of whom seem to somehow personify areas of the city above, such as the Earl of Earl's Court, and an angel called Islington. Débuting in 1996, the six-part BBC drama featured an impressive cast and some stunning visuals (notably the opening title sequence, created by Gaiman's friend and frequent comics collaborator, Dave McKean), but viewing figures were, unfortunately, less than impressive. Although the BBC decided not to commission a second season, Gaiman's novel adapting the series quickly became a best seller, and the original six episodes have already achieved something of a cult reputation. The interview that follows was conducted not long after *Neverwhere* finished production, and may well be Gaiman's lengthiest (and most frank) discussion of the series to date. It also features some of the writer's plans for a second season and beyond, which will now probably never reach fruition. Still, with the possibility of future novels, as well as an upcoming feature film, it seems safe to assume that we haven't seen the last of London Below...

How did you make the transition from working in comic books to creating *Neverwhere* for television?

Lenny Henry[*], who was a huge *Sandman* fan, came and found me. He said, 'I've got a company called Crucial Films; we're going to be doing some TV, and I'd like you to do a series for me.' I actually found the original fax which was sent to Lenny — we had a conversation at the Groucho Club in the morning, and in the evening I wrote this fax — and it's odd how much of *Neverwhere* was there right from the beginning. In the fax, I began by talking about running into a girl who's just been made homeless, who was scared that she was going to have to go back on the streets. She was worried about whether or not it was going to be a cold winter, because she knew that she was not going to be able to survive a cold winter, and I pulled some strings and got her a job.

---

[*] *British comedian, actor and producer.*

Here's what the rest of the fax said: 'I've had a few ideas already, many of which are contradictory and in an abbreviated form, so I'm throwing them all at you. It might be interesting to begin this story with a normal guy with a settled job, girlfriend and so forth. One night, on his way to something like dinner with his boss, accompanied by his girlfriend, they find a young homeless girl unconscious on a pavement and he realises he can't walk away. He has a tremendous fight with his girlfriend, who says, "Let someone else handle it, it's not our problem!" ending with her walking away and him trying to get the girl to a hospital. She comes around enough to stop him calling for any aid, but she's obviously terrified of something. He initially takes her back to his flat to recover, and finds himself being sucked into her world and her problems. He also finds that because he's befriended her, his life has fallen apart: he's lost his girlfriend, and possibly his job and home. Which means we get to go into the world that she inhabits as an outsider, and we learn things along with the guy who's our initial viewpoint character.

'The above is very loose and just a possible way into the storyline. Various questions that suggest themselves to me out in front include: are you looking at the series as a vehicle for you, as something for you initially that you can move out of after a season, or something that you simply create and wind up and leave without ever appearing on screen? I like the idea of having London itself as one of the focal characters in the story, in the way that the town of Twin Peaks is one of the major characters in

Twin Peaks, possibly even personifying London in some way; for example, an elderly man dressed in an incredibly filthy and tattered version of a 17th century red frock coat, wig and everything, who sleeps rough on the streets, not because he's homeless but because he's home, he *is* London, and if anything happens to him, then that's it for the city,' — which basically turned into the Marquis, I suppose.

'If we do want a SF/fantasy element, which would give us leeway to do a number of things, one possibility would be making our initial homeless girl (if we go with that beginning) a girl who can open doors in things, open doors to places, open doors where there shouldn't be doors, doors that let things into the world that shouldn't be here, or doors that open into places that never were. I like the idea of explaining as little as possible as a general rule. Any impossibilities should simply be part of the

∏EIL GAIMAN

Date/Place of Birth:
1960, Portchester, Hants, UK

Home Base:
Minneapolis, Minnesota, USA

Education:
Ardingly, Whitgift

First TV work:
Neverwhere

TV Career Highlights:
Neverwhere, Babylon 5: 'Day of the Dead'

fabric of what we're doing, almost taken in our stride. I also like the idea of something that could go anywhere from a genre viewpoint, possibly within one episode; it can be funny, quirky and terrifying and heartwarming and weird.'

I then ask the questions: 'What kind of mood are we after? What kind of feel? Film or video? Large cast or small? There you go, a bunch of random thoughts, any or all of which can be thrown away. They are jotted down randomly; see you Friday,' and that was the original outline.

So you asked where it began. It really did begin with me knowing the first ten minutes and not having a clue what happened after that, which is a very odd position to be in. It's not necessarily the way that one normally tells a story, but it definitely wasn't all plotted. It sort of arrived bit by bit, so having that beginning, I basically had Door, the Marquis, Richard and Jessica, and then I threw Croup and Vandemar into the mix. After that, a lot of it was walking around the garden at Lenny's place and throwing London place names at each other. Sometimes I'd say things and wasn't sure if they were good ideas or not, and he just loved them, which is where the Black Friars came from. I mentioned the idea of Black Friars, and he thought that was so wonderful that it was a case of, 'If you like it, then I'm doing 'em.'

I spent a couple of months with Lenny, making up these characters and telling him about them. I started with the characters and then wrote an outline for episode one, which basically said, 'And then stuff happens, and these are the kind of characters we'll meet on the way.'

How long did it take to write the scripts for all six episodes?

I wrote the outline for it in March 1991. About a year later, I got a commission to write the first episode, and in December 1993, I got the go-ahead to write episodes two and three. I wrote episode three while I was in Finland, near the Arctic Circle, and I was reading a book on the Orkneys at the time, which is why Earl's Court is filled with people with names like Halvard and Dagvard. I think it was January 1995 that I got the go-ahead to write four, five and six; I wrote episode four at Tori Amos's house, which was built over a canal, and I suppose that's the reason there is so much water in that episode. I handed in episode six in the summer, and at that point we were finally given a green light.

Let's talk about some of your major characters in *Neverwhere*. The series is seen through the eyes of Richard Mayhew, the 'normal guy' you alluded to earlier, who's played by Gary Bakewell.

Richard was easy. I just did me, as Gary correctly observed a few days in. He said, 'That's you, isn't it?' and I said, 'Yeah, basically.' Richard was very easy, because I took many of what my own reactions would be, but Gary didn't play it in the way that I would have done it. Richard was a delight. What I think is an amazing achievement of Gary's, which will be underestimated because he is the grey-jumpered bit of normality in the whole thing, is it would be very easy for Richard to be Arthur Dent [Douglas Adams's often bewildered human protagonist in *The Hitchhiker's Guide to the Galaxy*]. His function in the plot is mostly to walk around saying, 'What?' and getting in the way.

If you remember the *Hitchhiker's* TV series, Arthur Dent — who in the radio series and book is vaguely likeable — becomes profoundly irritating; it's like, 'Shut up, grow up, and take that stupid dressing gown off!' Simon Jones is a good actor, but Arthur Dent becomes a profoundly irritating character. Writing Richard, whose function in the plot is an Arthur Dent function, to be a little bit of normality and our point of view going into a place of strangeness, the most important thing I had in mind was likeability. I knew that if you liked and cared for this character, everything else would work, and if you were irritated by him or disliked him, then nothing would work. When I was writing Richard, there were three people I had most in mind — I say he's me, but it's not only me. The first person was Richard Curtis, the writer. It's interesting that *Four Weddings and a Funeral* [written by Curtis] made Hugh Grant, but as he's said in a number of interviews, the character he plays is Richard Curtis. Hugh Grant in anything else doesn't work, but in *Four Weddings*, what he does with the spectacles, the whole body language; it's all Richard Curtis. The second was Alan Cumming,

DON'T PANIC!

Originally conceived as a drama for BBC Radio 4, Douglas Adams's wickedly satirical work of SF, *The Hitchhiker's Guide to the Galaxy*, became a best-selling book (followed by several equally successful sequels), a play, and even a towel. In 1981, the BBC aired a six-part TV adaptation that brought Adams's ideas to visual life. In *The Hitchhiker's Guide to the Galaxy*, mild-mannered Arthur Dent discovers that the impending demolition of his house is largely irrelevant, when the entire planet Earth is vaporised in order to make way for a hyperspace bypass. Arthur manages to escape the planet's destruction along with Ford Prefect, a field researcher for the Guide, eventually finding himself on a stolen spaceship, along with two-headed con man Zaphod Beeblebrox, Zaphod's girlfriend Trillian, and Marvin the Paranoid Android. This bizarre group embarks on a series of adventures, involving Life, the Universe and of course, Everything. A classic of the genre, the TV *Hitchhiker's* managed to rise above its modest budget by means of a cracking story, a stellar cast, and ambitious FX work (including hugely effective computer-style animation to bring the Guide to life). A *Hitchhiker's* feature film, in the works for some time, may now remain unfilmed following Adams's untimely death in 2001.

particularly his performance in *Bernard and the Genie**, where he plays this incredibly likeable person; and when I was writing Richard, I had this vaguely Scottish lilt in the back of my head. So it's me, Richard Curtis and Alan Cumming, and sort of writing a character based on Richard Curtis with my reactions. There is a quality that Curtis has, which is this rumpled, corduroy likeability, and I wanted to give that to the character of Richard. He's the little steam train that chugs through the piece and keeps it all going. With a vaguely irritating Richard the whole thing falls apart; it just wouldn't work. And it was obvious from Gary's first screen test that, 'Oh look, there's Richard!' He read the lines, he *was* Richard, they had humour, they had warmth; the other Richards that I saw in the screen test didn't have that.

The other thing was that Gary was a fan of science fiction and fantasy, which made a difference, because he got it immediately. He knew who it was and what it was. I remember trying to explain the plot to Laura Fraser [who played Door] when she first came in. She sat down and I said, 'This is the plot,' and gave her a two-minute version, and she looked up at me and said, 'What drugs were you taking when you wrote this?' Whereas Gary knew what it was immediately, and that was lovely.

The Marquis de Carabas seemed to change quite a bit from the way you originally saw him. Is it true that the role was originally written for Richard O'Brien, of *Rocky Horror Show* fame?

That request came from Janet Street-Porter, who at that time was head of Youth [Programming at the BBC]. I was talking to Lenny on that first day, and I said, 'Is there anything that you want to throw into the pot? Have we got any thoughts on casting?' He said, 'No, nothing at all, except that Janet Street-Porter would like Richard O'Brien in it.' I said, 'I've got this character, this guy in the frock coat that I mentioned earlier.' The frock coat came along with the character from the beginning, so I said, 'Great, I'll do the character as Richard O'Brien.'

I knew I wanted a snide, sarcastic character, who was smarter than everybody else but not quite as smart as he thought he was, and who existed on favours; on checks and balances. I still wish that we had tried O'Brien out for the part, but I was overruled three to one by the time we were actually sitting around the table. But I remember seeing the video of Paterson Joseph trying out for the part and thinking, 'That's the Marquis!' His eyes glowed like the Marquis' eyes should have glowed, he smiled like the Marquis should have smiled, and he said the lines like the Marquis said the lines.

What's odd about the Marquis is that in the novel [written after the series had been filmed], the character is definitely black. I don't make a point about it, but the first time we see him we talk about this dark face, and these huge eyes and teeth in this dark face. A few pages later, he takes Door's small white hand in his huge black hand, and stuff like that. Despite the fact that it's stated explicitly in the book, people who

---

* Bernard and the Genie *(1991) was a one-off TV comedy drama, written by Richard Curtis, and starring the Scottish actor Alan Cumming as the likeable Bernard, with* Neverwhere *producer Lenny Henry as the Genie.*

have only read the book and then see the video are always surprised when Paterson is black, which I find odd. I think that's because the dialogue is a lot of things, but it isn't what you would think of as 'black' dialogue, it's just actors' dialogue. The joy for me of watching Paterson is, the Marquis' lines are not naturalistic. It is not kitchen sink, it is not mumbled *EastEnders*, soap opera kind of dialogue; it's dialogue that he sinks his teeth into. It's a question of who's going to get on top of lines like that, and whether you're going to relish it or have trouble with it, and he has no trouble with it, partly because he's an actor with classical training. The same with Hywel Bennett, who played Mr Croup; they're both people who happily 'get in there'!

Is it true that Mr Croup and Mr Vandemar, the main villains of the piece, are actually pinched from a story you wrote many years ago?

When I was about sixteen, I was down in Sussex in the little village I lived in. I was going for a walk when I passed these two people, and they were not much older than I was; they were maybe in their early twenties. There was a short, oily one and a tall, dull-looking one; this strange couple of men walking along in these oily clothes. I passed them and thought, 'Now there's Mr Croup and Mr Vandemar!' and the names just turned up in my head. The thing is, back then I'd begin lots of stories and I'd never finish them. So they were in at least one story I wrote — I think I did a song or a poem about them — because I was fascinated by these characters, and then never used them. That was partly because I didn't have anywhere for them to go, and partly because I didn't want to give them away. I didn't want to put them in a DC comic, because they were mine. DC had an enormous number of characters I've done things to that they've spun off, but Mr Croup and Mr Vandemar were mine, and I was going to wait until I was doing something that was mine to bring them out. They just seemed perfect for *Neverwhere*.

So they could appear in something else?

They could turn up in something else; I'd love to do a science fiction story with them in it. The thing about Croup and Vandemar is there are lots of different ways to bring them back, but they're like the Daleks from *Doctor Who*: you don't bring them back in every story. You want it to be a special event when they turn up, you want the front cover of the *Radio Times*: 'The return of Croup and Vandemar!' It should be something exciting.

One of your strengths as a writer is that you've always written well for women. But would you agree that some of the female characters in *Neverwhere* don't have the same sparkling dialogue as, say, the Marquis or Croup?

I don't know, I think Lamia's lines are as good as anybody's. She gets some killer lines in episode five. Hunter doesn't get many lines, she gets one amazing speech, which is her big speech, and she gets her great end scene, but she doesn't talk very much; she's not chatty. What I like about Hunter is, in many ways, it could just as well have been a man, except that it's much cooler and more interesting that it's a woman. Hunter is a fascinating little mass of contradictions.

Door is not cooked yet, she's not fully formed yet, as with most of the story. As a character, she's unbaked dough; she's still very young. In my head, Door is not over sixteen, but I think she's a good character, and an interesting one. Also, you get very little from her point of view. She tends to exist on the outside. I don't know if I was right or not, but I wanted a story with a male and female lead where there was not a romance. There was obviously a friendship and some kind of relationship, and maybe in a different situation there could have been something there. But I didn't want a romance, because at that point they start to define each other by each other. I'm pleased that Door isn't defined by Richard, she is not the romantic interest. That was what I wanted, but I think we were only partially successful, because there were some places where Dewi [Humphreys, the director] tried experimentally to do it a different way, but he wound up cutting them all out because they didn't work.

It's interesting, you saying there are no strong female characters, or they don't get great lines or whatever. If you actually look at who there is, we have pretty good gender parity, tending to weigh on the side of the women. We have Anesthesia, Serpentine, Hunter, Door and Lamia, and particularly when we get to Down Street, where the characters have to cross a chasm, we have Hunter and Door and Lamia. Richard is the wimp on the plank, while you have three fairly sensible women who just managed to cross it with no problems at all.

If you've got a character that's a hunter and then you cast Tanya Moodie, a black actress, and then give her a spear to carry, is there a real danger of negative stereotyping?

The only thing that was silly and tacky and wasn't in the script — and I still wish they hadn't had it — is the spear. I don't know why they put it in, but it was put in over my protests. She never uses it, so it seemed rather silly to give her a spear when the whole thing she's after is the particular spear she needs to kill the 'beast'. And when she comes on stage, it does kind of say 'Oh look, a warrior woman!' which was not the intention. You're not meant to say that at least until the point where she takes out Varney. And in the book, she's dressed in much more flowing leather stuff, has longer hair and a staff, because I wouldn't have done it like that.

But other than that, no. When Tanya got the part, there were lots of different people from lots of different backgrounds. I find it very hard to think of things like that, because in the case of her and Door and the Marquis, particularly those three, lots of auditions were done. We saw lots of audition tapes and saw lots of people who were black, white and Asian, and the people who got the parts — Tanya, Paterson and Laura — got them because they were the best. In none of those three cases — one white Scottish actor, and two black actors — did they get the parts because of skin colour. They got the parts because they did the coolest reading. There were white and Asian people on the audition tape I saw for Hunter and nobody was anywhere near as good. We had Asian, black and even some oriental Doors trying out, and we also had lots of Caucasians — loads of different people — and Laura was the one we liked best as Door.

Let me throw the other thing in on Hunter — and this was not something I intended to have, this is simply something that I have noticed — that women and men respond to Hunter as a very different character. The feedback I get is that a lot of women are saying, 'Hunter is such a cool character,' and I think that's because there aren't that many characters like her. There aren't that many roles like that given to a woman. She's not butch, she's not a Xena Warrior Princess or whatever. She's a very single-minded, very dedicated hunter, with her own rather strange agenda.

Some of the most interesting characters in *Neverwhere* only have a few scenes, whether it's Old Bailey, who trades in birds and information, or Serpentine, who obviously has a very big back-story to be told at some point.

In this series, the only character that turned up because I needed something to happen, and promptly wandered into the story, was Old Bailey. I don't think there's anyone else; maybe Serpentine a little, but she sort of came in from a different kind of direction. Originally, there was a whole scene set in somewhere called The May

BABYLON 5: 'DAY OF THE DEAD'

When Gaiman was told that the BBC would not be picking up a second season of *Neverwhere*, he finally found time to write an episode of *Babylon 5* for his friend, J. Michael Straczynski. 'I was in LA for the signing tour of the *Neverwhere* novel, where I had dinner with Joe and told him I finally had some time to write an episode if he still wanted one. He said yes, so I went home and jotted down some ideas, which became 'Day of the Dead'. I then phoned Joe and told him my idea about the Brakiri Day of the Dead, which he liked, and I wanted to do Rebo and Zooty and he said fine. I never thought we'd be lucky enough to get Penn & Teller to play them. Writing an episode of *Babylon 5* turned out to be astonishingly easy and pleasant. When I asked Joe if he wanted me to write an outline, he asked if I particularly liked writing outlines, and I said, "No, I actually hate writing them." He said, "Good, so do I; I'll just send the commission off to your agent; write me a script." It was as easy as that.'

Fair, but we costed out episode four, and that was the one scene where I was told, 'Look, you've done this whole huge marvellous scene which is going to cost us the earth. You've already got the Black Friars in that episode, you've already got the ordeal, we cannot do The May Fair; can you do something cheap instead?'

By that point, I'd been to Down Street tube station, and had this idea of setting a dinner party on that little area of platform. I'd also been playing with the idea of the Seven Sisters, so that had been floating around in the back of my mind for a while, and I thought, right, I'll do this strange Miss Havisham [from Dickens's *Great Expectations*] enchantress character, and I can also do some of Hunter's back-story with it. Once I'd written Serpentine, she also turned up at the end to take Hunter's body away, and her entire family becomes very important with the way I see *Neverwhere* and what I'd like to do if we did a second season.

When you first started writing the series, were you trying to use the homeless as a metaphor, or do they actually act as a catalyst for your story?

I think it's using *Neverwhere* as a metaphor for the homeless, or the dispossessed, the people who fall through the cracks. That's what it's about to some extent, because those are the people you don't see. The one point while filming *Neverwhere* that was the most heart-breaking and strange for me was when we were filming on The Strand, and we were sitting in those little dining coaches having food, and there were 200 people sleeping rough outside. I went over afterwards and said, 'Can we give these guys the leftover food?' and was told, 'Actually, we came down early and we fed them all,' which I didn't know and was very pleased about. But it was heart-breaking; it's London and it's for real. We're in one of the most advanced cities in the world, and we were behind the Adelphi Theatre, next to the Thames, and next to the Savoy, one of the plushest hotels, and there are all these people sleeping rough in February and it was fucking cold. We had to throw people out of the doorways so we could film in them. It was a case of art trying to dramatise life to make a point. As is made very clear, if you're part of London Below, they don't notice you and they forget about you. It's not that they don't see you, they just don't look at you, and they don't want to know.

After *Neverwhere*, there are probably a lot of people who will never look at underground railway stations in the same way again.

I wanted to recreate some of the magic that I used to get as a kid. The quote that I start the book with is G. K. Chesterton's *The Napoleon of Notting Hill*, and I remember the magic of Ladbroke Grove and Notting Hill and Shepherd's Bush, so I'd like to do a bit of that for people. I'd love to get Londoners to look at their city and the people and the things in it again. There's a strange level on which *Neverwhere* exists, by which I mean that was where we were filming. We were in places that you can't go. We were in the old St Pancras Hotel, we were on the rooftops, we were deep beneath the ground, we were in abandoned underground stations — we were in these places. I found it fascinating to be talking to these guards and the people in these different locations, because they all have a story to tell, which is part of *Neverwhere*. I was talking to the station manager at Down Street, the disused tube station we filmed in, and he was telling me about the time he chased somebody into a dead end, and there was nobody there, and how the guy couldn't have gotten back past him down in the tunnels…

You've also touched on some of London's great urban myths.

The boar in the sewers is a London urban myth that dates back to the 17th century, which is when it happened. This piglet got into the sewers, and they used to send in hunting parties after it, and it grew to be a huge boar, and for many years after that it was believed that it was still down there. It's a real London urban legend that predates alligators in the sewers of New York by 400 years. But because we couldn't find a giant boar, we made it a bull, or a 'beast'.

One of your frustrations when you were a journalist was that you'd hand something in, which would then be changed and was no longer your work. With *Neverwhere* you've entered the television arena, which is basically a medium of compromise.

During the course of filming, I kept saying, 'We'll ask for the moon and maybe we'll get some asteroids.' I discovered an Indian saying recently, which I thought was lovely, which was, 'Shoot your arrow at the stars, and you may hit an eagle. If you shoot at the eagle, you will hit nothing but the rocks.' So you're up against practicality, but sometimes you're just up against differences in aesthetics and differences in opinion. When it's simply those differences, at the end of the day, it's my opinion and my aesthetic, so I don't see any reason why I shouldn't win on that level.

What got me through the filming of *Neverwhere* with my sanity intact was that I knew I had the novel coming up. What was great about the novel is I stole everything I liked from the TV series that other people threw in. And I reacted against everything that other people threw in that I didn't like for one reason or another, whether it was a set or a way of shooting a scene or changing a line of dialogue. Back in the novel, it's the way that I wanted it to be.

Now that the series is finished, you can look back at the experience with a certain amount of objectivity. Knowing what you know now, what would you have changed if you had the opportunity?

There isn't an easy answer to that, but if I could do that, I would have fought for another week. Knowing what I know now, I would do whatever had to be done, including turning around and saying, 'Okay, I will kick in this or forego this fee if the money winds up here and I get a little more control for it.' But basically, I would have wanted another week, because that's what we needed. There are places there where my notes would say, 'What about this scene? We needed a close-up here, and a long shot there and we don't have it.' It's not necessarily stuff that other people will see, but I saw it.

The big battle that I'm still pleased that I fought and won was getting Dewi as director. I think he was by far and away the best of the directors we talked to. It was actually a three-person short list, where the first guy was very good and very brilliant, who said, 'I'd love to do it, I don't think I could do it in eight weeks, so could I have twelve weeks?' That basically took him out of the running. So it came down to a guy whose stuff I thought was singularly boring, and Dewi. All of Dewi's stuff that I've seen, including *Neverwhere*, has two things going for it, one of which is that he's very good at getting nice performances out of actors, and the other is it looks pretty. He also didn't have a problem with the mixed tone. I wanted to build *Neverwhere* like a layer cake. I wanted it to be funny and scary and touching and filled with a sense of wonder. So I finally won the battle, and that's the one I'm proudest of.

The answer to your question is, in a communally created work of art or entertainment, by definition, there are going to be a million compromises. If I wrote a scene in a field with a tree and a horse, and two people sitting under the tree talking and having a picnic, when I came to film it, it would not be the film I saw in my head. In *Sandman*, I could get very close, because I would describe the field and somebody would draw it. But in terms of going out and actually finding a field and an oak tree that looked like the one in my head, if I was lucky, somebody would give me three to pick from and I'd pick the one that was most like it. But more likely, you'd turn up on the day to simply a field with a tree. Then again, as I've said a few times, with *Neverwhere* I had the benefit that once the TV series was done, I got to write the novel, and there is something very nice and upside-down and wonderful about that. Instead of creating a work of art and watching somebody changing it into something for film or television, I got to take everything that had been done and say, 'Okay, this is *my* way,' and put it back the way I wanted to. It was the joy of writing a novel, which is something I really wanted to do, rather than just 'making' a novelization.

When you began writing the novel, were you still seeing the actors from the TV series in your head?

The strangest thing I found is that some characters from the TV series turned up and some didn't. It had nothing to do with how good the actor was or anything like that; it was some kind of odd head space thing. For example, the Marquis in the novel is definitely Paterson Joseph; there's not a doubt in my mind. Tanya Moodie is a fine actress, but she isn't Hunter in the novel. When I created Serpentine in my head, she was originally Siân Phillips and very Livia [from *I, Claudius*], but is now Julie T. Wallace. Richard is definitely Gary Bakewell. Door isn't Laura Fraser, which is interesting. In fact, Door is built up around a comment from Sheelagh [Wells, the show's make-up designer], that she wanted strange-coloured eyes. She wanted Door in weird contact lenses, which Laura never went into, but I thought it was a lovely idea that Door had incredibly strange-coloured eyes, so that's how she gets described.

One of the criticisms of *Neverwhere* was that perhaps it was too ambitious for the time and the money available. Are there any scenes or moments from your original scripts that you particularly regret losing?

We really did aim very high and very strange. And — I keep repeating myself, so it almost becomes a mantra — the things that I really regret, I fixed in the book. I wish the ending wasn't so fast; which is partly because we ran out of time and there were little scenes that didn't get shot. It's also because a number of people in the hierarchy were of the opinion that everybody knew Richard was going to get back to London Below, so let's get it over with, and anyway, we're running out of time. Given twenty-nine minutes per episode, we already had to lose Old Bailey's goodbye scene from episode six because there wasn't enough time.

What I got to do in the novel was a good fifteen pages with Richard back in the real world, so the reader gets to see him being really happy coming back, and then gradually becoming dissatisfied. As he begins to work his way back through his life, he realises he made the wrong choice, and the reader gets to see that. Right at the very last page, we send him back, which was the feeling I had wanted, but the BBC viewpoint and many other viewpoints tended to be, 'Get on with it!' So I did. But I got to end it the way I wanted to in the book.

What sort of stories would you still like to tell in this universe, whether it was on television or a future series of novels?

What I tried to do with *Neverwhere* was create something that goes off at the edges. I wanted you to feel that if you carried on to one side or another, there are other people with other histories and other stories going on in other places. We've done the story of somebody discovering another London and going into it and coming out, which is very much one story. I think if we did another *Neverwhere*, we might have several different storylines for different characters. I'd love to do a one-off story on how the Marquis got his coat back; we'd find out a little about the Marquis' family, and his brother, and stuff like that. The next storyline I would like to do for *Neverwhere* would be the Seven Sisters, where you find out about all the strange internecine struggling going on between these seven strange, very different women, of whom Serpentine is the second oldest. Putney is the youngest, I think Olympia is the oldest.

Anyway, it would be the story of the Seven Sisters and we would also find out a bit more about Hunter and her back-story, because she was working for them back when they were still on speaking terms, and they haven't been on speaking terms for thirty years now. I like knowing a lot more about *Neverwhere* than I put in. In the next book or the next series you will find out more, but I don't see the reason to tell you everything up front.

If I was doing *Neverwhere* as a series of books, book two might be Portico's story, or even the story of Door's grandfather — who's actually a much more interesting character than Portico — the one who built the House Without Doors. I don't know that I could do that on TV, because we're not at the point where *Neverwhere* has entered the culture so you can take it for granted and stop fucking with it. It's very easy to say, 'It's a story about time travel or space travel or lost continents,' things you can do as shorthand. *Neverwhere* isn't shorthand yet.

What aspects of *Neverwhere* still work for you even after you've seen them a hundred times?

There's one moment, which was not filmed as it was in the script. They went off and were creative with it, and I love what they did. I think I actually changed it in the book to go along with that scene, and that's when the Marquis gobs blood into

NEVERWHERE: THE MOVIE

Although the BBC version of *Neverwhere* wasn't a ratings success, Gaiman's novel quickly became an international best seller, so it was just a matter of time before Hollywood began calling. Henson Pictures snapped up the movie rights, and at the time of writing are still in development. Gaiman wrote several drafts of the screenplay before finally turning his attention to other projects. 'I had to do things differently, because the TV series was three hours, but here, I have less than two hours, so everything is up for grabs. One of the lovely things about having written it so many times in so many different ways is, like most writers (including me) who mostly tend to say, "This is sacred; how dare you touch it?" nothing in *Neverwhere* is sacred anymore. I've written it enough that it's all up for grabs. There are no characters left in there that are precious to me, partly because anything I didn't like in the TV series, I fixed in the book. I think it's very unlikely, for example, that Anesthesia will be in the film. There's only so much room in the plot, and she's a lovely character, but she's five minutes of stuff where we could be doing other things. I could start Richard and Hunter earlier, so I'll probably kill off Anesthesia before she ever hits the page and not miss her. I've already seen what she looks like, and I got her scene right in the book, so between those two, I don't have that, "She's my character, she must be in there" feeling anymore.'

Mr Croup's face, followed by Hywel saying, 'Naughty!' I don't know how many times I've seen that, I still laugh. It is a perfect scene, and the way I wrote it in the script, I had him gobbing into Mr Vandemar's face, but the way they shot it instead was just lovely.

The knife through Vandemar's hand, I could watch a million times. That lovely little scene at the end, with the Velvets walking past Richard; I just think it's magic. There's something about the expression on Lamia's face, the real dreamlike feeling, it's a moment of complete magic, and even the other Velvets, who sometimes look strange and other-worldly and sometimes don't, managed it in that scene. I always stop and watch a few Islington scenes: him singing 'Heaven,' and his final big scene; I think he's marvellous. Stratford Johns' speech [as Mr Arnold Stockton], and the Angelus stuff. Jessica and Richard's final scene, I think it's quite beautiful; it's funny and it's heartbreaking, and there's something nice and true about it.

It's a pity, but I think episode one is by far the weakest of all of them. Part of that is my fault, because I wrote a forty-five minute episode one, and the process of cutting it to a twenty-nine minute episode meant that it went a bit wonky. Because of the scheduling, it was also the first episode we shot; most of what goes on in there was done in the first week to ten days of shooting, so we really weren't up to speed yet. So, on the one hand, it's the first thing people get to see and it's the weakest, on the other, it's nice that it gets better from there. I think if you like episode one, then you have glories untold ahead of you. It's the weirdness of having people say to you, 'Are you happy with *Neverwhere*?' and there are two distinct answers, one of which is no, and the other is, 'God yes!' It's only seventy-five per cent of the *Neverwhere* that it could have been, but it's still 150 per cent more than anybody's seen on British TV or possibly any TV in terms of fantasy. ∎

JONATHAN GLASSNER

I t seems hard to believe that Jonathan Glassner, who never planned on working as a writer, let alone an SF writer, has spent the better part of a decade creating some of the best genre fare on television. After early jobs on *The Wizard*, and cop shows *Street Justice* and *21 Jump Street*, Glassner turned to SF, moving to Vancouver to help launch the revival of *The Outer Limits*. Then came the co-executive producer job on a certain other Vancouver-produced show which, whether he liked it or not, confirmed his reputation as an 'SF writer' — *Stargate SG-1*. It should be a broadcasting truism that good movies don't always make good TV. The television battlefield is littered with the corpses of TV shows based on box-office hits that just never made it on the small screen. Most of them, mercifully, don't even progress beyond the pilot stage. Others limp along for a few episodes until an embarrassed network finally admits defeat. *Stargate SG-1* is an exception. Based on the 1994 feature by director Roland Emmerich and producer Dean Devlin, the TV series took the film's concepts, expanded them, and devised a complex, ever-growing mythology. Developed by Jonathan Glassner and his long-time *Outer Limits* collaborator Brad Wright, *Stargate SG-1* quickly became a huge success. Glassner moved back to LA after three years on the show, but has remained active in the SF field: his most recent challenge was revamping *The Invisible Man* into an offbeat series that combined elements of buddy comedy, action-adventure and nifty visual FX. This conversation took place during the final weeks of production on *I-Man*'s second season...

Is it true that you actually went to school to become an actor, and then went into directing?

Actually, it even goes a step beyond that. I originally went in as a theatre major to be an actor, and very quickly realised that I wasn't so talented. I went to Northwestern University, which has one of the best theatre departments in the country, and was thrown in with an amazing array of actors that included Julia Louis-Dreyfus [*Seinfeld*], David Schwimmer [*Friends*] and Marg Helgenberger [*CSI*]. It was an unbelievable list of people, and I soon realised that I wasn't up to their level. So I switched majors to television and film, and decided to try and become a director. One day, Robert Thompson, who directed *The Paper Chase* [TV series], came and spoke to us. He said,

'If you want to be a director in Hollywood, the best way to get there is by being a writer first.' That's when I started focusing on writing and found I was pretty good at it, so I pursued that and ended up going up through the ranks as a writer, until I could assign myself as a director, and then did both!

So how did you get your foot in the door as a writer?

I wrote a spec *Moonlighting* script, and did a lot of legwork. I spent a lot of time on the phone and sending out letters just begging people to read it, and eventually I got it read at Universal. I went in to meet them about *Alfred Hitchcock Presents* [the 1980s revival], and sold them a script. They liked it so much that they gave me a blind commitment for two more scripts, so that was the start of my career, and I just kept going from there.

Did you freelance for a while or did you land a staff job?

I went on a show called *The Wizard**. I'd just written that first *Hitchcock* and they gave me a contract for two more, and then I got *The Wizard* at the same time. So I went on staff on *The Wizard* and wrote the *Hitchcock*s at night. I did *The Wizard* for a year, until it got cancelled. From then on, I was on staffs.

At what point did you make the jump into SF television?

I wasn't really intending to be a SF writer. I was always a big fan of SF and certainly had a liking for it and an understanding of it, but at the time, there really wasn't much SF on television. *Star Trek: The Next Generation* came on after I'd already started my career, and that was about it. But then the genre started getting hotter and hotter, and I ended up falling into it.

As a writer, don't you start getting identified for a particular genre?

In a way. I was basically a cop show writer — no, that's not true, I had a very varied career at first. I did [the *Nightmare on Elm Street* spin-off] *Freddy's Nightmares* for a year, which was my first producing job, and from that I went to cop shows for a long time. I

JONATHAN GLASSNER

Date/Place of Birth:
1961, Roanoke, Virginia, USA

Home Base:
Los Angeles, California, USA

Education:
Northwestern University

First TV Work:
Alfred Hitchcock Presents

TV Career Highlights:
21 Jump Street, The Wizard, Street Justice, Island City, The Outer Limits, Stargate SG-1, The Invisible Man

* A light-hearted, gadget-laden adventure/espionage show (1986-87) starring the diminutive David Rappaport (the late actor best known as Randall in Time Bandits).

then got a call from Lee Rich's company at Warner Bros, who wanted to figure out a way to do a SF version of *Rat Patrol*, which was a show he created years ago about a US desert patrol squad in the Second World War, and that led indirectly to *Island City*. So I created *Island City**, and that script was so well received all over town that everybody suddenly thought I was a SF writer, which was not really my goal. I fell into it that way, and ended up getting hired to go up to Vancouver and do *The Outer Limits*, which I did for four years, and then I did *Stargate* for three years, one of them overlapping. I also did a story for *Star Trek: Voyager* at one stage, but before they could get around to committing it to script, I got another staff job, so I didn't write the script [which ended up as the first season episode 'Faces']. So you're right, now I'm kind of pigeonholed as a SF writer.

What happened with the pilot for *Island City*?

Actually, it did very well in the ratings. The reason it didn't go to series was because of very bad luck for me in a business situation. *Island City* was done by an *ad hoc* network at the time called PTEN [Prime Time Entertainment Network, which had launched *Babylon 5* a year earlier], which was a partnership of Warner Bros and Chris Craft. While we were in production, Chris Craft and Warner Bros had a falling out and disbanded. Chris Craft went with Paramount and formed the UPN Network, and Warner said, 'The hell with you, we're going to form our own network!' and they formed the WB, and everything that was developed for PTEN just disappeared.

How did the opportunity on the 1990s version of *The Outer Limits* come up, and did the fact you'd done *Hitchcock* help in doing a new anthology series?

I guess somebody at MGM or [*Outer Limits* production company] Trilogy read my *Island City* script, so they called me in and hired me off that. Doing an anthology is basically like writing a pilot or a movie every week. If you can write anything with new characters, and set up a whole new environment each week, that's anthology writing. The only real difficulty or challenge is to set a tone that is *The Outer Limits* or *Alfred Hitchcock Presents*, and be able to define it, and stick to it. That was actually the biggest challenge on *Outer Limits*, because all the freelance writers would always try to pitch up *Twilight Zone*s, which are not the same thing. It was a subtle difference that was very difficult to communicate to people, especially people who were not SF writers by trade. *The Outer Limits* was a pure SF series; we only did scientifically based stories, things that are scientifically possible, not metaphysical things. *The Twilight Zone* dealt with metaphysical ideas. Sometimes they'd do SF but more often than not, a guy wakes up and he's in a box with a bunch of other people, and it turns out he's a toy. They were very out-there stories. We didn't do any like that. We only did pure SF.

Did you watch the original version of *The Outer Limits*?

I watched it as a little kid, but it scared me so much that I didn't really remember it

---

* Island City *was a TV movie that aired in February 1994. It took place in 2035, ten years after a fountain of youth vaccine began to mutate, turning people into monstrous 'recessives'. Island City, a genetically controlled metropolis, is built to protect its residents from the hostile recessive population.*

very well! I went back and studied it when I got the job, and it doesn't hold up. There are about three or four of them that are still really powerful episodes — to the extent that we actually tried to remake a few of them — but the majority of them are guys in rubber suits.

Were there tonal influences on the new series, or were you going in a different direction?

Oh no, we were trying to stay true to the original series, which was to do scary SF, so that's what we did. We told freelance writers that it had to be scary, it had to be SF, and it had to be a good story regardless of either of those factors. It had to have good characters, and good emotional drama. In other words, don't just come in with a cool idea that has no substance to it. We preferred episodes that had a strong ethical/moral dilemma, or a strong metaphor for something meaningful in today's world.

Didn't Joe Stefano, who helped create the original series, get involved in the revival?

He was very happy with it. He came up to Vancouver quite a bit and hung out with us, and went to dinner, and generally sat around and gave us his thoughts. He's quite an interesting guy.

Would the writing staff work together to 'break' all the episodes?

JOE STEFANO

One of the classics of SF television is the 1960s incarnation of *The Outer Limits*, which was created by Joe Stefano and Leslie Stevens. Stefano, who's probably best known as the screenwriter for Alfred Hitchcock's *Psycho*, still regards the original series as the centrepiece of his career: 'I'd never have dreamed that I would have that great an opportunity to communicate with the audience. I always looked at things from the audience's point of view, and in all our conferences, we were always saying, "How will it affect the people who are watching it?" That was what I wanted to provide: something that would be provocative and make you want to watch again next week. We had no 'star', nothing to draw you back except the fact that you had just seen a show that you liked. People would often mistake *The Outer Limits* for *The Twilight Zone*, but they were different kinds of shows. The only thing they had in common was they were both anthologies. I don't think I ever saw a *Twilight Zone* that I would have bought for *The Outer Limits*. They just came from different places in the psyche.'

Almost always. There were a few writers — Alan Brennert comes to mind for example — who didn't need our help at all. Alan is an amazing SF writer, and he would call us with an idea, and we would say, 'Yeah, go do it!' and generally his scripts would come in and we wouldn't have to do anything to them. There were a couple of them that the studio didn't agree with us on, and made us make changes, much to our dismay, but for the most part, Alan would just turn it in and we would shoot it. I think he was the only one that was the case with. We had to work out stories and rewrite stories for just about everybody else.

Alan Brennert wrote for the 1980s *Twilight Zone* revival too, didn't he?

He's a SF professional. He's done a lot of it, and he's a student of it as well, so he really understands the genre. I think he probably taught us more about 'What is an *Outer Limits*?' than we would ever have taught him. He was a huge fan of the original and of the new series, and he would call us every now and then and say, 'Guys, what are you doing? This isn't an *Outer Limits*!' This was in the first season, when we were all still trying to find the right approach.

What was the actual writing process of an episode?

Somebody, either on staff or a freelancer, would have an idea, and they would come in, and we would talk about it, and turn it into a one or two-page pitch document, which would then get sent to the Trilogy and MGM people in LA. They would approve it, or put in their two cents' worth, and we would adjust it according to what they wanted. And then we would beat it out into an outline. There were two ways. If it was a staff writer, we'd sit in a big boardroom with a big wipe board and we would write all the beats of the story up on it. If it was a freelancer, we would have them write an outline and send it to us. We would then give them notes and have them do another draft. We would usually rewrite that draft of the outline and send it back to them, and then they'd start writing the script.

Where did you come up with your own source of inspiration for stories?

People ask me that about everything I ever write, and I never know the answer! Maybe I'll read an article about some new scientific discovery that's being worked on, and something will click in my head and that will become something else which becomes something else, and by the time it's turned into a story, it has nothing to do with that scientific thing I originally read about. I was always fascinated by genetic engineering. One of the themes that *Outer Limits* had a lot of, and which occurred in probably eighty per cent of the episodes, was the message of 'Be careful playing God.' There were a lot of stories about scientists doing things that they probably shouldn't be doing, and the consequences thereof.

When did you get to start directing?

I was lucky on *The Outer Limits*, because I'd become rather entrenched there. I was the one writer/producer who started in the first season and stayed for the first four years. Brad Wright came in as a story editor and moved his way up the ladder very quickly and was also there most of the time, but not meaning to sound cocky, they really needed me. At one point I finally said, 'I won't come back next year unless you let me direct one,' and they reluctantly said okay.

Was that reluctance because you couldn't be writing and directing at the same time?

Not really, because the way we ran things on *The Outer Limits*, we were hands-on on the set as well. It was literally like doing a pilot every week. There would be all-new sets, all-new characters, new wardrobe, visual FX; we would be creating these things from whole cloth every week, so we never left that up to the people who were doing it. We were always there. The way we ran the show, there would be two writer/producers rotating being on set every other episode. In the second and third season, it was every third episode, once we put Brad into the rotation. So, I was on the set anyway for every third episode, sitting over the shoulder of the director, and I figured I might as well be directing one of them myself. I did offer that they didn't have to pay me my producing salary that week if they weren't happy with what I did; that was one of the incentives I gave them. They said okay, but I don't think they would actually have done that to me. They were actually thrilled with the first one I did, so after that, they let me direct three more.

How did *Stargate SG-1* come about? I understand you and Brad Wright both came up with the idea of developing a weekly series based on *Stargate*, independently of each other.

I was kind of a baby on *Outer Limits*, and I think I annoyed everybody, because they sent me up there for one year to get things going. After that, I was going to come home and do all the writing from LA, but we quickly realised that wouldn't work, for the reasons I just explained. So every year, I kept saying, 'I want to go home!' and the studio would say, 'What can we give you to make you stay another year?' In the third year, John Symes, the president of MGM, came up to Vancouver to sit down with me, and later with Brad, to persuade us again. I'd literally said, 'This is it, there's nothing you can give me that will keep me here another year!' and I was wrong, because he said, 'Do you want to do another series? Just tell us what you want to do.' I said, 'Well... you have this movie in your library, and if you will let me develop that as a series, I'll stay.' I didn't think they would, and at the time, Symes said, 'I don't know if we can do that, but let me look into it.'

I guess on the same day, Brad had said the same thing to the studio. Brad is Canadian and lives in Vancouver, so he wasn't planning to leave, but he'd had the same idea, and really wanted to do *Stargate*. A couple of weeks later, Symes called us back and said, 'How would you guys like to do it together?' and we were both thrilled. Brad and I were really getting along, so it worked out well. It turned out the reason Symes was hemming and hawing, and didn't say yes right away, was they were already in secret negotiations with Devlin and Emmerich. I guess it fell through, and Devlin and Emmerich weren't going to do it, so that's when they came to us.

Was it difficult as a writer to feel you've trespassed on somebody else's patch? It doesn't sound like the studio had any intention of doing a series of _Stargate_ films anyway.

MGM didn't, and that was a very frustrating thing for me, because I was a fan of Devlin and Emmerich, I thought they made great movies. But they were constantly bad-mouthing _SG-1_ in the press without ever seeing a lick of film we had shot, or reading our script or anything, and that really wasn't fair. And there was nothing we could do about it, because we didn't want to argue with them in the press. MGM never had any intention of making more features. It was too expensive, and they didn't think they would make as much money off of it. But MGM did offer Devlin and Emmerich the series. They apparently didn't want it, or they were asking for the moon — which MGM couldn't give them — so they ended up stepping away from it. On top of that, Devlin and Emmerich actually get paid for every episode of _Stargate SG-1_ that's made, so it's not like they're suffering because of it. It was disheartening that people I had been such a fan of were bad-mouthing us in the press for no reason, when they hadn't even seen what we were doing. I can understand them saying, 'We wanted to make movies, and the damn studio wouldn't let us, and they're making the series instead.' That's fine, but to then say the series is bad, it's awful, it's an atrocity, and it's ruined their vision, when they hadn't even seen any of it...

Even though you and Brad had separately pitched the idea of a _Stargate_ series, did you find you were of one mind in how to approach it?

We always are; that's one of the great things about working with Brad. If we were still in the same city, we would probably stay partners for the rest of our careers — at least, I would be up for it. We really didn't have any disagreements at all. The biggest battle was finding solutions to the problems that, at times, we both thought there might not be solutions to.

Was it a complex process, adapting the film into a series?

You've seen how many television series that are based on movies have failed. Most of them have, with the exception of _M*A*S*H_ and a few more that I can't think of off-hand, but very few. In the case of _Stargate_, I didn't think it was as much of a challenge, because the reason I was pushing to make _Stargate_ into a series was that I thought it should have been a series in the first place. I thought the movie had so many loose ends, because it should have been a series. Now, Devlin and Emmerich would probably say they left those loose ends on purpose because they wanted to make a series of movies, but nonetheless, you've got this device that has thirty-nine symbols, and it takes a combination of six of them to go somewhere — so why do you need that many symbols if it only goes to one place? To me, it was obviously set up to go other places, and was ripe for the picking to be a series. The only thing that was really a challenge in adapting it was creating characters that could go on from there. The characters in the movie were designed to be just in that movie and not really have a life beyond that, especially the character of Jack O'Neil, who was suicidal in the movie and ready to blow himself up. Nobody wants to watch a TV series where the lead character's ready to kill himself every week. It would be too depressing, so we had to completely redesign his character. The only character that really translated directly from the film was Daniel Jackson. And then the other characters were created from scratch.

Did you and Brad sit down at the beginning to work out the solutions to some of those problems you alluded to earlier?

That was the biggest challenge. Brad was in LA with me for about a month when we were breaking stories for *The Outer Limits*, because both of us were doing the third season at the same time as we were writing the pilot for *Stargate*. Then we did the fourth season of *Outer Limits* while we were doing the first season of *Stargate*. So Brad was in town breaking those stories, and in between those story meetings, the two of us would literally go out in the courtyard at MGM and pace. We'd say, 'What do we do about this? How do we fix that?' I think it was Brad who said, 'The reason the Stargate was buried in the movie was to keep the Goa'uld from coming, or to keep Ra from coming back through it. We've unburied it, so what kind of idiots are we? We've got to find a way to solve that plot hole!' I think one of the secrets, for any good SF to work, is that what you create within the far out world that you're saying exists, is grounded as much as possible in a reality. You make the rules and then stick to those rules. For example, if you're saying this giant Stargate exists, and we've put it underground inside a giant mountain, you have to consider things like, are we stupid for leaving it open there? We can do stories where bad guys come through and teach us a lesson, but then we have a choice: we either have to re-bury the gate or we solve the problem. So we did that. We had the bad guys come through the gate at the beginning of the pilot to teach us a lesson, and then we solved the problem [by equipping the gate with an iris to prevent any further surprise attacks].

Had you decided to create a recurring bad guy for the series right from the beginning?

One of the things we decided early on was to change one 'fact' that was in the feature. We pretty much stuck to all of the facts in the feature and tried not to change any of them, but the one thing we changed was that the film's villain, Ra, was the last of his race. We said he wasn't. Maybe he thought he was, or maybe the people thought he was, so maybe we're not even breaking the rules in that regard. But we said there were more of them, and we gave them a name, the Goa'uld. Then we created the whole biological basis for how they exist, and how their larvae are grown in Jaffa, and all of that. When you look at the movie and see Ra's guards, they seem to have powers that they never explain. That's what made us say, 'Maybe they're another form of alien,' and that's where we came up with the Jaffa. One of the goals of the pilot was to bring everybody back together and fill all of the holes.

Was there a long-term plan mapped out for *Stargate SG-1*, or did you just wait and see where it went?

A little bit of both, to tell you the truth. I did have a long-term plan for the first two seasons, for what was going to happen with the Goa'uld and our recurring villain Apophis in particular, but we didn't want every episode to be about them, because that would get old. One of my favourite shows growing up was *Battlestar Galactica*, but I think one of its flaws was that every week, it was, 'The Cylons are coming! The Cylons are coming!' and we wanted to avoid that pitfall. That's why we don't have the Goa'uld every week. By the way, one of the interesting things we came up with for the Goa'uld was when we said to ourselves, 'They're supposed to be this big powerful force, but how powerful can they be if we keep beating them?' That's when we said, 'Well, what if they're not? What if they're feudal, and they're not getting along with each other, so we're only dealing with them one at a time?' I think that decision worked to our advantage. For example, Apophis and Ra were archenemies, and Hathor and Apophis hate each other. They're all little kingdoms, trying to steal the other's kingdom, so if they're fighting each other more than they're fighting anybody else, they're not as much of a threat to us. It's not one glorious leader being followed by millions, who could easily wipe us out. I think we've probably met eight different Goa'uld leaders, who *all* hate each other! And then there are the other alien races, some of which are more powerful than the Goa'uld, while others have just managed to avoid them.

Did you create a series bible that outlined all these races?

They weren't mapped out, at least originally, but as we continued, they became part of the bible. For example, the Asgard became a big part of the mythology of the series, but we didn't even dream of the Asgard until we first met them. One of the things we did, particularly in 'The Torment of Tantalus' (which was an episode I directed and Robert Cooper wrote), was to say that there was a group of four alien species who were obviously very powerful — they used to meet in this place that the team found in 'The Torment of Tantalus'. One race is called the Ancients, and they're the ones that built the Stargate network. The Goa'uld didn't build it, they just took it over and started using it. Within that framework, we decided, let's gradually meet the other three races. The Asgard are one, the Tollans are another, and we also decided that we can't make all Goa'uld necessarily bad, which gets too one-dimensional, so that's why we introduced the Tok'ra. They're 'good' Goa'uld, who have become a very big part of the mythology, especially when we made Samantha Carter's father one of them.

You've gone on record saying that *Stargate* is a particularly difficult show to write. Could you explain why?

With any show that has as highly woven and complex a mythology as *Stargate*, the longer the series goes on, the more difficult it becomes to have freelancers come in and write for it. Unless they're a big fan of the show, and have watched every single episode and really studied it, they won't get all of the mythology, and how the various characters and species interact. The other part of it, which is true with any television series, is that 'getting' the voices of the characters is always a challenge. The biggest challenge we had on *Stargate* during the first two seasons was with everybody taking their rejected *Star Trek* ideas out of their files and pitching them to us! The show is not *Star Trek*. It's completely different from *Star Trek*, but people have trouble seeing that. They think it's *Star Trek* without the ship, it's a gate instead, but if that's what you pitch to us, it doesn't work. *Stargate* is set today, with people that are not the brilliant know-it-alls of whatever century the various *Enterprise*s are. More often than not on *Star Trek*, they would teach the guest stars that week a lesson. On our show, we generally learn a lesson from the guest stars. Our people have no idea what they're about to step into every week, unlike *Star Trek*, where they take out their little tricorders and they know everything before the show starts. It's a big difference.

Was there a lot of attrition in the writing staff during the early months?

Not a whole lot. One of the things that's suicidal about Brad and I is that we tend to roll up our sleeves and do it ourselves, so we would have people pitch to us and they would strike out, and we would end up writing every third script ourselves. I think I wrote four scripts with my name on them in the first year, and probably five more that I had rewritten from page one. Brad probably did more than that, because he's even more of a lean mean writing machine! Thank God that Robert Cooper showed up. He wrote an early episode of the series as a freelancer, and nailed it, and impressed us so much that we hired him on staff and he's still there. We also had Katharyn Powers on staff, and between us we probably wrote three out of every four scripts.

How did the script writing process on *Stargate* differ from *The Outer Limits*?

You adjust it and move it around a bit on each series, but it's basically the same process. The big difference on a continuing character series is you have to make sure you're servicing your characters. We would have that moment where we'd say, 'Okay, it's all beat out, that's four acts; only one problem: Teal'c doesn't have anything to do in this show!' So we'd have to go back and redo the whole story to use Teal'c, or any of the characters, with the exception of O'Neill who was always in the forefront. That's the biggest challenge in episodic television: you want to make sure you give everybody something to do, so they're not just standing there holding the horses.

Since you don't usually have subplots, or 'B' or 'C' stories in *Stargate* episodes, does that make it difficult to get all your characters into the main story?

Yes, but in *Stargate*, the four of them go through the gate together, so you can't really have an 'A' and 'B' story, unless you have the rare occasion when we would have one of them staying behind that week. Their story then becomes the 'B' story, while the other three are off on the 'A' story. Generally if we do that, the 'A' and 'B' stories dovetail in the end when they get back together to solve the problem.

What kind of lead time would you try and get on your scripts?

The one advantage we had on *Stargate* was that we didn't have a lot of bureaucracy to deal with. The studio would approve everything and that was it: the network trusted us after having done three years on *The Outer Limits*, and they were very happy with what they were seeing on the first year of *Stargate*, so they just left us alone, and that helped. But one of the big challenges on *Stargate* is that it's such a huge show to mount every week, we had to have the scripts at least a month in advance. We tried to have them ready six weeks in advance of shooting if we could. On a normal television series

BRAD WRIGHT

Jonathan Glassner's long-time production partner Brad Wright had written for such series as *Neon Rider* and *Highlander* before demonstrating his gift for thought-provoking SF ideas on the 1990s revival of *The Outer Limits*. After a successful collaboration on that series, Wright approached MGM about creating a TV spin-off of the popular feature *Stargate*, little knowing that Glassner had just done the same thing! After creating, and working together on *Stargate SG-1* for three seasons, Glassner left the show and moved back to Los Angeles, leaving Wright in Vancouver as executive producer. *SG-1* continued to flourish under his guidance, through its fourth and into its fifth year, which included celebrations for the show's 100th episode; a rare landmark in television. Things continue to heat up on the *Stargate* front, with the Sci-Fi Channel stepping in to buy a sixth season. According to Wright, it acts as a springboard for a possible *Stargate SG-1* feature film, which would resolve some of the major elements of what will apparently be the show's final season. The feature would in turn act as the launching point for a new spin-off series, tentatively titled *Atlantis*. So it appears that Wright will have his hands full for some time to come, as he continues to explore new worlds beyond the Stargate.

like a cop show, the script usually shows up on the set the day it starts to prep, sometimes even the day it shoots. But we would have five rotating sound stages with sets being built on them, and some of those sets would take a month to build. Visual FX would then take three months after the show was shot, so we had quite a lot of lead time on every episode. It was a killer.

How difficult was it to direct on *Stargate*?

It was hard, which is why I only directed two episodes! In the first season, I did 'The Torment of Tantalus' fairly early on, and the reason I did that was because I wanted to set an example. I wanted to demonstrate how I thought the look of the directing should be on the series, and show it could be done on our schedule. It probably wasn't necessary, because shortly after that, we found two directors that we used almost every other episode; Martin Wood and Peter DeLuise, who are great and certainly didn't need my help. But at the time, we were still looking for that, so that's why I did it. The other one I directed, 'Serpent's Lair', was done at the end of the first year [and shown as the opening episode of season two], so all the scripts were finished by then.

Do you generally write in the office all the time, or do you try and take your work home?

You don't get the luxury of being able to write everything at the office. I'd write three lines and then have a meeting with the art department, write two more pages and then the visual FX guys would wander into my office with things to show me, so that's the way it worked. It was a challenge. I'd work long hours, and usually do 'clean up' on all my scripts at home on the weekend.

At what point did you feel the series was running relatively smoothly?

Fairly quickly, actually. It really clicked when we hired a new line producer named John Smith, who's still there, who is a god of organisational skills. After he had been there for maybe a month, everything was working like a well-oiled machine. It was a little more chaotic before that, except the art department under Richard Hudolin. Richard basically oversaw all of the art department, and the wardrobe, and he also dabbled a little bit in the visual FX side, to make sure their look was consistent. So because of him overseeing all of that, it helped provide a certain cohesiveness right off the bat.

What made you decide to leave *Stargate* at the end of season three?

It was a life decision. As I said earlier, I'd originally told my wife we were going up to Vancouver for a year to do *The Outer Limits*. Every year I'd come back to her and say, 'How much money do they have to pay me before you think it's worth staying for another year?' and we just kept staying and staying. We had a baby up there, which was not a pleasant experience, because the socialised medicine is a frightening thing, and our families are in LA, so our whole support network was down here. We finally said six years is enough; either we're going to move to Vancouver permanently or we're going to go home. It was a hard decision for me, because I love *Stargate* and the people up there, so it was difficult to walk away from. Sometimes you just have to choose your life over your career.

Do the various studios and production companies in LA forget about you when you're in Canada for several years?

That hasn't been a problem, because *Stargate* is very well known. My only problem was what you were talking about earlier, that I've been pigeonholed as a SF writer. I'll go in and pitch a medical show for example, and the networks will say, 'Why are you bringing us a medical show?' My agent has to explain to them that I wrote *21 Jump Street* and *Street Justice*, and I was a cop show writer for a while, so I'm not just SF. That's been my biggest problem, because the only networks buying SF right now are Fox and UPN, and even UPN isn't really buying because they've got too much of it. When I came back from Vancouver, I wrote two pilots, one for Fox and another one for Showtime, so I was busy. Of course they were both SF; that's all they would look

THE INVISIBLE MAN

When USA Networks approached Matt Greenberg (then best known as the writer of *Halloween H20*) to create a new TV series based on the classic Invisible Man story, he wasn't very interested: 'When my agent asked if I wanted to take this meeting, I was ready to say, "Screw it, I can't come up with anything really interesting!" but then I had this weird brain flash, and started getting excited about the idea. I didn't want to do invisibility the way it had been done before, such as bleach injected into the skin, or weird radiation. One of my favourite movies was *Predator* — I loved the way the creature in that became invisible by bending light. I thought, why can't we do invisibility in an organic way, and that's when I came up with the idea of quicksilver, and giving a guy a synthetic gland. Once I had that concept, I thought we could do it as a subversive satire, taking some of the clichés of SF, and turning them on their ear. At that point, it suddenly became interesting to me.' Quickly establishing itself as a witty and enjoyable show, *The Invisible Man* starred Vincent Ventresca as Darien, the reluctant I-Man, who along with Hobbes (Paul Ben-Victor) and scientist The Keeper (Shannon Kenny) works for The Agency, a shadowy government force, combating the even murkier group known as Chrysalis.

at. The one I wrote for Fox was the same year they had one from James Cameron [*Dark Angel*], another one from Chris Carter [*The Lone Gunmen*], one from the creators of the *Blair Witch Project* [*Freakylinks*], and one from Jonathan Glassner; which one do you think is not going to get made? The irony is they then talked to me about coming in and doing *Freakylinks*, which at the time was called *Fearsum*, and I ended up not doing the job. After that, they turned it into *Freakylinks*, which sort of says it all in terms of the direction they were going, so I was thankful I hadn't done it.

How did you get involved with *The Invisible Man*?

When I got back from Vancouver, I was doing a pilot for another SF show for Showtime when I was contacted about doing *The Invisible Man*. I initially turned them down, because I was too busy with this pilot, and then USA Networks convinced me to just consult on the show for a while, which I agreed to do. Showtime never made the pilot, so USA Networks kept asking me to run the show and finally I agreed to it, about halfway through the first season. I'd just been too busy, and didn't want to do a halfway job just because I was working on the pilot at the same time.

Did you set out to create a mythology for *The Invisible Man* in the same way you had on *Stargate*?

I believe that good SF in television has a certain degree of serialisation to it, especially in terms of the protagonists. I think having a group of villians like Chrysalis is a valuable tool, because you don't have to keep explaining, it's not always the Russians or the Chinese who are trying to do bad things for basically inexplicable reasons. It's more interesting to have a fictional group with even darker, more bizarre motives.

Is it a constant challenge for the writers to find new and different ways to use invisibility as a story device?

That's one of the first questions that I asked of the writers when I came in. And I still ask any writer who comes in with an idea, (A) why does the story require an invisible man, and (B) what can we do differently with the invisibility this week that we haven't already done? He can't just go invisible and sneak in somewhere, because that gets old after a while. That's a challenge, but to me, what carries any good television show season after season is not the gimmick, ie the invisibility. It's getting to know the characters and caring about them. I think the relationships we've built up are strong, and if Darien couldn't go invisible at all, I think the show would keep being fun.

What do you see yourself doing as a writer, say, five years from now?

If I can, I'll keep running television series. I'd love to segue into directing features one day, but I don't particularly want to write them. I don't know if I'll be able to do that, but I'm really happy doing television. ∎

ROB GRANT AND
DOUG NAYLOR

Former schoolmates Rob Grant and Doug Naylor began their long-time
collaboration in radio, before working on the TV comedy show *Carrott's
Lib* in the mid-80s. After becoming head writers on the satirical puppet
series *Spitting Image,* they eventually decided to create their own television
project. Remembering an old radio sketch they'd written about a guy going
slowly space crazy with only his computer for company, they began to develop a series that would mix SF with laughs. Like oil and water, comedy and SF
tend not to mix well. There are a few notable exceptions, such as the movies
Dark Star and *Galaxy Quest,* and the TV series *Lexx* (covered elsewhere in this
book). And then of course, there's Grant and Naylor's creation — *Red Dwarf.*
A demented fusion of anarchic comedy and SF parody, *Red Dwarf* first aired
on British television in 1988 and quickly developed a loyal cult following.
Eight seasons later, it's become a phenomenon, with episodes airing around
the world, and a big-budget feature film in the offing. Grant Naylor (the
hybrid name by which the pair were often referred) wrote six seasons of *Red
Dwarf* together, as well as a pair of best-selling *Red Dwarf* novels and the
comedy series *The 10%ers,* about the behind-the-scenes activities at a talent
agency. Unfortunately, the partnership ended after *Red Dwarf*'s sixth season,
under circumstances neither writer has been willing to discuss. Grant went on
to create two new comedies, *The Dark Ages* and *The Strangerers,* while Naylor
stayed with *Red Dwarf* for two seasons thus far, and is now working on the
aforementioned feature. This in-depth and ultimately rather poignant interview was conducted before the duo split up following *Red Dwarf VI...*

**This may sound like a strange question to begin this conversation, but do you
consider *Red Dwarf* a SF series with elements of comedy, or a comedy series
with elements of SF?**

Rob Grant: I think that's the kind of thing that's been evolving over the entire run,
so I'm still not sure we can come up with the answer. When we started out, it was
intended to be comedy with SF, but we tended to find during the first season that the
more science fictiony shows were more successful, and funnier, surprisingly.

Doug Naylor: We were actually told not to make it science fiction. People were always put off by SF, and we always knew that if we were going to do SF, we would creep in and slowly increase that factor when we were on the air, as opposed to when we were first commissioned to do the series. I think we wouldn't consider doing an episode that didn't have a SF idea now, which wasn't true of the first season.

Grant: I think it's always had a base line, but obviously the series has developed as it's gone on. Holly has changed, the characters have developed, Kryten was introduced, and he made a big difference in season three, so it's changed in that way.

Was the idea for *Red Dwarf* a long time in development, or did it just spring full-blown into the series we're watching now?

Grant: When we actually sat down and had the idea, we started with the central concept of the last human being alive, and then tried to populate it with non-human characters. They were the criteria, and we also didn't want any aliens in it, because we thought that would make it different from the other SF shows.

Naylor: The whole point of SF is generally to get aliens in it, so the idea of doing SF *without* aliens —

Grant: — was perverse, but it forced us to tell different stories than were commonplace.

Basically, your idea began with the character of Dave Lister and went on from there?

Grant: Actually, it was a sketch for a radio comedy sketch series we used to write called *Son of Cliché*. There was one recurring little format which used to last about two minutes every week, and it was about this guy who was slowly going space crazy, and his only companion was his computer*. That was the starting-off point for *Red Dwarf*. But we thought we couldn't have just a guy and his computer; it would be too boring. So we then added the hologram and the Cat.

Why did you make the last human alive such a slob?

Grant: There's a Kurt Vonnegut element about it, that the lowest, slobbiest human

GRANT
NAYLOR

Place of Birth:
Salford, Lancashire (Grant)
Manchester, (Naylor) UK

Home Base:
London, UK

Education:
Liverpool University

First TV Work:
Carrot's Lib

TV Career Highlights:
Spitting Image, Red Dwarf, The 10%ers, The Dark Ages (Grant), *The Strangerers* (Grant)

* *Ironically, the voice of Hab, the ship's computer, was played by Chris Barrie, who played Rimmer in* Red Dwarf.

being is the one who survives last.

Naylor: You wouldn't want some dashing hero in it; it would be terrible for comedy, anyway.

Did the character of Rimmer start off as a hologram, or did that fall into the 'clever idea' category?

Grant: No, we started off with the idea that he was a hologram, but in the first half of the pilot episode he's alive. Apart from that, he's always been a hologram. That was the idea entirely.

Naylor: We just didn't want him to start off as a hologram. We wanted him to start off as a human being. We didn't want aliens, and at the time, we didn't want robots, so we thought, 'A hologram!'

So 'mechanoids' — like Kryten — were okay, but not robots.

Grant: Er, we eventually relaxed that rule —

Naylor: — when we realised how difficult it was going to be. Nobody could actually

SF COMEDY

Comedy and SF are like the oil and vinegar of television. They rarely mix well, because it's so difficult to capture the delicate balance between them. In most cases, the comedy tends to dominate, with the SF often becoming nothing more than a few decorative touches. In the 1960s, sitcoms such as *I Dream of Jeannie*, *Bewitched* and *My Favorite Martian* featured a SF or fantasy element, utilising the still-emerging science of special FX to create visual punch lines. Decades later, *Mork & Mindy* would follow the same basic template. In more recent years, SF or fantasy-based sitcoms have usually been relegated to children's programming. Shows such as *Halfway Around the Galaxy and Turn Left*, *Luna*, *Kapatoo*, *Metal Mickey*, *Mike & Angelo* and *Watt on Earth* were usually produced with low budgets and little imagination. To date, pretty much the only comedy/SF series that have straddled both genres successfully are *The Hitchhiker's Guide to the Galaxy* and *Red Dwarf*. In both instances, imaginative ideas and skilful writing were able to transcend meagre budgets. There have been other attempts at SF sitcoms, but the results have usually been painful viewing. The less said about *Come Back, Mrs. Noah*, the better. Or *ALF*.

touch anything. The computer couldn't touch anything, or Rimmer. Only Lister had the ability of touch, so it was really difficult to get anything done. That was why we introduced Kryten!

So you've got Lister, who is arguably not one of the greatest human beings around, and you compound the problem by introducing Rimmer, who's not very likeable either...

Grant: The idea of making Rimmer unlikeable was that it was supposed to be a decision made by the super intelligent computer, in that having your friends with you would be a frustration, and actually creating conflict is the grist of life. The computer designed Rimmer to be his companion in order to get on Lister's nerves, in order to drive him further.

And how did Holly the ship's computer factor into your initial equation?

Grant: We wanted to play against the cliché of having a super intelligent computer who knew everything. In the TV series, we didn't really feature Holly in the first half of the pilot, as we did in the book[*]. In the series, you've basically only seen him demented. When we came to do the back-story for the book, he was super intelligent, but then his terminals had rotted, and he had gone a bit mad being on his own.

At what point did he start to become more human? Was that when Norman Lovett actually started playing the character?

Grant: That's right. In the beginning, we were originally going to have a straight computer, but we saw Norman, who'd actually come in to audition for Rimmer. We didn't pick him for Rimmer, but we were all fond of him because he was so funny, and so we said let's give him the computer voiceover, which is what Holly was at the time. We recorded two shows with Norman just doing a voiceover, and he was moaning all the time saying, 'You're wasting my assets, not putting me on the screen!' We then went back and re-recorded bits of the first two shows, and put him on a monitor. After that I think Holly really developed because we had Norman playing it.

Naylor: Very much so. It kind of worked, because when his face was in repose, it was sort of credible that he could be brilliant, but as soon as he opens his mouth...

Grant: There was always meant to be something of a mystique around Holly; was he putting them on, or was he really insane?

According to Danny John-Jules, neither of you really knew what you wanted to do with the Cat at first.

Grant: We rewrote his first scene about seventeen times, and I still don't know if we

---

[*] Red Dwarf — Infinity Welcomes Careful Drivers, *by Grant Naylor. This was followed by* Better Than Life *by Grant Naylor,* Last Human *by Doug Naylor and* Backwards *by Rob Grant.*

got it right; in fact, I know we didn't. The Cat as a character didn't really come into his own until the second series, and even more so in the third series. In the second series, he started cooking a bit. We liked the heart of the character, the basic idea of a guy who's evolved from a cat, but we couldn't decide what cat-esque qualities to imbue him with. We didn't want to make him like a character from the Andrew Lloyd Webber show and have him creeping around in leotards. We wanted him to be more kittenish: vain and self-centred, but those things were very hard to portray originally. In the early episodes, we made him totally self-centred, so that he barely interacted with the others.

At this point you've got your cast of characters together, and you start taping the first episode of *Red Dwarf*. You've both gone on record that you weren't happy with that first episode, so what were some of the problems that had to be addressed?

Naylor: It's very strange, because the script got an incredible amount of good feedback. Everyone who read the script really liked it, but in the end, we wound up rewriting quite a lot of it because it wasn't working for the guys who were doing it. The thing we were trying to avoid was making it look like *Blake's 7*, and it didn't. In my opinion, it looked worse, that first season. It looked so deeply bad, the sets shook, and everything just looked terrible. It was everything that I hate about science fiction on TV. For example, there was originally a whole sequence in the first episode where Lister was burying the crew that wasn't meant to be funny at all. It was pathos; it was really sad. He had the ashes of each crewmember, and he was supposed to be putting them into this thing that flushed them out into space, which was actually a kitchen bin painted grey. The ashes go in with a CLANG, and it's a sad, sad moment. But it was a flip top bin! He picks up another one, clang, and we finally said, 'We can't have this! We've got to drop this piece because it looks ridiculous,' and of course Craig [Charles]'s performance was terrible because he couldn't get into the part at all, not with this terrible flip top bin to work with. So it was lots of things like that.

Grant: It's very hard to get SF right. It's hard to get television right the first season. We were constantly rewriting all the time saying, 'That doesn't work!' Apart from the pilot, the next two shows we wrote contained almost no SF, or just 'wallpaper' SF that was already introduced in the pilot. We had imagined the show would be like that, a sitcom in space. The first SF script we submitted was the second episode that went out, 'Future Echoes', where they break the light barrier and see images of themselves in the future. It was one of my favourite episodes of the first series, and when we delivered the script, everybody had a curious expression on their face, and nobody really knew what it was about. It wasn't something that they had dealt with before. We didn't have a lot of SF brains on the show. Ed Bye, who was directing, said he didn't understand what was going on with some of the sequences, such as the ones with the mirror. Nobody had given us any feedback about that script, and we were beginning to think, 'Is it really that bad?' When it played, it was all perfectly straight-forward and everybody understood it. It played so much better than some of the other episodes, we thought this was the way we would take the whole series. Better to fail in glory than to try and be ordinary.

From a technical point of view, making one of your characters a hologram must have been a real nightmare.

Grant: It was awful, and we were always reminding each other that Rimmer 'couldn't do that' because he was a hologram.

Naylor: The first series was constantly, 'Oh, if Chris [Barrie] could pick that up,' followed by, 'Oh no, he can't because he's a hologram!'

Grant: It was very difficult for Chris, because he could never figure out what to do. He couldn't touch or fiddle with anything, he couldn't eat; all these things help with one's comic timing.

At what point did things really start to gel with the series, so you were both happy with the way it was going?

Naylor: We're still waiting!

Grant: By season three, we'd all started to loosen up a bit and it all clicked for us.

Naylor: Season two was much better than season one, but the sets still looked awful, and the production values were still pretty awful. By then, we knew that (1) we wanted to do SF for sure, because they offered the best plots, (2) we wanted to have some kind of OB [outside broadcast], and (3) was basically to try and lose the original drive room set, because it was terrible. We wanted to try and get a new, more colourful drive room, and get rid of all these greys and the shaky sets. That's what happened, and we made it happen quite quickly after season one.

In season two, you introduced Kryten, who at the time was played by David Ross. Did you develop the character as one to bring back as a regular at some point?

Grant: No, and we had a big decision to make later on. Doug was really for having him in, and I kept saying, 'It's going to screw up the chemistry!'

Naylor: We'd worked with David Ross before, and we knew he was a really fine actor. It was just a guest spot, but it worked so well, we thought, 'Maybe we'll bring him back when we get to season three.' David Ross wasn't available, so Paul Jackson[*] recommended that we have a look at Robert Llewelyn, and he became Kryten.

---

[*] *The show's original producer, who first sold the series to the BBC.*

Grant: That was really when things began to click for us, because Kryten gave us that extra dimension we thought had been missing. He could pick things up, and he was also brilliant at carrying exposition, so we felt we could tell more complex stories. You feel when you listen to him that he has that quality; it's a very rare quality.

Going back to series two for a moment, did you feel that things had at least _started_ to gel by then?

Naylor: No. We as writers always knew what the characters were, but we were still trying to get it on screen. The cast was quite inexperienced, and didn't give very three-dimensional performances. It was a constant battle to make them underplay it. It was all, 'Let's belt it out to the audience.'

Grant: It was really the fashion in alternative comedy at that time, that there was always a lot of shouting going on, in terms of crude dramatic performances.

Naylor: It was very difficult being the writers, because you were only allowed so much time to actually say, 'If you try the line this way and do less...' — 'Okay, he's tried it; now go away and write!' That's why we were very keen to produce as well, because Paul was extremely busy, and [director/producer] Ed Bye was handling quite a lot of it by himself, so we were very keen to produce season three.

THE STRANGERERS

A decade after co-creating _Red Dwarf_, Rob Grant turned his attention to another SF comedy, this time *with* aliens. In _The Strangerers_, Mark Williams and Jack Docherty star as a pair of displaced alien space cadets who land on Earth, and have to masquerade as humans when their mission goes horribly wrong. 'Their leader is incapacitated,' explains Grant, 'and the two novice trainees are not of sufficient rank or status to actually know what their mission is. They haven't completely mastered walking yet, much less eating or sleeping, but they have to survive, avoid detection and get back to their rendezvous point.' The idea for _The Strangerers_ was inspired by a quote from legendary SF author Arthur C. Clarke: 'He said, "There are only two options: either life exists out there, or we are the only living thing in the universe, and either alternative is equally incredible." So I thought, what if they _do_ exist and they _do_ come down here? In _Red Dwarf_, we were doing a space series that didn't have aliens, which forced us to do unique stories, because we couldn't have the blue thing of the week come in and give us a plot. I wanted to do an alien show, but with aliens that you really hadn't seen before.'

Grant: As writers, they respected us well enough as individuals, but we had to say things four times before anyone would do anything.

Naylor: And then it would only be a suggestion...

Going into season three, it seemed like everything was thrown out the window and you started fresh. The look was different, the direction and so forth. What sort of changes did you consciously set out to make?

Grant: We got a new set designer and a new costume designer. Everybody thinks season three got a massive cash injection, but we actually did it for less. We just spent the money differently. We piled loads of money into special effects, and then said we'll write around what's left.

Naylor: The visual FX had slightly increased on the second series, but what we now had was a library of model shots. So instead of the first two series where we had model shots which were *Red Dwarf* just passing by, we had new extra shots, so it was starting to get richer and richer.

Did you get any objections from the viewers over the new look and direction of the series?

Naylor: You had your die-hards, the ones who were real fanatical fans, and obviously their favourite show was the pilot; the worse the show was, the more they liked it!

Grant: We also got objections to Kryten because Robert plays him with a Canadian accent, and we got a lot of English viewers saying, 'They're catering to the American market now,' and it wasn't true. We simply thought that the Canadian accent was funny.

You mentioned earlier that there was some discussion about adding Kryten to the mix. Was that because you thought you had a successful equation going, and you didn't want to ruin it?

Grant: Well, I did. Doug always thought that it would be better with Kryten in it, and as a SF purist, that a robot, you know... We soon changed our minds when he came on and sort of filled all the gaps for us. The other thing we were worried about was that it was a very male-oriented series. If we were going to bring in another character, let's make it a woman, but then we were worried about that altering the chemistry, because there was an important air of sexual frustration about the ship.

But Hattie Hayridge came in to replace Norman Lovett as Holly, so you did have a woman in there.

Grant: That's why we got a woman to replace Norman when he went. It was a natural redundancy thing. He went, we didn't want him to go. He moved to Scotland and got married, and he'd had a heart attack a couple of years earlier and was worried about his health and jetting down to record the show in Manchester, so we had to let him go. But, we realised, this will solve our problem. There will be a female presence on the ship, and it will stop it from being so 'sweaty socky'. In the beginning, if you'd had the original Holly scripts, you would not have cast a blonde woman to play a thick computer, because then you start to get into stereotyping and bimbos and dumb blondes.

Why did you decide to begin season three with a *Star Wars*-type crawl, which explained all the changes, but so quickly that it would have to be played back several times to read it?

Grant: We'd started writing an episode which linked seasons two and three, where they move into the officers' quarters, Holly changes sex, and Lister has the two children, but it just didn't work and we thought, 'We're locked into this now!'

Naylor: And we didn't want the first show to go out in the new season to be an explanatory kind of episode.

Grant: We let this problem drag on and on, and we'd actually recorded all the shows before we came up with the crawl — we were just going to do nothing, but Paul Jackson said, 'You can't do that!', didn't he?

Naylor: No, it was us that said 'We can do this!', and at the last minute that afternoon, we got the idea and rushed up and typed this thing in.

Grant: If you check that actually, there's a printing error in there where the bottom line is repeated. We couldn't get it out in time because we were doing it so quickly!

At what point did you decide to start parodying well-known SF films, like *Alien* and *RoboCop*?

Grant: These were films that we adored. I adore *Alien* and *RoboCop*. I actually think *RoboCop 2* is a much better film; I really like Frank Miller's work. As Woody Allen said, 'If you're doing parody, you have to adore it.' In season three, we started saying instead of just doing it ordinarily and pretending these things hadn't gone on, we would refer to them, and I think it actually enriched the whole thing. We used to occasionally slip them in, but we were very self-conscious about it. There's a supposed *Citizen Kane* parody when Rimmer dies and says 'gazpacho soup' instead of Rosebud. We actually got quite a lot of response to that.

By season four, were you relatively happy with the way the characters were established?

Grant: We felt that we'd gotten them pretty much as we wanted them, and everything looked pretty much the way we wanted it to, so we now felt free to go in and do the stories.

Naylor: It's very peculiar: season four was by far the most successful season in the UK. The general response was that the writing was the best, but we felt season four wasn't the best by any means.

What would you have chosen?

Grant: Season three.

Naylor: 'Dimension Jump' and 'Justice' aside — I quite liked those two — there just seemed to be something missing from season four. We had to write more quickly than we would have wanted to.

Grant: I think 'Justice' is as good an idea as we've had, and the same with 'Dimension Jump'. I feel the rest of them were a bit pedestrian in terms of their original ideas. We've never really done two *Red Dwarf* episodes that you can put side by side and say they're the same. We were trying things that hadn't been tried. In 'Polymorph' [during season three], we were trying to get it a bit more movie-esque, and I think it came off to a large extent. I really liked the quality of ideas better in season three than season four on the whole. Having said that, I think 'Meltdown' was a funny show, and 'Justice' was very funny. What we then tried to do in season five, and I don't know if it came off or not, was not concentrate on the comedy at all. We were trusting that the stories were good enough so that when we actually got to the comedy, it was a natural product of the story, rather than saying, 'When we get to this funny point...' In 'Justice', the whole thing leads to this fight where everything you do to the other guy happens to you. We didn't do that in season five. We were just trying to tell good SF stories, and let the comedy take care of itself.

Do you feel you were successful?

Naylor: We made a conscious decision to sacrifice some of the comedy for the sake of some of the stories, but then you get into the edit and you go [burying his head in his hands and groaning loudly]. Ultimately, I liked the kind of direction it was starting to take.

Grant: I really liked 'Terraform' an awful lot. The thing about it was, at the script stage, we started with Kryten cutting his hand off and the business with Lister thinking it's a tarantula, but it's difficult when you're scripting visual stuff: the hit rate isn't terrific when you're relying on a prop to do the comedy for you. But I thought it came off very well, and I really like the look of the stuff when they were in Rimmer's mind, and the weird bit with the gravestones. It doesn't end terrifically, because the actors never really got that scene right, the part where they pretended to like Rimmer.

Naylor: It's interesting, because nobody seems to be able to agree on what the good shows were and what the bad shows were. We did a poll in the official mag, the *Red Dwarf Smegazine*, and 'Holoship' was deemed to be the weakest show. 'Back to Reality' was the strongest, 'Terrorform' was one of the weakest, and yet in America during rehearsals for the US pilot, everybody adored 'Terrorform'. They thought it was the strongest show we had ever done.

During season five, you had a problem with Juliet May, who was supposed to direct all six episodes. Did she get in over her head with *Red Dwarf*, which has so many technical aspects to overcome, or did she just not have the same feel for the show that Ed Bye did?

Grant: Both are partly true. The worst thing, that compounded the problem, was that she wouldn't ask for help. She wanted to take it on her own shoulders really, and I think we basically didn't see eye to eye.

Naylor: She was around for the first four, and then we kind of had to do some re-shooting, and spent a lot of time in the edit. In the end though, her name is on four episodes and it's the best-looking series, so I think she came out of it very well.

Grant: It really is a hard show to do.

Naylor: It's one of the most difficult shows to direct. Unless you realise this going in — quite how difficult it is — you're going to be in big trouble. Ed had a hell of a time, if you look at some of the early shows he directed, so this is no slight to anyone. It's just one of the most difficult shows with our budget, which isn't big, to direct on British television.

You had to step in. How did you split up directing chores on the remaining episodes?

Grant: Nominally, people expect to see one director, so I was the one in the box actually calling the shots with the knuckles going white, but we did everything together.

Naylor: There was one very funny section where the whole shoot finished, and we had the end of season party, and then asked everybody to come back so we could re-shoot as much of 'Demons and Angels' as we could before we got kicked out of the studio. That was the plan, but we had no time to rehearse, so it was a matter of 'Okay, we'll start the first scene, and we'll go along and try to pick up all the worst scenes, and do as much as we possibly can!' There was this very funny scene where Rob was in the director's chair and I was right behind him writing and passing the stuff to him. He would read it, and we'd dash down to the floor and say, 'There isn't enough time to get this photocopied; here are your lines, we'll block it now, and shoot it one scene at a time. Right, let's do it!' and we would dash back up to the box. Everybody had a hangover, and did not want to be there. That's why it's quite interesting people think 'Demons and Angels' — which in my opinion was *so* bad — was any good.

Grant: We always have a terrible time at the end of the series choosing which one is going to go out first because they do transform dramatically in the edit.

Naylor: You can have an episode that looks good, and then is terrible before the sound dub, then goes through the sound dub and is okay. It's really bizarre. I wanted to kill myself after 'Back to Reality' before they dubbed that. I just thought, 'This is so hopeless!'

During this period, you also went to America to work on the pilot for a US version of *Red Dwarf*, which ultimately wasn't picked up by NBC. What happened with that project?

Grant: There was this guy called Linwood Boomer, who understood the show, and we got on with him tremendously well. We went over as creative consultants for the pilot, and arrived the day before the third rehearsal. The pilot was made, and NBC saw the pilot, and felt they wanted a few changes to be made. Weeks went by, and ultimately Linwood left the show[*], and we came in as executive producers. At that point, NBC was still very much interested in the project, but they wanted it to be more like the British series than the pilot was.

That seems a bit ironic, considering the amount of time spent trying to Americanise it.

Grant: Yes, but I feel that the pilot was taken a little bit in the wrong direction. They tried to play down the SF angle, which was actually what we tried to do over here. It wasn't all it could have been though, and I don't think they made the proper adjustments for the cast. They cast Craig Bierko as Lister, and basically he wasn't a loser and a lowlife and a slob; he was a handsome hero, and we felt that if they were going to proceed with that, you would have to change Lister's character substantially.

Naylor: Which was fine, but that wasn't tackled the way it maybe should have been. Anyway, we came in and our brief was basically to change it back. They didn't believe the Cat worked in the pilot. Although they bought the premise that there didn't have to be a female cast member to begin with, after the pilot they felt there should be a woman somewhere, and they wanted the cat to be a woman. Our initial reaction to that was, you've got a lot of 'Catwoman' problems, and how it would radically alter the chemistry between them. We went away and thought about it, and much to our surprise, we thought it could work. We were then asked to re-cast two of the parts, one of them was the Cat and the other was Rimmer.

---

* *Boomer later went on to create the wildly successful sitcom* Malcolm in the Middle.

There wasn't a problem with Robert Llewelyn playing Kryten?

Naylor: Or Jane Leeves[*], who was playing Holly. Everybody was very happy with Craig Bierko, who tested well: the reaction of the American test audience was very positive. Even though he was a different kind of Lister to the British one, we thought he was going to be terrific when the show was written for him and to his strengths. We then cast Terry Farrell[†] as the Cat, and Anthony Fusco from New York as Rimmer, and wrote two scripts, one of which was based on 'Camille' and the other on 'The Final Day'. Everything was looking pretty good, and we came back home, and were here for about three weeks when we were asked to come back to LA again to make a promo for the marketing people.

Grant: This was the week of the LA riots.

Naylor: We flew out on the Sunday when the riots were calming down. On Monday, we wrote a fourteen minute promo with some old material and about eighty per cent new, and got hold of Terry Farrell. She arrived on Tuesday; we got together with the hair, make-up and costume people, and shot it on Wednesday in a tiny studio. We had a corridor as a set and a couple of flats, and the crew were just brilliant, absolutely fantastic. We did all sorts of things, like shooting through a radar screen with a ceiling piece over the top of it so it looked like we were looking through a radar screen, and the whole thing cost about $40,000. We shot it on Wednesday, edited it by Friday, and everybody said it was far better than the pilot was. It looked great, it looked expensive, and it worked. Everybody was incredibly confident. The guys in the suits, who never give anything away, were absolutely *convinced* we would get a series of thirteen. It was then tested; we actually had a guy who found out where the testing was and went to it, and he said everything went terrifically. Then, right at the very last moment, NBC chickened out. So we went to Fox, who wanted to make it 'more Fox,' which seems to mean stupider, make it more character driven, make it...

Grant: Whackier.

Naylor: And emptier. We weren't interested in that.

At what point did you feel the project was getting away from you?

Naylor: When we were there during the pilot, you could see it was too late.

Grant: But we went in thinking, 'There isn't a chance that this is going to be picked up by an American network! We're going to have fun going over; let's play a long shot.' The more we worked on it, the more we thought it had a chance.

Moving on to season six, what was the motivation for taking your stories out of *Red Dwarf* and setting them on the shuttle, *Starbug*?

---

* *Leeves subsequently appeared in a memorable two-part* Seinfeld *episode as Marla the Virgin before being cast as Daphne in* Frasier.
† *Who then went on to play Jadzia Dax in* Star Trek: Deep Space Nine.

Naylor: It was to take it in a different direction and to give it a new energy. We felt if they were forced into a much smaller craft with low supplies, it would give a whole new, fresh feel to whatever the series was. Obviously you don't know in advance if it's going to work or not, but we had to make a decision quite early on to say, 'Okay, *Red Dwarf* is out.' To that extent, it gave it a different feel. Whether it's better or not, I don't know, but it's certainly different from the other series. It's much simpler, being set on *Starbug*. The whole thing is more vital, and because of that, the jokes are buzzing together, whereas in season five, we deliberately set out to lose some of the comedy to see what would happen. In six, we wanted to put more of that back in, and I think it worked. We were very determined to really go back to basics. The big thing, I think, was transferring from *Red Dwarf* to *Starbug*, because it's very hands-on, and 'real' in a way. The danger is in your face, as opposed to being on this giant space freighter.

Grant: I remember in the American pilot, where the final scene was that Lister pressed the buttons on *Red Dwarf* and it spun off into space. The rest of them didn't understand that he didn't steer the ship, didn't understand about some of the weird things he did. Essentially Doug is right. It looks much better with them steering around things. We also felt in series five that when we were in *Starbug* and they were more hands-on and in control, the excitement was more... exciting. They could run away from things, they could be fired at in a way that you can't really do with an enormous ship. And they were under more privation, and having to suffer more. We also felt, and this was reflected in the fan opinion we were getting, that we were under-using Holly and the Cat. We thought that by getting rid of one of them, at least temporarily, the function of the remaining one would be enhanced, and I feel that has worked. The balance was split more evenly in the sixth series.

Naylor: Also, the American pilot had been able to come at everything from a new angle, so we could say, 'Where did we go wrong with the English version?' We were able to re-think the format, and it was quite refreshing to be able to go back in, having already made all our mistakes and having to live with them. When it looked like the American version was going to be a new start, one of the things we decided was it would be much better for it to be on *Starbug* for all sorts of reasons. The only reason we had *Red Dwarf* as a ship that size was to explain the evolution of the cats. And also, we were scared, and if we ran out of plotlines, we could always go down to the fifteenth deck and find something.

In season six, you also gave Rimmer the ability to touch, something that had been a problem in the early days.

Naylor: Yes, that gave him a whole new dimension, a whole new area to put the character into.

Grant: When we made the decision in 'Legion' to give him a hard-light drive, it was a function of the plot, and we'd originally intended to go back to the status quo at the end of the show, but then we thought, why? It's a nice idea that we've got the option of the hard-light drive when we need it, so we kept it in.

With your sixth-season ender 'Out of Time', you changed the ending at the last minute and made it a cliffhanger in which the *Starbug* is seemingly blown up. What was your motivation for altering the ending in that way?

Naylor: Because everybody said, you've got to finish it there! All the people in the editing room were saying, 'That's where you cut it, right there; kill them all off!' It meant having to shoot an extra sequence to blow up the ship, but it was a much more dramatic way to end the series, and it gave us all sorts of scope for series seven. [To Grant] Do you still feel —

Grant: — that it was a mistake? You never know if there's going to *be* a series seven. I felt that. *Blake's 7* was so churlish really to leave it like that at the end of a series[*].

Naylor: It does say 'To Be Continued'! Joking aside, I never thought in a million years that we would end it the way we ended it at the time we were doing it. It was partly

RED DWARF CONTINUED...

After Rob Grant's departure following *Red Dwarf VI*, Doug Naylor took over the series as sole executive producer. Season seven saw big changes, including the departure of Rimmer, and the return of Lister's love interest Kristine Kochanski (Chloë Annett, replacing C. P. Grogan), who becomes a regular member of the crew. The look of the show changed too: while *Red Dwarf* had previously been shot on multiple cameras in front of a live studio audience (like most sitcoms), season seven switched to shooting with a single camera, and no audience — a far more filmic approach. Fans were unsure about the results. The season climaxed with the rediscovery of *Red Dwarf*, which had been dismantled by a group of Kryten's nanobots. This led neatly into *Red Dwarf VIII*, in which the nanobots restore *Red Dwarf* to its original state, complete with its entire crew complement, all unaware of the accident that had killed them all. (The live studio audience and multiple cameras were also restored, following the previous season's experiment.) Lister is thrown into the brig, where he's soon joined by a newly rebuilt Rimmer, the Cat is examined as a scientific curiosity, and Kryten is re-classified as female! Their escape attempts result in a few run-away viruses and a rampaging T-Rex, as well as another season-ending cliffhanger. Naylor and Co went on to gear up for the long-gestating *Red Dwarf* feature film, showing there's still plenty of smeg in the concept yet...

[*] *The classic BBC sci-fi series famously finished its fourth season on a cliffhanger, with all the main characters seemingly dead. There never was a fifth season.*

written that way because, for some reason, Craig got it into his head that we were going to kill them off, and I think as a joke, we thought we'd better write something into the last episode where we killed Lister off. We called the original script 'R.I.P. Dave Lister', and that was the script we gave to him, saying, 'We don't know where you heard this rumour, but it's absolutely untrue; here's the script!' But we'd always intended to kill them all off and bring them back. Also, the solution is there in the episode. They can't possibly be killed off.

You were also under tremendous time and budget pressures at that point, weren't you?

Naylor: The whole series was just insane, and the pressure went from show one all the way through to the end. In the end, I'm not sure the most pressure was on the last show, where at least you're thinking, 'This is the last show!'

What sort of improvements do you want to make in future seasons?

Grant: It takes us a while to be in a position where we can be that objective about it. Since series two, I've always thought, it's going to be hard to get as good as that again. Then you start writing the new series, and by the second show you start thinking, well...

In an ideal world, how long would you like the series to continue?

Naylor: I want to take a look at season six and see what it's like.

Grant: I still feel excited by the whole thing. When it starts getting pedestrian for us...

Naylor: I thought this season was going to be pedestrian and that we were starting to run out of ideas, but now I don't know what the answer is.

Can either of you see *Red Dwarf* going on without you?

Grant: Not without us writing. I think we'd always write it. ▌

DAVID GREENWALT

These days David Greenwalt is, by his own admission, a bit of a Hollywood veteran. His first job in the industry was in the mailroom at Universal Studios in the summer of 1968, where he fell in love with the idea of becoming a writer. He duly built a career as a writer, and latterly director, of feature films: he co-wrote the 1983 Rob Lowe/Jacqueline Bisset comedy *Class*, and co-wrote and directed 1985's *Secret Admirer*, for example. But after making the simple discovery that 'TV was better than movies', he moved towards the small screen, writing, directing and ultimately producing shows, including *The Wonder Years*, *The Commish* and his own co-creation, the critically acclaimed but little-seen series *Profit*. So it was that when, in 1997, Fox was making plans to put a TV show based on Joss Whedon's half-forgotten movie *Buffy the Vampire Slayer* on the air, they asked Greenwalt to work with the less experienced Whedon in launching the series. Greenwalt joined *Buffy* as co-executive producer, marking the beginning of a creative partnership that has brought out the best in both writers. When *Buffy* quickly became an unqualified success, a spin-off series was not long in coming, and *Angel* débuted in 1999, with Greenwalt acting as executive producer and show runner. That series has now established itself as interesting, offbeat, and a huge hit in its own right. This conversation took place while Greenwalt, having finished production on *Angel*'s second season, was just beginning on its third...

Let's start by talking about the creation of *Buffy*, and how you got involved in the development of the TV series.

Years ago, Joss had this idea for *Buffy the Vampire Slayer* (I think his original idea was actually Rita the Underpaid Waitress!) and the core of his idea was: wouldn't it be great to see a small, petite, vulnerable young woman go into a dark alley and beat the living shit out of a bad thing? That was his core idea, and then he married that to another very key, core, mythic notion, which is, 'I'm a girl, people don't pay that much attention to me, but I discover that I have this incredible power. I'm a Slayer, how do I find my place in the world?'

Joss tells a really interesting story about being on a scary carnival ride in one of those cages where it goes up and around, and there was a little nine year-old girl sitting across from him. She was so scared she couldn't even open her eyes. She's shaking, and Joss is making jokes, trying to get her to relax, and gradually she begins to open her eyes and look around. By the end of the ride, she's yelling and screaming and enjoying herself. It's that journey of — and I'm going to use a crappy new age word — 'empowerment', from 'I'm small and fragile' to 'I'm big and strong and can take care of myself!' while asking, 'Where is my place in the world?' And then Joss added another terrific layer to it, which is basically adolescence and the pain of high school. I've often said that if Joss had even a single date in high school, none of us would be here today, in our great big homes and our fancy cars.

Well, then they made a crappy movie out of his very good movie script. They completely botched the humour and the action, and misunderstood what he'd intended to do with it. Although the movie did very well on video, you sort of forgot about it. Then Gail Berman, who's currently the president of Fox Broadcasting, but was then working at [production company] Sandollar, said, 'This is a great series, we've got to do it!' She'd originally said, 'This would make a great series!' back when the movie script was written, and they ignored her. She said it again once the movie was out, and they ignored her again when the movie came out on video. Finally, they said, 'Well, if you can get Joss Whedon (but you never will) we might consider it.' So she went and got Joss, who said — and this is the revenge of the writer — 'I want to see this thing done correctly.' So anyway, they decided to make this little show.

So where did you come in?

My entrance into the story is that I was a reasonably successful movie writer (and not terribly successful movie director) throughout the 1980s, and sort of began dabbling in television in the 90s. I'd co-created a show called *Profit* with John McNamara the year before *Buffy* came on, and even though it tanked abysmally in terms of the ratings, it was a huge critical success: we were on the top ten list of every critic in the country. It was a very interesting, black comedy kind of show — the sort of thing the BBC might do in the UK. It was a very dark and somewhat amusing story about a psychopath, who lived in a very beautiful penthouse apartment. But, you soon learned, the apartment had a cardboard box in a hidden compartment in the wall, because this guy had been

DAVID GREENWALT

Date/Place of Birth:
1949, Los Angeles, CA, USA

Home Base:
Los Angeles, California, USA

Education:
Cal State Northridge;
University of Redlands

First TV Work:
Help Wanted: Kids

TV Career Highlights:
The Wonder Years, Doogie Howser, M.D., Profit, Buffy the Vampire Slayer, Angel

raised in a cardboard box by his crazy psychotic father... Now he worked in a giant corporation, and did incredibly mysterious and horrible things, but all from the point of view of improving productivity. It was a show that maybe seven people saw in America and loved, but it was critically acclaimed! There were only four episodes and it was yanked, but both John and I got a lot of attention from it, and it afforded me some new opportunities in TV. I met Steven Bochco [the legendary creator of *Hill Street Blues*, *LA Law* and *NYPD Blue*] and a lot of the great executive producers of the business, and in a way, I had a bit of a sense of writing my own ticket that next year. At the end of that season, I had the opportunity to have my pick of shows, in terms of the fact that I could certainly meet all the people who were getting new shows ready. I had a stack of ten or twenty pilot scripts, and when I read *Buffy the Vampire Slayer*, I remember saying to my wife, 'This is far and away the best-written pilot this year. Who is this guy?' So I met Joss, who looked about nineteen or so, a very cherubic-looking fellow, and I think there was a mutual liking there. I adored his writing, but I don't know if we knew what to make of each other.

Meanwhile, I was in the middle of negotiations to go and be a co-executive producer on *Profiler* for NBC, but Fox came to me and suggested a deal, which was, 'Listen, you're a bit of a veteran. This is Joss Whedon's first TV show; come here and be a co-exec, and help him get the show going. We're only doing twelve episodes this first

FROM FILM TO TV

One would think that a successful genre movie should easily translate into an equally triumphant television series, right? Actually, it almost never happens. Maybe it's the fact that TV is a much more demanding medium, where time and money (two of the most valuable commodities as far as good SF is concerned) are frequently in short supply. Perhaps TV producers just don't understand the underlying concepts behind a particular film. Whatever the reason, for every *Stargate SG-1*, there are a dozen *Planet of the Apes*. Most feature-to-TV concepts never make it to the end of their first season. That casualty list includes *Starman* (TV's Robert Hays didn't have the quirky charisma of the film's Jeff Bridges), *Logan's Run* (no budget), *Beyond Westworld* (no Yul Brynner), *Timecop* (no Jean-Claude Van Damme, although maybe that was an advantage) and *Total Recall 2070* (no clue about much of anything, really). Thankfully, the exceptions that help prove the rule are *Alien Nation*, *Highlander*, and the aforementioned *Stargate SG-1*. In each case, the TV creators were able to reinvent and expand the original concepts, while bringing in different but equally talented lead actors to build the new series around. Future producers should learn from their example.

season, so help him get his show started, and then you can go to *The X-Files*, and if you do well on *The X-Files*, you can write your own ticket.' From the studio's point of view, Joss had worked on both *Roseanne* and *Parenthood*, so he'd done some television, but he'd never run a show. So the deal was proffered to me as, 'You start with *Buffy* and go to *The X-Files* and that's where you'll make your mark.' Of course, in a day, I fell in love with Joss on all creative levels: his generosity, his work ethic, all these extraordinary things about him, and the pure, unadulterated freshness of his writing.

So Joss had made a presentation of some of the scenes from the pilot, and then he completely revamped it and we re-broke it. When I say 'we', of course, I give him eighty per cent of the credit. The first two episodes were a two-parter, and he hired a bunch of other writers and we started work breaking the stories.

Did you have much experience writing for genre shows at that point?

I'd done a little bit of genre, but I don't really have a comic book background. I'm not wild about SF, whereas most people here have a big genre, horror and comic book background. I very quickly appreciated the reason why *The Hobbit*, or *Dune*, or Batman, Superman, all that genre stuff, is so popular, and it's this: you can tell a story in a bigger way. The classic example from *Buffy* (and it was one of the original ideas that Joss pitched when he sold the series to the studio and the network) is the girl at Sunnydale High School who feels so insignificant that she literally turns invisible[*]. We've all felt like that. But my favourite story arc ever, and I think we'll never achieve this again because it's a one-time thing, was 'Innocence', in which Buffy finally gives herself to Angel on, I believe it was her seventeenth birthday, and they have sex. Unbeknownst to her, there's a curse that kicks in if Angel knows perfect happiness, and sex with her *was* perfect happiness, so he turns evil again. But the metaphor you had was, 'I sleep with a guy, and the next day he's an asshole and turns his back on me.' He's so mean and awful to her, and she doesn't know what's happened to him, but emotionally, she has this experience that everybody has. When we did those two episodes, there's not a man or woman from fifteen to fifty who couldn't relate to them. There's not a guy who hasn't been a dog to a woman, or been hurt in a similar way, and there isn't a woman who hasn't been hurt like that.

To me, this is pretty terrific art. A silly little show, with a silly little title, flying under the radar, but it's capable of touching us on a very deep level. Genre touches us on a very deep, mythic level, and I'd hesitate to go all the way to the Bible with this kind of thing, because I wouldn't insult people. But, 'in the beginning was the word', and the word is capable of inspiring and comforting and sending people into battle. Words are a powerful thing. So anyway, I realised, 'My gosh, I've hitched my wagon to a rising, shooting, soaring star here.' Also, a great deal of personal affection developed between Joss and me over the early years.

But then you left to go and work on *The X-Files*...

---

[*] *The premise was used in the episode 'Invisible Girl' in season one.*

Yes, and by the time I had to go to *The X-Files*, we were all very sad about it. I only went to *The X-Files* for three months at the end of *Buffy*'s first season, and just struck out miserably. I couldn't write *The X-Files* to save my life, and came scrambling back to work with Joss just as soon as I could. I re-upped with Fox with a much better deal than I would have gotten had I been successful at *The X-Files*. And then we just started plugging away; I was the number two guy for him. And then of course, Marti Noxon* came in that second year and was a huge find for us, and we just threw everything at her, we had her writing everything! Every second or third script was Marti, and the three of us became the triumvirate of evil here, as we call ourselves. Whenever possible, the three of us still get in a room together when we're stuck on a story or there's something amiss, because each of us brings something very specific to the table.

Why did you have a problem writing for *The X-Files*?

Howard Gordon is a great guy, and he became a terrific friend and was very sweet to me at *The X-Files*, but the show makes no sense to me. I don't understand *The X-Files*. Are there aliens or aren't there? Is there a conspiracy or not? When is Scully going to say, 'You know what, every week you say it's a supernatural thing and I say it can't be a supernatural thing and we've been on about 150 of these adventures now,' so when is Scully going to say, 'Hey, I bet it's supernatural!' The show is just not in my bones at all, and it's a very tough show to write; a lot of people more talented than myself

HOWARD GORDON

Originally writing with partner Alex Gansa, Howard Gordon landed several freelance TV assignments before becoming a staff writer on *Beauty and the Beast*. His work with Gansa on an ABC pilot called *Country Estates* caught the attention of *X-Files* creator Chris Carter, who invited them to work with him on the series. The duo collaborated on a number of *X-Files* scripts before Gansa moved on to other projects (including *Wolf Lake* for CBS). Gordon remained on the series for several seasons, moving up to executive producer before leaving the show in 1997. While developing new properties for Fox, Gordon became a consulting producer on *Buffy the Vampire Slayer*, writing (or co-writing with his friend David Greenwalt) several episodes, such as 'What's My Line, Part I'. When Angel was spun off into his own series, Gordon contributed a number of episodes, including 'Hero', 'Expecting', and 'The Ring'. Gordon's more recent genre projects were an American version of the UK's gritty vampire drama *Ultraviolet* (unfortunately unsold), and a pilot based on the comic book series *Ball and Chain*, about a married super-hero couple, which may yet be picked up. The 2001/2002 season saw him working on the Fox real-time drama *24*.

* *Now an executive producer on* Buffy.

struck out there. *Buffy* and *Angel* have metaphors, they're funny and serious at the same time. They just appeal to my peculiar talents. My talents are limited, and I'm fortunate to have a place that I can express them, and make a lot of money to boot! *The X-Files* is a big tease of a show. It's a show where you say, 'Oh, you think it's this, but now it's this,' and I could not connect to that show, nor could I write it. So I'm in awe of people like Howard Gordon and Chris Carter and the guys who *can* write that show, because I was over there for three months, and it was incredibly painful.

Do you think the first season of *Buffy* had more of a 'monster of the week' feel to it before the introduction of Angel?

Sometimes you need a monster of the week, sometimes you don't. You always need to ask, 'What is Buffy's journey, or Angel's journey? What are they going through?' and we craft the monster of the week to the metaphor, to what the person is going through. Occasionally, you'll come up with the idea for something really cool. The idea of 'Teacher's Pet' for example was, 'What if a guy literally becomes the teacher's pet and is left in a cage in her basement?' And so in fact, a story like that does grow out of what could be considered a more 'exterior' idea. But the 'interior' idea of that is, 'I'm a virgin, I have a crush on my teacher; what if she had a crush back on me?'

But Angel did change the chemistry between the characters, didn't he?

Joss had introduced the character in the *Buffy* pilot. He was this dark, mysterious character in the shadows, and Joss said, 'He's a vampire, and they're going to fall for each other,' but we really didn't know how big that would be. We had to hunt and hunt for an actor to play this character. We had no money, so we needed somebody who was a star, but who wasn't a star yet. To the great credit of Gail Berman and Marcia Schulman, who was our casting person at that time, they brought this guy David Boreanaz in, who was very impressive in the room, but very low key. Joss and I weren't a hundred per cent positive, but Gail and Marcia were like, 'This is the guy. This is the guy!' And boy were they right.

So Buffy is the Slayer, and here's this vampire whose name is Angel — there was some hokiness to it. But I volunteered to write episode seven the first year, which is when Buffy and the audience find out Angel's a vampire, and when Buffy kissed him for the first time. So I volunteered to write that episode, in the same way that one sometimes volunteers to write the Christmas episode — 'I'll do it, it's probably not going to be that big an episode,' but it was *gigantic*. The chemistry between them and the mythic possibilities of that first story were just huge, and then it took off with a power of its own. There were so many great episodes dealing with the hate-love relationship that they had, and how they suffered through it. The other great thing about working with Joss is, we don't do 'This couple kind of like each other, and for five years, they're going to almost maybe get married some time...' We take it to a place where we can turn it around.

Do you feel the writing for the show went into a different direction when Angel left?

No, I disagree entirely with that statement. Joss always knew what the show was, and the show never went in a different direction. There is nothing more 'high school' than your first tragic love. Joss found the single greatest metaphor for that, of any episode of any show ever, which is, she loses her virginity to Angel, and because of his curse, he turns evil. In fact, the metaphor is simply: he won't call her the next day. When she finally does talk to him, he treats her like shit. So it's all about the pain of growing up, and it has nothing to do with Angel himself. It's like if you do a story about a student who has her high school photo taken: the story is not about the photographer at all, it's about how the student feels, the pain of 'How do I look in that picture? Was I even there the day they took the picture, and does anyone even care about me?'

Did the writing staff work out most of the early episodes as a group?

We plotted everything out on big charts. Joss, during his days writing *Waterworld*[*], would buy little figurines and set them up all over his bed and desk in Hawaii and figure out where everybody was. When we worked on 'School Hard' together, we'd put huge diagrams of the school up on the wall and decide exactly where everybody was at every moment in that episode. The other thing I learned from Joss was how to plot out action. You have to physically plot out each step really clearly and really closely.

Of those early shows, are there any scripts that particularly stand out for you?

I think my first show was 'Teacher's Pet', which is an idea I'd pitched to Joss, and he liked it and it went really well. And then we were looking for the first story where Buffy and Angel kiss, and we had no idea that it was going to be such a gigantic episode, so I said, 'Oh, let me write that one.' Obviously any story that you see on *Buffy* or *Angel* has been broken substantially by Mr Whedon, if not entirely. And then the Buffy/Angel thing was just gigantic; people couldn't get enough of it, and we were all a little surprised.

Is it fair to say that Joss had a very specific tone in mind for *Buffy*, which may have been difficult for some writers to understand at first?

From where I sat, I think that's very accurate. I'm going back to the late 1980s, when if you came to TV from movies, you did one-hour shows, which were usually turgid dramas, with a few minor exceptions like *Northern Exposure*. If you didn't do movies, you went into half-hours and that meant comedy. The idea of really mixing the two wasn't done. But if you look at comedy shows like *Friends* or *The Dick Van Dyke Show*, the best of those series usually have some very painful things at their core. They're wickedly funny, but the core is something painful or dark, and — you just said the word — tone was so key. For some reason, and I think it's because I came from movies that had humour and drama in them, I seem to be able to do that. And by the way, I worked harder on *Buffy* and now *Angel* than anything I ever did in my life. That's because I was so in awe of Joss and his talent, and these aren't just shows you crank out in a week and throw on the air. Fourteen hours is a minimum day here, but what makes it worthwhile is we're all involved in something good.

I think the tone of *Buffy* is a hard thing for people to get. We had a lot of attrition here in the early days, even though there were a lot of very talented, hard-working people — but most shows are like that. I'm sure the people on [the children's puppet series] *Mr. Roger's Neighborhood* were saying, 'We can't find anybody who can write our show!' I think it's endemic in our business. But when you read, and even when you physically look at a Joss script — I think of the musical notes on a staff as if I'm reading Mozart — it looks very simple. It feels like nothing else could happen but what is happening, it feels inevitable, and you have these really funny absurd occurrences, melded with tragic, moving, heartfelt experiences. There is a little bit of magic in there as well. We all read Joss's scripts and say, 'How does he *do* that time after time?' But it's just finding the heart and the core of the story, and the question he asks all the time is, 'What do we need?' Frequently when people want to build a story, they say, 'What if we had a giant monster come in? What if we had a monster who was like a tumour?' Instead of that kind of thinking, you have to be saying, 'What if I felt so insignificant that I literally turned invisible?' You have to find the emotional core of these stories, and that's where the bulk of our work is done. The rest is just putting it together. Breaking the stories, finding what the core of these stories are, I would say that's certainly more than half of our workload.

So it was a matter of finding writers who could fit in to that very specific tone.

A lot of it is finding that fit. Sometimes it takes a year to train a writer in this kind of writing, and if you're lucky they get it. I think the secret that Joss had in his pocket was that if he had to, he could do the whole thing by himself. In that first year, he *lived* here in these offices. I'd come in at seven in the morning, and he'd have spent the night here. I think he directed five to seven episodes a year, he wrote five to seven, and of course he rewrote all the episodes in the early years, so it was extraordinary the amount of work he was doing. But it was always exciting, and every eight days, you'd get a wolfman show, a vampire show — well, obviously a vampire show, but look at the episode where Dracula the 'real' vampire came back last season[*]. That's what I love about *Buffy*. What a film school this has been. They call me a Hollywood veteran in my bio, and I'm about to turn fifty-two and I've been doing this for twenty-seven years, but I've never had so much fun, and I've never learned so much about film-making. In the last five years, we've done 160 episodes, and there's a new challenge every week, some new monster, some new thing, and you keep learning. It's like the old studio days; I'd like to think in the 1930s, I would have been one of those studio guys making three movies a year. And nowadays, you

---

[*] *In the aptly-titled 'Buffy vs. Dracula' in season five.*

can't learn anything in film-making. You can wait five years and make one film; what the hell can you learn from that?

At what point did you talk about launching Angel into his own series?

I think it had to be year three that Joss came to me and said, 'What do you think about spinning David/Angel off into his own show?' I said, 'I think it's a great idea, but I think we must take Cordelia with him because Angel is such a dark and power-ful character, and we need a bright and sunny character to balance that out.' That was my big contribution to *Angel*: bringing the character of Cordelia along with him. So we broke the pilot, and it was not easy. With *Buffy*, even though all the stories were difficult to break, Buffy always seemed very clear cut. She is a small girl in big situa-tions. She's also somebody who's slightly worried about her hair and nails while she has to go fight evil, so the juxtapositions are very clear, because adolescence is so strong. Now we were suddenly saying, 'Let's go to the big city, LA, and let's have a darker, more urban, slightly more gritty environment.' Originally, we thought *Angel* would be more of an anthology show, that we wouldn't be trying to find out 'What is the 'Angel' of it?' With *Buffy*, we had to figure out what the 'Buffy' of it was; what is she suffering, what is she learning, what is her arc, how is she growing? Early on, we discovered we *did* have to know what the 'Angel' of it is, or what the 'Cordelia' of it is.

What we do best is explore characters, and it's basically a heightened melodrama with broad strokes of comedy. That's what we do, and it reflects that fact that life is terri-fying and full of tragedy, and then silly comedy. Both shows are frequently confused, and people think they're camp because our guys might quip with a demon or tell a joke in a very serious situation, but the shows are in fact the direct opposite of camp. One thing I learned from Joss is that sentiment is fine. You need sentiment. In some of my movie background, I had written... not necessarily romantic comedies, but clever, witty and somewhat psychologically disturbing stuff, as you go up to *Profit*, but I always hated sentiment. I always thought television was just full of crappy senti-ment. But the way Joss taught me to see it was that we crave sentiment, and senti-ment is fine, but you have to earn it. I'd never really thought of it that way; that you can really earn sentiment, and you can have a big feeling. You can have a scene with-out a joke in it, but you have to earn it. It can't just be, 'Well, Johnny's dog died.'

Is it true that you'd intended *Angel* to be a much darker show, until the stu-dio pulled you back?

This is a somewhat complicated answer, but believe it or not, it's the truth. We'd imag-ined *Angel* as a pretty dark and gritty show, and as we began making it, Joss and I began feeling, 'Oh God, what is this turning into? We're in warehouses or dirty, dingy streets all the time, and we're not feeling the fun coupled with the redemption.' At the same time, we said to the network that what *Buffy* is to high school and college

— that metaphor of being a beleaguered adolescent and a beleaguered very young adult — we will continue, and find great twenty-something metaphors for *Angel*. This will be the metaphor for what it's like to be a young person in your twenties in the big city. In fact, we didn't find nearly as many of those metaphors as we wanted to.

We were actually in total agreement with the network and their concerns. I think we were coming at it from a story standpoint and they were coming at it from the kind of images they wanted to broadcast on their network, but in terms of the result, we were in complete accord. We didn't only want to see warehouses and dirty alleys and downtown streets, which is certainly part of LA. But there's also Bel Air, there's Hollywood; there's an endless list of things that are peculiar and nice to LA, and still carry the metaphor of LA as a place that people come to in order to start over. One of the things we did was introduce Gunn, who was definitely from the street. He was in fact leading a pack of young folks who were hunting vampires. In that same episode, we also had wacky billionaire David Nabbit and his life, because we wanted to contrast the two lifestyles, and one without the other wouldn't have been interesting.

So how has the tone of *Angel* developed from your original conception?

Sometimes we look at what we did over a period of a year and say, 'Oh my God, Cordelia and Angel, I should think somewhere deep down inside, even if they don't know it, they must have feelings for each other. Look at how much they've been through!' so there are some things that you do that come out of the show itself.

As I was saying before, we pitched *Angel* as a dark, gritty urban show. There were going to be female undercover cops who got hooked on crack and in fact became real prostitutes, so it was going to be *really* dark. One of the things we did in the original pilot was a scene in which Angel fails to save this girl. She's been bitten by a vampire, and Angel has her blood on him, and he suddenly starts licking the blood off his hands. That was a pivotal, key moment in the pilot, and if you don't remember what I'm talking about, the reason is because we cut it the hell out of the show! It was suggested by Marti Noxon and we thought it was brilliant, so we wrote it into the pilot. But when we put the episode together, we said, 'We haven't earned the darkness of this moment, and people won't understand it. Angel is battling his darker forces.' You might have understood it better by the time you got to episode ten of year two, where he fired his staff and really went dark.

We'd certainly written one very dark episode, which had all those elements I was just speaking of, with the lady cop going really bad, and the network got kind of scared. They said, 'Look, we're the WB, we don't want a show this dark!' If we (being Joss and me) had thought in our hearts that we were on the right track, we would have said, 'Go fuck yourselves! This is the show we're making, and we'll go somewhere else if you don't like it!' But in fact, we agreed with them, because something was missing from the show, some central, core part of it. Either we'd lost our metaphors, or the metaphors were too dark, so we revamped the show. In that first year, they were still in dark offices, tiny spaces, and every time we tried to do downtown LA, it just looked lame. Also, 'LA' is really just a place in people's minds. You can physically live in LA, but what the hell is an LA landmark — Griffith Park, Disneyland? It's not a city like New York or Chicago or Philadelphia. So our original idea, that the *place* was important, changed; the whole show really did change, and we went with the changes in a way, I think, that's to our credit.

In our weird way, *Angel* was a tougher show than *Buffy*. We thought it was going to be an easier show but it's not, because the metaphor isn't so simple; but ultimately, we've finally figured out that *Buffy* is about how hard it is to be a woman, and *Angel* is about how hard it is to be a man. Those are really the core values of the two shows.

Is that really the basic core premise when all is said and done?

It seems to be. The original notion of *Angel* was that it was sort of an alcoholic metaphor; 'I must never 'drink' again, and one day at a time, I must try to do good and make up for my horrible past!' but you kind of get sick of that after a while. You know he's going to do good anyway, and then it becomes the larger issue of saying, 'it's hard to be a guy in the world. It's hard to be gentle when you should be, and sometimes you have to be violent. Sometimes you have to beat on the head of bad people, so how do you balance that all out and not become evil when you fight evil?' I love writing the shows because you get into such deep, sometimes biblical references, and a lot of metaphysical places, but you can also tell jokes, and those are some of my favourite areas.

How quickly did you manage to put together a good writing staff on *Angel*?

Actually, the only person who's remained on my staff from season one is Tim Minear, discounting Joss Whedon and Marti Noxon who are our *Buffy* people, who were very helpful. Of course Joss's involvement is essential to the show, and obviously he breaks all the stories with us. But of my first year's staff, only Tim Minear is still here. In a sense, Tim is to *Angel* what I was to *Buffy*, and in another sense, what Marti Noxon is to *Buffy* now. He's a kindred spirit who appeared and who could write, produce, direct and do everything. He could break a story, which is really the key thing. There was also another in-house person, Mere Smith, who was our script co-ordinator [on season one], and we threw scenes and ideas at her because we knew she was brilliant — a hard worker and a talented writer. She was also one of those very rabid stalker *Buffy/Angel* fans, and by God, she wrote a *Sopranos* that knocked our socks off! When it came to the end of the year and we were talking about who we wanted to hire, we were interviewing all kinds of people, and we said, 'You know what? We're going to hire Mere,' and she's worked out terrifically.

There were also people like Shawn Ryan, who was on last year who did great, but went off to make a pilot. There was Jim Kouf, who happens to be an old friend and former movie partner of mine, who came in to consult, and learned a little bit about TV just for his own career. He's really busy writing now. And Howard Gordon from *The X-Files* was here in a consulting capacity, and he's now gone on to other things. So there are people who came into the orbit and went away for other reasons. It's true that in two years, I think we've built a pretty effective staff on *Angel*, whereas it took four years on *Buffy*. It's a lot of luck, who walks in the door. You can read a script that's great, but maybe they're not great in the room.

Looking back, what worked on the first season of *Angel*?

I think the biggest highlight is the fact that we were all still breathing by the end of it! The first year was unbelievably hard. Out of those twenty-two, I think we did eighteen pretty damn fine episodes of television, which is pretty great batting on my part. I loved when Spike visited the show and then Buffy, and later when Faith visited the show. I like when Angel made a mistake and misjudged something, or did something funny; there are certain things that are very big for me, and one of them is that we make a little fun of Batman! Angel is our hero, but a hero doesn't have to be perfect, he can make mistakes. He's struggling to do the right thing against great odds, so maybe he doesn't always succeed. I actually have a pretty special affection for most of the episodes, and I could go through all twenty-two and say, 'I'll tell you what I like in this one.' I think we finished out the year with a bang. It feels complete and three-dimensional to me, what we did, and I think people worked unbelievably hard on it.

After what you've done at the end of season two, the audience really doesn't have a clue what you've got up your sleeve in terms of story, do they?

I certainly hope not. I guarantee at the end of episode one of year three there is a huge surprise of gigantic proportions that will turn everything on its head, and in a way, will map out the next two years of the show. Again, you're speaking of something near and dear to my heart, which is tone, and how Joss likes to shake things up. What happened in season two, our characters were in new offices. We had a new character in Gunn, played by J. August Richards, so we were kind of in a new world. Just when we became sick of the 'We meet in the hotel lobby, Cordy has a vision, we go solve the crime' stories, we came to about episode ten, which is usually our last episode broadcast before Christmas. There's usually a break at that point, so we try to think of episode ten as the 'Act II' break of the season if you will. Sometimes we like to put a cliffhanger in there, so Joss said, 'Let's let Angel lock Darla and Drusilla in this room full of terrible lawyers who have made his life a living hell and walk away from it.' It's a brilliant scene, and if you just had that scene, it would be a great ending, but then let's have his people say to him, 'Hey, that's crazy, you're going back to your old ways. We are all that stands between you and darkest night.' He says, 'I know you're all that stands between me and darkest night,' and of course you're expecting him to say,

'And that's why I need you,' but instead he says, 'You're all fired!' So he fires them, and it immediately sets the show on its head and suddenly we're not in a formula anymore. Suddenly I have my three characters — Wesley, Cordelia and Gunn — in a new environment, trying to fight crime and trying to continue. We have Angel living in the sewers and going to a very dark place, because he knows if he has to hunt down Darla and Drusilla and kill them, he has to go to a very dark place. So that was the first great twist of the season for me.

The second great twist was when Angel set Darla and Drusilla on fire and got them out of town, so he did go very dark. He actually had sex with Darla at one point, but he basically had his soul restored, and came back and made amends to his people, and he didn't want to be the leader anymore. He wanted to be a worker among workers, which is a beautiful thing. So they made Wesley the titular head, and Angel even gave Wesley his office. That was around episode sixteen, and in fact emotionally, in one sense, the work of the season was done. It was a very unusual structure: Angel has gone through the dark night of the soul, he's made up with them and now he's come back.

We were out to dinner one night and we said, 'What the hell are we going to do for the rest of the season?' and Joss basically said *Wizard of Oz*. I forget how he put it, but he basically said, 'They should all get sucked into another dimension. They should all get the thing they're looking for, so we'll make Cordelia a princess, Angel will be in a

CREATING A NEMESIS

Sherlock Holmes had Moriarty, Doctor Who had The Master (as did Buffy, for a while at least); every hero needs a signature villain to square up against. Perhaps with that in mind, a major new adversary for Angel is introduced in the show's third year: Horst, a vampire hunter who tracked Angel and Darla across Europe in the 1700s, and has now arrived in the twenty-first century to continue his mission. The character is played by Keith Szarabajka, probably best known for his role in Stephen King's 1991 series *Golden Years*. 'Keith and I go way back,' notes Greenwalt. 'He was also in my show *Profit*, and now he's playing a vampire hunter from Angel's past. He's human, but he figures out a way to get into our time from the past, and he's going to hunt Angel down and kill him. That's his goal, so he's going to be an over-arcing villain for the year, which is going to add a lot to the show. He's a villain with a good point of view — 'Hey, Angel killed countless people, and he should be punished!' Angel, in a way, almost agrees with him; he's not simply going to say, 'If you come near me, I'll kill you.' He's actually more likely to think, 'Well, he kind of has a point…'

noble land of clear black and white, and Wesley will become a general. Gunn will have to deal with incredible racial inequities in this world where the humans are the slaves and the indigenous demons are the power, and we'll meet this wonderful new character Fred. So we kind of went out on the season with what we like to call a gay romp, but underlying all of this stuff were some very dark things. For example, Angel turns into a more vicious vampire, a primal vampire because there is no balance in that world, he's either all good or all evil, and he's terrified that he's going to stay a vampire, that he won't be able to get back to his human side. So this year people are going to say, 'What the heck are they going to do?'

So how is season three going to develop the characters?

All I can tell you right now is that things are going to get weirder! The first episode deals with the fact that Buffy is dead and how Angel is going to deal with that; how he's going to go on with his life, and what that means to him. The second episode is just heart-rending, with Cordelia getting stigmata from her visions, so she's literally suffering in her body the sins of the demons, of the evil of the world. It nearly kills her, but at the same time, it deepens her character. We're going to do an episode where Gunn is forced to choose between his old world with the guys on the street, and his new world with Angel. And then in episode four, an old guy changes bodies with Angel, and you have this crazy fake Angel drinking martinis and trying to screw everything in sight!

Are you going into the third year with the same enthusiasm and excitement you had in the beginning?

Remember *Quantum Leap*? I used to love that show, because you just didn't know what you were going to get each week. It could be serious, it could be an episode dealing with civil rights, or it could be plain silliness. Season three of *Angel* is like that — and yes, it's really exciting. ∎

MICHAEL PILLER

After he was discouraged by a particularly vindictive creative writing professor while at college, Michael Piller seemed resigned to a career in journalism. But, one 'religious experience' later, he rediscovered his faith in his abilities, and found himself in Hollywood, writing spec scripts which eventually led to commissions for such popular 1980s shows as *Simon & Simon* and *Cagney & Lacey*. He went on to work on the SF-tinged series *Probe*, but by then there was another SF show that had really caught his eye — *Star Trek: The Next Generation*... In television, it's damn near impossible to capture lightning in a bottle twice, and that thought had doubtless crossed the minds of Paramount executives more than once as they green-lit *TNG*. Would the studio be able to tap into the same fan enthusiasm that made the original series a cult phenomenon, or was their latest effort doomed to failure? Although *The Next Generation* turned out to be a ratings success, all was not well behind the scenes. There was a high turnover of writers, many of whom found it difficult to work within the constraints of Gene Roddenberry's universe. Enter Piller, who joined the show as head writer during season three, and began building a solid writing staff that would continue into the subsequent spin-offs he co-created, *Deep Space Nine* and *Voyager*. Unfortunately, there was also a down side to being the caretaker of Roddenberry's vision. As Piller reveals here, some of the young writers on *Voyager* eventually began to chafe under his strictures, much in the same way the *TNG* staff did under Roddenberry during that show's early seasons. So maybe history *does* repeat itself...

Is it true that you took a creative writing class in college, and were basically discouraged from pursuing it as a career?

That was back when I was a student at the University of North Carolina — it's one of my favourite stories to tell! My father had been a writer, so I'd gotten some encouragement from him. I was a fairly successful high school writer, but then you get into college and start finding new challenges, and sometimes you over-challenge yourself. To be fair to this professor, I was not writing well in college, but he would open the class by saying, 'There are enough bad writers out there. I have no interest in sending any more bad writers out into the world, so if I think you're a bad writer, I'm going to do everything I can to discourage you from becoming a writer.' Unfortunately, I was one of those people that he decided didn't cut it. It was the 1960s when everybody was doing a lot of drugs and I wasn't, and everybody had this new consciousness and open liberalism. Although I was liberal, I was a Kennedy liberal, so I was trying to stretch my writing into directions that I knew nothing about. I learned the hard way that when you start writing about the horrors of war and don't have anything but old war movies to draw on, you're not going to be able to bring anything new to the table. This was the kind of teacher who read students' work to the class and made fun of it, and the others would laugh, and by the time this course was over, I was emasculated as a writer. I didn't want to go near creative writing for years, so I went into journalism.

You've talked about having a 'religious experience' some years later, after going to see a performance of *A Chorus Line*.

There's a song by the character of Morales called 'Nothing', which is about her struggles to become an actress. She sings in the song that the teacher on her drama course at school basically told everybody that they had to feel 'the wind on the toboggan' and 'feel the snow' — but she didn't feel anything. The teacher says, 'If you don't start feeling something soon, you're going to be transferred,' so she's frustrated and lost and confused. This teacher keeps telling her she's no good, and I'm sitting in this theatre, surrounded by hundreds of people, thinking, 'This is my story!' So Morales goes to church to pray for guidance, and Santa Maria speaks to her and she says, 'This course is nothing. This man is nothing; go out and find a better class!' and I thought, 'Why didn't I think of that?' From that day forward, I started writing again, and found what I was meant to be doing in this life.

You went to LA and began working for CBS in the 1970s. Were you writing spec scripts in your spare time?

I got hired out here as a censor when I left the news business, and I started writing screenplays too. I was eventually moved upstairs to the entertainment division as an executive, and the more screenplays I read, the more confident I got writing my own.

MICHAEL PILLER

Date/Place of Birth:
1948, Port Chester, NY, USA

Home Base:
Los Angeles, California, USA

Education:
University of North Carolina

First TV Work:
Simon & Simon

TV Career Highlights:
Cagney & Lacey, *Probe*, *Group One Medical*, *Star Trek: The Next Generation*, *Star Trek: Deep Space Nine*, *Legend*, *Star Trek: Voyager*

I recommend to anybody who wants to be a writer in this business to read lots of screenplays, both good and bad, because the good ones are remarkably simple and straightforward; but then you look at the bad ones and see the overwriting and purple prose and bad dialogue, and seeing the difference gives you great confidence. So I wrote a *WKRP in Cincinnati* and a *Lou Grant* on spec, and a two-hour TV movie — and didn't sell any of them. Plus I wrote probably another half dozen scripts that weren't even worth showing to people because they were so bad, just me learning my craft. But the three scripts I mentioned were the ones where I said, 'Look, I can write!' and I showed them to people, who responded to the material. Ultimately, it was Barney Rosenzweig at *Cagney & Lacey*, and Richard Chapman and Phil DeGuere at *Simon & Simon* who gave me my first assignments. I said, 'If I left the network, would you give me a writing assignment?' and when they said yes, I basically cut my lifeline off, with my wife's support, and with just two assignments became a writer. If I had any sense, I probably wouldn't have done it, but I felt very confident.

Previous to your work on *The Next Generation*, you hadn't been in the SF genre to any great degree. Did you have any hesitation about signing on to a well-established SF series?

I was interested in *The Next Generation*, not because it was SF but because it was good. My family and I watched the first two seasons together, and every once in a while, they would put a gem of a story in place and you just got blown away. I happened to have lunch with Gene Roddenberry, [producers] Rick Berman and Maurice Hurley the week after 'Measure of a Man' ran — I was so impressed with that episode [in which the android Data's rights as a sentient being are questioned during a tense court case]. I didn't get the job on the writing staff I was after, because they hired my old friend Mike Wagner, who I'd worked with on *Probe**. But Gene and Mike did not get along. I wrote a *Next Generation* script for Mike, and it was about the only one Gene, Rick and Mike all agreed on, so when Mike quit, the other two asked me if I'd be interested in taking over as head of the writing staff. It was intimidating, but I went to Gene and said, 'Look, I've got to tell you right up front, I don't consider myself a SF writer. I consider myself a character writer. I can make the characters grow, I can get beneath their skin, but I'm going to need help with the SF.' Gene said, 'Don't worry about it, the SF will come through the door. If you can execute scripts like this one and give us the character work we need, then it will work,' and obviously he turned out to be right.

When you took over on *The Next Generation*, was the writing staff in bad shape?

It was in complete turmoil. The reputation that *Star Trek: The Next Generation* had in town was not good. It was basically considered the worst place to work in Hollywood, and the reason for that was that Roddenberry had very strict rules. His vision was sacrosanct, and he didn't care about excuses or explanations, he didn't want to argue about it. He wanted you to do it his way, and a lot of writers couldn't see his future his way. Gene really didn't want any conflict between the human characters, so the

---

* *A short-lived (lasting four months on ABC in 1988) sci-fi tinged mystery series, created by Isaac Asimov.*

problem that Mike Wagner and every writer on staff was having was that they were feeling constrained and restricted, and unable to move within this box that Roddenberry had created. My problem was very simple: I didn't have any scripts to shoot next week, and the writers were saying, 'The reason is that Gene won't approve anything!' My attitude was, 'Roddenberry has obviously done something right, because *Star Trek* has lasted three decades. I'm here to find out what makes *Star Trek* work as Gene Roddenberry created it, and execute it to the best possible ability that I have.' With the very first material I started to develop, I said, 'I need to see every script, every abandoned story, and every submitted piece of material that's sitting around because I have to have *something* to shoot next week.' Somebody gave me a script called 'The Bonding' by a guy named Ron Moore[*], who was about to go into the Marines. It was an interesting story about a kid whose mother goes down on an away mission and gets killed, and the kid is obviously torn apart by the death of his mother. Seeing how much he's suffering, the aliens provide him with a mother substitute. The writing was rough and amateurish in some ways, but it had real potential to tell an interesting story.

So I went to Gene and pitched him the story, and he said, 'It won't work. In the 24th century, death is accepted as a part of life, so this child would not be mourning the death of his mother. He would be perfectly accepting of the fact that she had lived a good life, and would move on with his life.' I went back to the writing staff and told

RICK BERMAN

When Rick Berman joined the *Next Generation* production team back in 1987, he didn't realise that he would become one of the most influential voices in the *Star Trek* universe for many years to come. Berman, now an Emmy Award-winning producer, originally came to Paramount in 1984, where he performed a succession of different roles for the studio, from director of current programming to vice president of long-form and special projects. After overseeing the new *Star Trek* series for just a couple of weeks, he was invited to lunch by Gene Roddenberry, who asked him to sign on as supervising producer. It was the beginning of a long and rewarding relationship for Berman that continues to this day. In addition to his work as executive producer (as he ultimately became) on the various *Star Trek* shows, Berman co-created *Deep Space Nine* with Michael Piller, *Voyager* with Piller and Jeri Taylor, and more recently, the 'back to basics' prequel series *Enterprise* with Brannon Braga. He's also maintained the same hands-on role with all the *Trek* films since *Star Trek Generations*, including *Star Trek: Nemesis*, which reunites the *Next Generation* cast for the fourth and possibly last time.

* See page 234 for more on Ron Moore.

them what Gene had told me, and they smirked and said, 'Now you know what we've been going through!' I said, 'Wait a minute, is there any way we can satisfy Gene's 24th century rules and at the same time not lose the story that we have to shoot on Tuesday?' I finally thought, what if this kid has been taught all of his life not to mourn the death of his loved ones, because that's what society expects of him? He's taught that death is a part of life, so he doesn't have any emotional reaction to the death of his mother. Well, that is freaky, and that's going to feel far more interesting on film than if he's crying for two acts. What if the aliens, who feel guilty about killing his mother, provide him with a mother substitute — and the kid bonds with this substitute? And what if it's Troi (who had not been playing a very important role in the series up to that point), who goes to Picard and says, 'We have a problem. The kid isn't going to give up this mother substitute until he really accepts and mourns the death of his real mother, and we're going to have to penetrate centuries of civilisation to get to the emotional core of this kid in order to wake up his emotional life.'

Well, Gene loved the idea. It respected his universe, and at the same time, it became a far better episode than it would have if Gene had simply signed off on the original pitch. From that experience, I learned that 'Roddenberry's Box' forced us to tell stories in more interesting and different ways than we would have in any other typical universe. Ironically, I became dedicated to preserving the box as much as I could, and as time went on, it sort of became 'Piller's Box'.

You finished *TNG*'s third season with 'The Best of Both Worlds, Part I', still considered one of the best episodes in the show's history. Is it true you wrote the cliffhanger without knowing how it would be resolved?

When I started writing that story, I wasn't planning to come back the following year, so all I had to do was write part one, and it was somebody else's problem to write part two! I was exhausted, and it had been the best and worst year of my life. The story of how the cliffhanger came about is one that Rick and I argue over, but I remember it very vividly. The head of the television division at Paramount came to us at the tail end of the season and said, 'Guys, we might have a problem with Patrick Stewart's contract, so you've got to come up with a cliffhanger that gives us an opportunity to kill him if we have to.' So we said, 'Okay...' I loved the Borg; Maurice Hurley had come up with them for one of the Q episodes*, and we decided to bring them back. Our first take on it was that Data *and* Picard were both taken and Borgified together, so you had Data and Picard merged as an entity built by the Borg. I think it was Rick who said, 'Why make it so complicated? Just let Picard be taken!' By that time, I was so tired from writing twenty-two episodes — we spent the season what [fellow writer] Ira Behr called 'riding on the rims' like our tires were flat — so I would sit there and say, 'Okay, just write one more page.' When it came out and everybody reacted so strongly to it, I was delighted. And then Roddenberry came in while the season was winding down and said, 'Listen, the series needs one more year to really catch on, and I'd really like you to come back next year.' With that in mind, I was forced to go back

---

* *The second season episode, 'Q Who'.*

and write part two without knowing how I was going to get our people out of this disaster, and get Picard back from the Borg. I discovered how to do it virtually the same time as our characters did, when they came up with the idea of using the Borg hive mentality against itself. I can remember feeling very pleased with myself, because there's nothing quite as nerve-wracking as not knowing where you're going. I've often been quoted as saying, 'Being a writer is like being on the crew of the *Enterprise*, because we're all explorers, going off into the unknown every time we sit down at the typewriter.' I certainly felt that way in that circumstance.

Did things begin to improve on the writing end with season four?

I think the staff I inherited on the third season were already disaffected and very angry. I don't think Ira was very comfortable in the Gene Roddenberry part of the universe, so he quit, along with everybody else. I was able to hold on to Ron Moore, who was beginning to show promise. He could write the best Klingon characters in the world, but still hadn't learned to write humans yet. When Ron wrote 'Brothers', where Picard comes home to see his brother, I had to do a lot of rewriting on that, because his human voices just weren't sparkling enough yet. I said, 'Listen Ron, you're doing a great job, but you still have some things to learn. Hang in there and pay attention to what I've done, and you'll see why I did it. Do you see what I've done to this character? The kid for example is better than what you had there. That's what we've got to find in these voices and these characters.' By the time I left, Ron was writing the best voices of anybody on the show.

One of the great contributions I can take pride in is the discovery and development of new talent that was capable of replacing me when I left. It's a painful process, because you have to fire some people that don't work. But then there are people you find who work out better than you ever thought they would. In the meantime, the head writer has to be prepared to carry a great deal of the burden, making sure that the scripts each week are as good as they deserve to be for the audience that tunes in every time. Mostly, as in the case of 'Brothers', I would take over the script with a week left before filming, and the structure would be in place, and I would put in my personal touch. There was quite a bit of rewriting in the fourth season, but in the fifth season, things really became easy for me because everybody had got the message by that time. I had a group of dedicated people who were working their asses off to make things better, so instead of taking every freelance script myself, I would farm it over to [staff writers] Jeri Taylor or Joe Menosky or somebody else, so I wouldn't have to rewrite those things myself.

At what point did Rick Berman come to you with the idea of doing a spin-off series, which would ultimately become *Deep Space Nine*?

The truth is, I'd been bugging Rick for two years to get the studio to consider a spin-off. I came out of the network world, and when you had a huge phenomenon hit like

The Next Generation, you did another show. There's no question in my mind that the audience was ready for another series. Rick agreed with me, and went to the studio, who said, 'We will never do another *Star Trek* series at Paramount! We're still negotiating the contracts with Roddenberry's lawyers, and we've got ten lawyers assigned to *Star Trek* now; we're not going to do this again!' And then, Brandon Tartikoff came in and took over Paramount, and the first thing he said was, 'I want another space show.' He didn't say *Star Trek*, he said, 'space' and then he said, 'I have a vision of *The Rifleman*** in space. I see a man and his son going through space, keeping law and order.' Ultimately, Rick said, 'You know, we've had great success with the *Star Trek* franchise, and you have a rabid fan base of people who will follow you to the next show.' Tartikoff said, 'I don't care whether it's *Star Trek* or not; if you think it's a good idea, we'll do *Star Trek*.' So Rick called me up and said, 'Guess what? Brandon wants to do another show. He thinks it's *The Rifleman* in space, he sees a man and his son, so let's create another show.' That's how it came about.

Did you both have a firm idea of what you wanted to do with *DS9* right from the start?

We pretty much knew that there were only three kinds of series that you could do in space: one was going to be on a ship, one was on a space station, and one was on a planet's surface. We talked about the planet's surface for a while, doing a 'Wild West' town, but realised we were going to wind up shooting on location up in the mountains above Hollywood and thought that was untenable, so we basically turned our attention to the space station idea. So where do you put the space station? The idea of putting it at a Gibraltar, or a key, critical spot in the Roddenberry universe where there was danger and threats and things like that, seemed to be a logical extension. And then you had to figure out what was in the Straits of Gibraltar that made it such a strategic location. We started looking at our universe and what elements we could use: the Cardassians, a wormhole, and so on.

How did you feel about suggestions by *Babylon 5* creator J. Michael Straczynski, that the concept behind *Deep Space Nine* may have been taken from ideas he'd developed for his show?

Joe who? The irony is, when we got the go-ahead to do *Deep Space Nine*, Straczynski's wife† was working for me as an intern. I walked into the office, and we were talking about something — I don't know what it was — and I started saying, 'Hey, we got the go-ahead for the new series!' I'm not sure I have a clear vision of this, but I remember her saying, 'Really, you're kidding; a new *Star Trek*; what's it about?' I said, 'It's going to be on a space station.' And she went white. She said, 'Oh my God, my husband has been trying to sell a space station series!' and I said, 'Gee, I'm sorry, but I'm sure there's room for more than one.' To me, it was a regrettable coincidence, but not only do these things happen all the time, but they also happen to *me and Joe* all the time. If you're paying attention to his career, you'll see that he's signed to create

---

* *A highly successful series that ran on ABC from 1958 to 1963,* The Rifleman *starred Chuck Connors as homesteader Lucas McCain, a widower bringing up his son Mark (Johnny Crawford) in the lawless Old West.*
† *Kathryn Drennan, who wrote the episode 'By Any Means Necessary' for* Babylon 5's *first season.*

a post-Armageddon series for Showtime [*Jeremiah*]. I did [the post-Armageddon-set pilot] *Day One* last year, so I *could* say that he basically saw *Day One* and is using all my ideas this year! Now that the situation is reversed, he'll know how it feels to be doing something that is along the same lines as what somebody else is doing.

Were the characters on *Deep Space Nine* relatively easy to construct, or were some more difficult than others?

There's no question that we had trouble with Dax from the very beginning. We had a very difficult time figuring out a way to communicate the duality of that character, and it wasn't until Ira decided to make her a wisecracking, Howard Hawks[*] kind of girl that she really found her voice. She was originally stuck with all the technical jargon, which Brent Spiner used to call 'Piller filler', and Terry Farrell was not well suited for that role, so we went off searching for that. With Bashir, I wanted to create a character who was somewhat unlikeable, so we could make him grow into something interesting, and we created this fellow who was rather full of himself. By the middle of the first year, we started getting research back from the studio saying, 'We've got to fire the doctor; nobody likes him!' 'Well,' we said, 'That was the idea...' but we then softened him up a little bit. Early on, Kira came across to us as a bit too hard, so I think we moved her into a more accessible kind of voice. With Sisko, we were having a difficult time matching our ambitions for the character with the actor. I've never actually talked to Avery Brooks about this, but in the Roddenberry world, race and colour really don't play a major role, except in terms of whether you're green or an alien. In terms of humanity, the role of the black man is no different from the role of anybody else. I always thought that was a problem, because I felt a great deal of what Avery had done in the past used black attitudes to define the roles that he created — but there was nowhere to do that in the 24th century. There was a certain anger that Sisko carried around with him, derived from the fact that his wife had died and that he felt a little bit lost in the universe. But that felt out of character for Roddenberry's universe, so we struggled with how to use Sisko in the context of the role of the builder. Ultimately, I think it worked out, but it was a struggle at first.

Who am I missing? Quark never changed, and Odo never really changed. Those guys were the most successful from the get-go. And of course O'Brien didn't change. I think there was concern, because with Keiko and O'Brien, we tried to tell stories about a real married couple. Some people found the arguing between them and the stress of the relationship crossed the boundaries, going into personal conflict that Roddenberry wouldn't like, so we pulled back on that as well.

Do you feel that the series came together relatively easily?

My goal for the launch of *Deep Space Nine* was to straight away start telling the kind of stories that we didn't start telling on *The Next Generation* until the third season. I wanted to tell character stories, to get involved in the personal lives of our people in

---

[*] *American film director, of such classics as* Only Angels Have Wings *(1939) and* The Big Sleep *(1946).*

ways that I felt had helped turn the tide of *The Next Generation*, but without waiting for the usual ramping up period. I was surprised when we started doing some of those stories, we were getting feedback from people, and they weren't happy with them at all. They felt the episodes were not big enough in scope, so that may have been a misjudgement on my part in the first season. Instead of creating stories that were there to illuminate character, maybe I should have created plotlines that were bigger in scope, but ultimately added to the characters. That was a lesson we took into *Voyager*, and we had somewhat better success in terms of storytelling.

What made you decide to create another ship-based *Star Trek* series, which eventually became *Voyager*?

The Next Generation was coming to an end, and the studio decided there would be another *Star Trek*. Rick actually felt the franchise could use a little breathing room and wanted the studio to hold off on *Voyager* for at least a year, but the studio more or less said, 'We're going to do this with or without you. We'd rather do it with you, but we are going to do it.' What happened with *Voyager* was that it coincided with the creation of UPN [United Paramount Network], so there was no putting it off. We were the instruments of launching UPN, so it wasn't a question of what was good for *Star Trek* at that point, but what was good for UPN and Paramount. With the edict of, 'We're going to do this whether you like it or not,' Rick came to me and said, 'Okay, they want to do another one.' Frankly, I was already tired, because I was creating and

LEGEND

One of Piller's proudest accomplishments to date is *Legend*, a light-hearted Western adventure series that aired on the UPN network back in 1995. Richard Dean Anderson stars as Ernest Pratt, a gambling, womanising rogue, who makes a living by writing a series of successful dime novels about a hero named Nicodemus Legend. Through a series of events, Pratt finds himself reluctantly taking on the real-life heroic persona of Legend. Joining him on his adventures are an eccentric Edison-like European inventor, Janos Bartok (played by *Star Trek*'s Q, John de Lancie), and his assistant, Ramos (Mark Adair Rios). Using Bartok's futuristic devices, including a steam-driven motorcar, the trio set off on a series of adventures in the old West. While *Legend* was a critical success, those good reviews didn't translate into huge ratings for the fledgling network, which cancelled the series early in the first season. Piller returned to *Voyager*, while his co-creator Bill Dial went on to write and produce the final seasons of *Sliders*. As for Richard Dean Anderson, he soon accepted the starring role in *Stargate SG-1*.

working on other projects by then; I had written *Legend* the year before as a TV movie with Bill Dial. So that year became the most extraordinary, demanding season I've ever had, because *Voyager* and *Legend* both premièred on UPN simultaneously, with *Deep Space Nine* running concurrently in syndication. When we were creating *Voyager*, I'd said to Rick, 'Look, I really think my time at *Star Trek* is limited. I'd love to help you launch this series with our partnership being as successful as it is, but I think we need someone else, too. You and I both agree we want a woman captain to be in the chair on this show; if we don't, we're certainly going to be questioned about that.' (We'd made a conscious effort to have an African American in the chair in *Deep Space Nine*, so the logical progression, now that we'd taken care of the racial issues, was to take care of sexual issues.) So I said to Rick, 'It really makes sense for us to ask Jeri Taylor to join us, because then we'll have a female point of view in the room, and it won't be the two guys being the creative forces behind the first female captain.' I was also very up front in saying, 'Look, I will probably only stay on this a year or two, and I want to put somebody into the creative development of this series who's going to stay with it for longer than I'm prepared to.' That's why we recruited Jeri.

When you began production on *Voyager*, how much of a problem was caused by the initial casting of Genevieve Bujold as Captain Janeway?

She was unprepared to play the part. Our *first* choice was actually Susan Gibney, the actress who played Geordi's virtual reality girl in *The Next Generation**. We felt so strongly about her that we shot the first scene from the pilot, where Ensign Kim reports to the captain, with her in the role, and we played that whole scene and showed it to the studio. But they were not swayed, and the decision was that we would not hire Susan Gibney. I should add that we were also reading men, because the studio was not convinced it was in the best interest of *Star Trek* to put a woman in the chair. But they were willing to listen to us, because we said our audience was enlightened enough for us to cast a woman. I remember a British actor, Nigel Havers, who was one of the last men to stand, but ultimately somebody said 'Genevieve Bujold'. We met with her, and she looked great and was eager to work, so we went with her, knowing that star power was going to be extraordinarily valuable to us. Kate Mulgrew was one of the last three or four that we interviewed, but Genevieve Bujold had a quality about her that we were really excited about. We also felt the international flavour of *Star Trek* would be enhanced. We'd had an American captain, we'd had a British captain, and now we were having a French captain, so I thought we were being extraordinarily open minded about it all.

So Genevieve Bujold started filming, but she was used to doing features and working in a very specific manner, with great preparation and great rehearsal. She soon realised that she was going to be working twelve-hour days, with none of the luxuries that come with acting for features — I don't mean luxuries in terms of perks, I'm talking about the luxury of time and preparation. It's also a very difficult proposition for any actor who's not particularly familiar with *Star Trek* — or writer, or director for that

---

* *Gibney played Dr Leah Brahms in the third-season episode 'Booby Trap'. She reprised the role in season four's 'Galaxy's Child'.*

matter — to come in and start work on the series. I think it was clear that Avery Brooks had problems when he started, and there's no question that Genevieve had a problem understanding what the 24th century human being was like, and what Roddenberry's vision of humanity was. Both actors would often bring approaches to their characters that would not feel comfortable within the context of *Star Trek*, and it took us time, saying, 'No, that's just not the way Roddenberry sees the future.' I think Genevieve bristled under that: I remember we had an argument about whether or not the captain would bother to brush her hair. She didn't think the captain would brush her hair in the morning, and we said, 'This is Starfleet, you can't just come in with your hair all over the place!' The bottom line was, she was just not happy about the working conditions and said, 'Thanks anyway...'

... enter Kate Mulgrew. What kind of tone were you trying to create for *Voyager*, as opposed to *TNG* or *DS9*?

It's true that the tone of *Voyager* was affected by what the studio considered to be a problem on *Deep Space Nine*. It was very simply this: on *Deep Space Nine*, we had created conflict, without changing the fundamental rules of Roddenberry's universe. We put our humans into circumstances where they would be forced to confront conflict everywhere they turned. We had a great deal of pleasure writing those conflicts, and we also wanted it to be grittier and darker. However, the studio felt that one of the things that had happened was that this conflict and grittiness in *Deep Space Nine* had pushed away some viewers who basically tuned in to *Star Trek* for its optimism and its bright future. There was no question that we were going to do another ship show, because one of the criticisms — and a false one, I believe — of *Deep Space Nine* was that it doesn't go anywhere. So, we put them on a ship, but obviously we didn't want to do a rip-off of *The Next Generation*. We wanted to do something new, fresh and original, and force ourselves to be creative, so we basically put the ship into parts unknown. I think I said in the room, 'You know how Q suddenly throws the *Enterprise* off into parts unknown and we meet aliens like the Borg and so forth, and we finally get back by the end of the episode to where we were? What if we didn't get back at the end of the episode?' I think that was the origin of the *Voyager* premise, and then you have the great mythical power of 'the search for home', that comes with sources as far back as *Ulysses* and even as simple as *The Wizard of Oz*.

In any event, the studio felt that the cause of dwindling ratings on *Deep Space Nine* was that it was dark and gritty and had conflicts, so they said, 'This needs to be a bright, wonderful, happy show!' Well, we created a set-up that inherently had conflict in it, whereby you had the Maquis, the terrorist ship, forced to become one crew with the people on *Voyager* who are chasing them, which I think is a terrific premise. But it was then decided that all conflict was going to disappear almost immediately. Everybody was going to wear uniforms, they were going to be Starfleet and obey orders, so everyone was going to join hands and have the common goal to get home, and we would not play the inherent conflict between the Maquis and Starfleet. As a writer, I seek out legitimate ways to tell stories about conflict, and frankly, I think we did a very good job of that on *The Next Generation* by finding ways of bringing conflict on board the ship through alien visitors. On *Voyager*, we had a very natural conflict that was being ignored, and it was very difficult to tell stories that made the characters come alive when you couldn't have them disagreeing about anything! Essentially what we had was a pilot episode that ended up leaving us unable to tell character stories as a result of the studio's feeling — and perhaps Rick's — that we needed to get past the 'Starfleet vs Maquis' premise as quickly as possible, and onto our journey home, where it's one for all and all for one.

What I think became clear is that once you brought Seven of Nine on board, you got cultural conflict that nobody else was able to bring. As a result, and I think Jeri Ryan's quality as an actress had a lot to do with it, she became the most interesting character on the ship, because she was the one person who disagreed with everybody. The other character who was successful early on was the Doctor, because he was in conflict with the rest of the crew. He was an outsider and he didn't like the way they were treating him, but because we played it for humour, you were able to see how that worked. The rest of the characters were sort of caught in limbo as a result of our decision to be fearful of conflict.

You mentioned earlier that at one point, you were working on *Voyager* and *Legend* simultaneously. What sort of problems, if any, did that create for you as a writer?

I essentially worked on the first thirteen episodes of *Voyager* before I had to turn my attention to *Legend*. I then did thirteen episodes of *Legend*, before coming back for year two of *Voyager*, and basically tried to reassert my authority after I'd been absent for half a year, and it was very difficult. I had watched a lot of contemporary television, to see what the latest tricks were in terms of how I was going to approach *Legend*, and I saw that things were speeding up. There were more scenes that were a lot shorter, and a lot more visual tricks. Coming back to *Star Trek* I felt, as a result of seeing what was out there, that we were stuck in a time warp. I felt we were still writing scenes that were too long, the shows were talky, and we needed to get it to the MTV generation, in terms of understanding that audiences were more impatient than they'd been ten years earlier when *The Next Generation* had been developed. We needed to push the envelope in our writing, ambition and visual sense, but I received resistance on every front.

In the middle of the season, Jeri Taylor and Rick came to me and said, 'You're making everybody miserable. The production people are crying because they don't think they can meet your requests, the scripts are too complicated to produce, and everybody is unhappy.' For the rest of the year, I continued to push for my vision of *Trek* and everything that I believed in, but Rick thought that I had been influenced in my approach to the work by *Legend*, which was light and fun, and wild and off the wall. Rick felt that wasn't what *Star Trek* was, and that I had to be reined in a bit, in order to get back to the solid values he believed the franchise really wanted. By the end of season two, the young writers went to Rick and said, 'Look, if Mike stays, we're going. He won't let us do the kind of things we want to do, and he has very strong opinions about what *Star Trek* is. We think *Star Trek* can be more than what Mike thinks it is, so if he stays, we're leaving.' Rick came to me and told me this, and of course I felt very badly about it all, but it was done with honour and friendship and no personal feelings. At that point, I'd really done all I knew to do in space and would ultimately have been frustrated if I had stayed, so I wished everybody well and went on my way.

How did you feel about returning to the *Next Generation* universe one more time as the writer on *Star Trek: Insurrection*?

That's a long conversation, and I've written a whole book about it, which unfortunately Pocket Books chose not to publish after a barrage of telephone calls from the studio. The irony is that the people at the studio who complained about it hadn't read it. It's basically a book for young screenwriters about how an idea turns into a movie, and all the changes that you go through. I talk about the notes from Patrick Stewart, the notes from the studio, a first draft of the story that we threw out and started over, and then the first disastrous draft of the script. We deal with what went wrong, and going back and getting a new vision, and how it really turned into a fine script, and

THE DEAD ZONE

Piller's newest project is a television pilot based on *The Dead Zone*, Stephen King's 1979 best seller, about Johnny Smith, a school teacher who awakens from a four-and-a-half year coma with psychic abilities. After discovering that a presidential candidate will eventually start a nuclear war while in office, Smith sets out on a mission to assassinate the politician, sacrificing his own life to change the future. King's novel was made into a feature film in 1983, directed by David Cronenberg, and starring Christopher Walken as the tragic hero. In Piller's pilot, Anthony Michael Hall plays Johnny, with *Deep Space Nine* alumnus Nicole deBoer as his girlfriend Sarah. Certain changes had to be made in the storyline to create an ongoing series, not least of which is the fact that Johnny lives! Although *The Dead Zone* tested higher than any pilot in the history of UPN, the network originally planned to pick up the series as a mid-season replacement. Piller went on to complete production on a second hour, which would be combined with hour one as a TV movie for the international market. At the time of writing, UPN has still not ordered any further episodes of the series.

then of course all the changes that were made before it went to the set, and the final version. And then there's what happens when you go through the camera and into the editing room.

I can tell you that I have mixed feelings about the way the picture ended up, although I think we reached many of the goals we tried to reach. It was decided early on that we wanted something quite different than *First Contact*; I think somebody at the studio said, 'What you want to do is 'Measure of a Man' here, that kind of thoughtful story.' About halfway through the process, fears began to arise that it wasn't going to be 'big' enough. The quote in *Entertainment Weekly* saying that the film was going to be 'softer, gentler' got back to the head of the studio, who started calling down, saying, 'Hey, everybody is talking about this small movie you're doing!' When I look at the picture now, I think it holds up very well, especially if you compare it to the other nine *Star Trek* movies. It's warm and funny and it's about something, and very much a tribute to Roddenberry's original vision of *Star Trek* and what the series is about.

After *Insurrection*, you worked on an American version of the UK series *The Last Train*, about survivors of a massive meteor strike.

That was our pilot in 2000. The WB ordered *Last Train*, which we called *Day One*, and we shot a thirty-five minute presentation reel in Vancouver. It was one of those natural premises for SF that I thought could be very special; a group of strangers come together, a post-apocalyptic world, a search for a safe haven — but what we did was Americanise it very effectively, and hopefully made it attractive to the WB. But they got worried that it wasn't consistent with anything else they had on their schedule, and felt they could not take risks. We're now developing it as a feature and hopefully you'll hear more about that soon.

You're now working on a TV version of *The Dead Zone*, which has already been made into a feature, back in 1983. What was it about Stephen King's novel that prompted your interest in adapting it?

I think what interested me about *The Dead Zone* was that it is, in essence, a story about a charismatic man who must find his place in a new kind of world, where he's not quite sure how to fit in. You couldn't have a more humanistic journey for any character in the world. Certainly when Mr King wrote the book, he was looking at Johnny as a Jesus metaphor, and I think that's a fascinating thing to look at in contemporary society.

I did make certain subtle changes that helped me to adapt it into a television series. For example, in the book, there's really nothing to keep Sarah and Johnny together, but if she was going to be a regular continuing cast member, I needed something to force them to be in proximity. So the child she has in the book, I made Johnny's child, which forces them to have a long-term relationship. There are other little changes like that, but fundamentally, I wanted to use the book as the basis of the whole first season of the series. I wanted to use every possible detail that the Master provided us with for story material, and really take a look at Stephen King's universe, and *The Dead Zone* universe, in meticulous detail.

At the moment, you're just waiting for a green light on the series?

If we get a call tomorrow that says, 'We're ordering you,' then we turn our attention to it. There's not much for us to do but wait for the phone to ring. We're in a business here, so we've developed several projects for the coming season, which we're taking to the networks shortly. That's how the game is played. You've got to keep selling so you have things in the pipeline. ∎

ENTERPRISE

How do you create a new *Star Trek* series that will offer something new and exciting, when just about every *Trek*-related concept has already been done? Let's face it, after seven seasons apiece on *Star Trek: The Next Generation*, *Deep Space Nine* and *Voyager*, not to mention the original series, nine feature films, countless books, video and computer games, where do you go?

Answer: back to the beginning, of course. *Enterprise*, which débuted in September of 2001, is the stripped-down version of *Star Trek*, before the halcyon days of holodecks, replicators, photon torpedos, the Federation and all those wonderful gadgets that make 24th century living so wonderful. This is the 22nd century, where space is still the final frontier. The fifth *Star Trek* series takes place 150 years in the future, about ninety years after the events seen in *Star Trek: First Contact*. In that film, Earth has finally developed warp drive capability, which in turn brings them into contact with the alien Vulcans. At the start of *Enterprise*, humans and Vulcans are working together peacefully, if not one hundred per cent happily. Mankind resents their alien allies for holding back their technology. Warp pioneer Zefram Cochrane had been working for years with the father of Jonathan Archer (Scott Bakula) to develop an engine with warp five capability, but neither man lived to see it in action.

When Earth encounters a new alien threat, Archer takes command of the *Enterprise* NX-01, a cutting-edge starship, equipped with the warp five engine. His hastily assembled crew includes chief engineer Charles 'Trip' Tucker (Connor Trinneer); security officer Malcolm Reed (Dominic Keating); helm officer Travis Mayweather (Anthony Montgomery); the ship's linguist and communications officer Hoshi Sato (Linda Park); and Dr Phlox (John Billingsley), an alien medic. There's also T'Pol (Jolene Blaylock), who initially joins the crew as a Vulcan liaison. By the end of their first mission, *Enterprise* is ready to go off into space and truly go where no man has gone before.

The task of creating a new *Star Trek* series went to executive producer Rick Berman, who became caretaker of the franchise during *Star Trek: The Next Generation* and went on to co-create *Deep Space Nine* and *Voyager*. As his number two man, Berman chose long-time writer/producer Brannon Braga, who had worked on several seasons of *TNG* and *Voyager*, as well as co-writing *Star Trek Generations* and *Star Trek: First Contact*. Together, the duo sat down and began hammering out the concepts for their new take on Gene Roddenberry's legacy.

'What I really wanted to do was to create a series about *The Right Stuff*,' Berman recently revealed to Titan's official *Star Trek* Magazine, "about the first guys to travel in space, the ones who were both in awe and a little bit terrified about what it was they were doing.' By going backwards, Berman explained, the fans would get to see all the elements that they have come to know and love, but in their earliest stages: 'At the same time, we'll be seeing humanity where they truly *are* going where no man has gone before. We are seeing people who don't take meeting aliens as just another part of the job. Nothing is routine.' Noted Braga, speaking to the Television Critics Association, 'It's a very terrifying place in that everything is unknown to this crew. Earth is in much better shape than it was in the movie *First Contact*, in that poverty, crime, disease and hunger have all been eradicated for the most part, but the Federation has not yet formed. That's a long way off. Starfleet is very, very young, and this crew has met very few alien species since the Vulcans arrived. So really, the landscape of the universe is virtually unknown to these people, and they will meet many friendly, and also many terrifying aliens.'

Because *Enterprise* is set in a time much earlier than recent *Star Trek* series, the characters don't have access to many of the technological devices that will become commonplace in the 24th century. That means the characters — and the show's writers for that matter — will have to rely on their wits a lot more often. 'We don't have shields,' Braga pointed out, referring the ship's armaments, or lack thereof, 'we have hull plating. Photon torpedos don't exist; there's some sort of a torpedo that is very much like a high-tech missile. And the list goes on. We do have a transporter that's just designed for cargo. It's been approved for people, Starfleet have approved it, but nobody wants to use it. They're all nervous about it!'

While it remains to be seen if *Enterprise* will become as successful and long-lived as its predecessors, the show's creators seem to be finally interested in taking a few risks. It would have been an easy matter to put together yet another ship show set in the *TNG/DS9/Voyager* milieu, but it's more ambitious to strip away all the comforting continuity, characters and gadgets of the past three decades and try to create something different. It is certainly refreshing to see, in the first couple of episodes broadcast, heated conflict between characters (Archer has little time for T'Pol), and a Starfleet officer (Hoshi) who screams at the first sign of danger! That said, *Enterprise* may well turn out to be the most direct descendant from Gene Roddenberry's original series, in terms of its overall tone and style, and more importantly, its focus on the ability of man to create a better world for himself.

'I think *Star Trek* is unique in two important ways,' Berman told the TCA. 'First of all, it's been around for thirty-five years, and it's become part of the American mythos. You'd be very hard-pressed to find somebody who doesn't know about 'Beam me up, Scotty!' or warp speed and things like that. I think it's comfortable to people because of its familiarity. I also think that in a world where there's a lot of SF that's quite apocalyptic and negative, *Star Trek* has always had a hopeful viewpoint of the future. As long as that exists, there's always going to be an interest in it.' ∎

J. MICHAEL STRACZYNSKI

Star Trek may have been the paradigm that SF television was measured against for over three decades, but *Babylon 5* is more likely to be the model these days. Its creator, J. Michael Straczynski, had started out in TV writing animation scripts. He later moved on to the live action toy tie-in show *Captain Power*, but all the while he was planning an epic space series, which would tell a story with a beginning, middle and end. No cute kids, no talking robots, and plenty of twists and turns. As G'Kar, the reptilian Narn ambassador explains with masterful understatement in an early episode, 'No one here is exactly what they seem.' Over the course of *Babylon 5*'s run, behind-the-scenes events were often as intriguing as the episodes themselves. Straczynski never knew from one season to the next if the series was going to be picked up, and it was only a last-minute jump from syndication to cable station TNT that allowed *B5* to finish its fifth and final season. Bizarrely, it was TNT that later purchased the *B5* spin-off series *Crusade*, only to dump it after just thirteen episodes. But revenge, as they say, is sweet, and Straczynski got to continue his saga, with a two-hour TV movie for the Sci-Fi Channel, *Legend of the Rangers*. The writer has now also made a hugely successful move into the world of comics, creating his own line of titles for Top Cow, as well as writing *The Amazing Spider-Man* for Marvel. The following conversation took place as Straczynski was juggling all of this with duties as show runner on yet another genre TV project: a post-apocalyptic drama called *Jeremiah*...

You started off as a journalist. How did you make the leap to television writer?

I actually started off in theatre. I was writing plays, and had my first play produced when I was seventeen. The problem was that you can't make much money in theatre. But I had an interest in journalism, and started selling articles when I was seventeen or eighteen years old, and began to discover that I could actually make a living at it. By the time I hit college, where you really have to have an income to help get through things, I was selling enough in my journalistic work to get my own place and subsist. So my first inclination was toward the dramatic arts, but by default and the fact that I loved reporting and being a journalist, I ended up doing that pretty much full time. I worked for a lot of different mags and publications, and basically came to LA riding on that. I came up to write for the *LA Times*, the late-lamented

Herald Examiner (back when we had a real two-paper town), was a correspondent with *Writer's Digest Magazine*, and finally ended up at Time Inc. I was hired by one of the magazines inside Time Inc — I don't want to say which one it was — but we used to gather in the office of one of the editors to pitch the stories we wanted to cover that particular week. The person to my right pitched an article about the new National Rape Hot Line, and the editor, who was female, said, 'Well, you know, rape's been very good to us, but do you have a new angle on the rape thing?' Now, I'm of the belief that under all of us there is a trapdoor, and that trapdoor is held in place by one very small pin. Anything at all can make that pin jostle out of place, and when I heard that statement coming out of someone's mouth, made in the interests of commercialism and selling magazines, the trapdoor opened. So when my turn came up, I said, 'I don't really have anything,' and after the meeting was done, I went to my desk, got my stuff, left, and never went back.

I decided that I had to do something to get 'clean'. How that got me into television is anybody's guess, but the actual transition point was basically being home one day and watching cartoons. I like to watch cartoons, I'm a goofball that way, and that was when the *He-Man* series was on, which I happened to like in a dopey way. It was fantasy with sword and sorcery, and in that first season, they were making a decent attempt to create a consistent world. So I said, 'Well, I could do that,' and just for fun, I wrote a script and did all the wrong things that you're not supposed to do. I wrote a spec script with no agent, sent it off in the mail with no contact, no phone call, no nothing, and to my surprise, the producer called and said, 'I love the script, why don't you come in and we'll talk about it.' That led to writing one script as a freelance assignment for *He-Man*, and then I did two more and they said, 'We're out of budget for freelance scripts for the season,' and I thought, 'Well, that was a nice ride!' It was more money than I'd made in a long time. But then they said, 'However, we do have an opening to come on staff,' and would I be interested in working on the staff? So I went on staff at Filmation and worked on *He-Man* for a year, and most of another year

J. MICHAEL STRACZYNSKI

Date/Place of Birth:
1954, Paterson, New Jersey, USA

Home Base:
Los Angeles, California, USA

Education:
San Diego University, CA

First TV Work:
He-Man and the Masters of the Universe

TV Career Highlights:
Jayce and the Wheeled Warriors, The Twilight Zone, Captain Power and the Soldiers of the Future, Babylon 5, Crusade, Murder, She Wrote, Babylon 5: Legend of the Rangers, Jeremiah

on *She-Ra* the follow-up series, and went on to other animated series. Along the way, I did a *Twilight Zone* episode for CBS and went on from there.

How did you actually learn the mechanics of writing a television script?

I knew how to write a script having done it in theatre, and also doing radio dramas working for KCBS in San Diego, but I didn't know how to do an animation script. I had friends who were working in animation at that time, but I've always been loath to take advantage of that sort of thing, I feel it's unfair to your friends. So they didn't even know I was trying to do this until after I'd sold the script. So I ended up going down to a store in Burbank and hunting for animation scripts, and I found an old *Spider-Man* script. It had the right format and it wasn't that much different really, so I took it home and read through it, and got it immediately, and wrote my script.

Was it easy to make the jump from animation into live action drama?

No it wasn't. There's a definite prejudice against animation writers; a stigma attached to those who work in that area, which is extant to this day. It's the perception that people are animation writers because they can't make the break, and there is some validity to that, but there's also something *not* true about that. There were people working in animation back in '84, when I did it, who are still there. They haven't made that break, and whether you say it's because of the stigma attached, or that they haven't got what it takes, is a point of some debate. It is difficult to make the jump, although I wasn't that interested at first anyway, because I was having a blast writing cartoons. I did *He-Man* then *She-Ra*, and then Larry DiTillio[*] (who also worked on the show) and I were denied the story editor credit that we'd earned. So we left Filmation and went to DIC, and did *Jayce and the Wheeled Warriors*, and then I got onto *Ghostbusters*. That basically happened because the story editors didn't want to be story editors all the time, so they commissioned thirteen episodes for ABC and sixty-five for syndicated, for a total of seventy-eight, to be done in one season. They knew I was fast, so the president of the company called me and said in his French accent, 'I tell ABC you are funny, so do not make for me liar!' So I said, 'Fine, I'll be funny.' It was doing that show which gave me some visibility with ABC, and doing a network show put me in a position to go in to CBS and say, 'I'd like to come in and pitch.'

Also, the SF circle in LA is somewhat incestuous, so I peripherally knew the guys working there, enough to finally get in. I sold one script, which got rewritten badly in-house, but that one credit was enough to get me in a position when *Captain Power*[†] opened up to get into that show. *Captain Power* was really a cross-breed between a cartoon and a live action series. It was the first show that had CGI and it was meant to be a kids' show, although Larry and I came in and made an adult SF show. But it was enough of a cross-breed that they figured it wasn't too much of a jump to have animation writers come in and try it. If it had been a different kind of show, it probably

---

[*] *Who later became Straczynski's script editor on Babylon 5's first two seasons.*
[†] Captain Power and the Soldiers of the Future *ran for a season in 1987, and though its primary purpose was to promote a line of toys from Mattel, it is still fondly remembered by many as an imaginative, enjoyable show.*

never would have worked. At that time, I tried to write a script for *The Next Generation*, which was just starting up, but was told that I didn't have the credits for it. I've never forgotten that comment.

In many ways, didn't *Captain Power* provide much of the foundation for what would later become *Babylon 5*?

Yeah, the idea of using CGI for the first time in a television series was pioneered over there. We were also the first ones to set up the virtual studio, where scripts were e-mailed back and forth, at a time when a lot of them were still being written on type-writers. We set up this whole system, later used on *Babylon 5*: the e-mail correspondence, which has been archived in a few places by a few people who captured the messages and kept them — for blackmail, I assume! In one of the more famous ones, John [Copeland, later producer of *Babylon 5*] explained to me by e-mail that we could not blow up the robots, the Bio Dreads' heads anymore, because they thought it was too graphic and grotesque. I wrote back a note saying, 'Is there any stricture against kicking them in the nuts?' That eventually got relayed to Mattel apparently, who weren't too happy about it. It was there that I saw a lot of the things that were wrong about how SF television was made. Granted it was done ostensibly for kids, but we never wrote it that way. We wrote it as something we would have wanted to watch — which is probably why they pulled the plug. But I saw there were opportunities to really do good stories in SF if you were willing to put your ass on the line and treat it properly.

During this period, were you trying to develop *Babylon 5*?

I was thinking about how I'd do a long-term saga, and not make the mistakes made with *Captain Power* and other SF shows. I liked *The Next Generation* to a certain extent, but I also saw that they were not pushing the limits; they had this great Porsche, but they were keeping it in the garage. So it finally became clear what I would do if I had the option. From that experience and everything that preceded it, came *Babylon 5*.

What was the inspiration for *Babylon 5*?

It's hard to be precise, because the way writers work is that you get a piece of some-thing here and something there, and they begin to coalesce over time. When I was still working on *Captain Power*, I began playing with the notion of a space station series, which is why I slipped the name 'Babylon 5' into an episode. So I had the name and the idea about the station, and that was as far as it went. The problem with most SF series in general is they're either the man on the run going to different places, or searching for something; those are the two major paradigms in SF. Either one involves going from place to place, so why not create a place where the stories would come to you? I felt the most logical choice was a space station of some kind, so that was the storyline I was developing on the 'keep it economical' feasibility track.

On the other track over — I'm usually running nine or ten tracks at the same time, which means I get derailed a lot — was this notion about doing a big, no borders kind of huge saga. It would cross many years and have a lot of different characters and different worlds. I thought that was a different show, because the requirements of something like that were huge, as opposed to this little space station story. It wasn't until I was in the shower one day, which is where I have my best thoughts, that the two stories collided in my head and I said, 'No, you idiot, it's the *same* story!'

Did you write the pilot script and then put together your key production people, or was it the other way around?

The series of events, as best as I can recall them — bearing in mind that recalling lunch last week is difficult for me — was that I wrote up a treatment first. And then I thought, 'Okay, who can I bring this to, to partner up with?' because I was still very much on the lower story editor level. When I had first started working for Doug [Netter]*, he said, 'Look, I'm not a writer, I'll never give you a creative note,' and never did. He always supported the written word on the page, so I thought, that's the guy I've got to go to. I'd either just left *Power* or just started on *Twilight Zone*, because there wasn't much of a gap between them, so during that period, I brought them the treatment and said, 'This is what I'm thinking about; what do you think?' They thought it had a lot of promise, and said, 'When you have more, bring it back.' So I then went out and wrote the pilot screenplay, expanded the treatment into a full bible and brought it back, and Doug and John both said, 'We like this, we want to get on it.' We talked to some of the people we'd worked with on *Power*, including Ron Thornton, John Iacovelli and a couple of other designers with whom we had some background, and had some preliminary discussions. I then hired Peter Leger to do some conceptual artwork; I knew Peter through his wife Christy Marx†, who worked with me on other projects including *Captain Power*. We made colour Xeroxes of the artwork and included that with the proposal, and then started taking it around to not just the networks and studios, but the agencies. There was one agency who said nothing interesting could be done in this kind of space station environment and it was a stupid idea, but that began the five-year period from 1987 to 1992 of trying to sell the damn thing.

Since you'd always intended to produce B5 economically, were you surprised that no one was interested?

I was taken aback by the fact they didn't get it, but more than that, I began to understand one of the real problems in television, which is that producers lie. Virtually everyone we went to saying, 'We can do this for a price,' said, 'We've heard that before,' and invariably it went over budget.' *V* was supposed to have been done for a reasonable price, and it single-handedly damn near killed Warner Bros Television with cost overruns. So either they didn't understand what we were trying to do story-wise,

---

* *Executive producer on* Captain Power, *and later,* Babylon 5 *and* Crusade.
† *Marx went on to write 'Grail' in* Babylon 5's *first season.*

or those who did understand, didn't believe we could do it, either for the money or at all. The few who got the story *and* thought we could do it for the money didn't think there was a market for it, so we were being banged back and forth between three different paddles non-stop for five years. We needed to find somebody that (A) got the story, (B) thought it could be done for the money, and (C) knew there was a market for it. It was the combination of those three things that took us five years to find.

How much was the *Star Trek* mind-set an obstacle for you?

It was a hideous obstacle, which is why I sometimes go ballistic when I hear fans say it made it easier to sell *Babylon 5*, when in fact it was the exact opposite. The spectre of *Star Trek* made it immensely more difficult to sell that show, because in America, the paradigm was created that 'there is only *Star Trek*'. That had some superficial merit in the sense that in fifty years of American television, how many SF shows have gone more than three seasons? Very few, particularly space shows. So we would bring the material to them and they would say, 'Well, there's already a space show out there, which has a corner on the market.' We would insist, 'No no, there is room for more than one space show,' but they would not get it out of their head, and this is a direct quote from most of them: 'The market will not sustain more than one show that's like *Star Trek*, period!' Even our guys from Warners said that, so it was a tremendous obstacle.

U

Writer/director Kenneth Johnson wanted to tell a sprawling SF epic, using the arrival of a group of aliens as a thinly veiled allegory for the growth of fascism. The result was *V*, an ambitious 1983 mini-series, in which a fleet of humanoid 'visitors' arrive on Earth pledging peace and co-operation, but are soon revealed as a race of vicious reptiles who plan to drain the planet of resources. That includes the human population, which will become their newest food supply. The original mini-series may have lacked subtlety in terms of its storyline, but it proved to be a ratings block-buster nonetheless. A follow-up mini-series, *V: The Final Battle* soon followed, but after some major creative differences, Johnson insisted on using a pseudonym on the project. He went on to develop the TV spin-off of Rockne O'Bannon's movie *Alien Nation*. In 1985, NBC unveiled *V: The Series*, which featured most of the original characters, but nowhere near the budget or production values of either mini-series. It lasted just nineteen episodes before being cancelled, but fan interest remained high, and several follow-up novels were published. Some years later, J. Michael Straczynski was approached about developing a revival, but the project was believed to be potentially too expensive and was shelved.

How did you feel when you discovered that Paramount was creating their own space station series, *Star Trek: Deep Space Nine*, at the same time?

It was devastating. I'd deliberately created something that was a whole different environment from *Star Trek*, which has always been a starship, so I thought, we're safe in this one area. I remember very specifically, it was two days before Christmas of 1992, and Walter Koenig called me at home. He'd just had lunch with Richard Arnold[*], and Walter knew about *Babylon 5*, and he said, 'Do you know what the new *Star Trek* show is going to be?' I had no idea, and he said, 'It's about a space station near a warp point, for businessmen and travellers to come in and out, and there'll be a lot of intrigue and political stuff.' I just sat there on the edge of the bed where I picked the phone up and felt the world evaporate under my feet. I thought, 'We're fucked, we have just gotten boned so seriously by this thing that we're not going to recover!' Sure enough, when Warner Bros heard about this, there was a huge movement on the part of certain executives to kill it. There were always a number of folks at Warners who weren't happy with us going ahead. They weren't the main guys who were our patrons, but a few off to the side would have preferred an in-house, Warners-owned project rather than an out-of-house project, which is what we were. They came to us and said, 'This is terrible, it was bad enough when we said the market can't sustain two space shows. Now you're saying there are going to be two space station series on at the same time, and if they [the fans] have to choose between them' — why they have to choose between them, I have no idea — 'they're going to go with the *Star Trek* name!' We came within a half-inch of having the plug pulled on the whole thing, but again, our angels in the form of [Warner executives] Dick Robertson and Evan Thompson refused to let it go. I think on some level, they were as morally indignant as we were about what happened, because they knew where it came from.

The reality is, in the last week or two of the previous October, it was announced in the trades what our show was going to be. The title was out there, it was going to be a space station-based series. There was a presentation at a big TV conference in San Francisco, so there was no big secret about it. It was the impression of a lot of people at Warners, myself included, that at minimum, it was an attempt by Paramount to co-opt what we were doing: to take the basic space station concept which is not owned by anybody, put the *Star Trek* stamp on it and undercut whatever else is going to come out and threaten their franchise[†]. Not only was there a vested interest financially in doing that, but let's also understand that Paramount and Warner Bros had a visceral hatred for each other, because they were both trying to get networks off the ground. That's what PTEN was meant to be, and Paramount knew they wanted to make a *Star Trek* show one of the foundations of their own network, whether it was *DS9* or something else. So they had every reason in the world to try and undercut it, to try and knock *Babylon 5* down somehow.

We heard reports from other journalists that they were telling the TV stations, 'It's going to be a crappy show.' They were telling advertisers not to advertise on *Babylon 5*

---

[*] *Former assistant to* Star Trek *creator Gene Roddenberry.*
[†] *See page 168 for DS9 co-creator Michael Piller's take on this period.*

because it was going to be terrible and cheap looking. Rumours even came to us that they went to certain TV stations and said, 'You can have their show or our show, but you can't have both,' to try and pressure us off the market.

It was trench warfare for about two years. Every non-illegal dirty trick that could be pulled, was pulled on us. We went to hire one of the directors from *Star Trek*, Rick Kolbe*, who agreed to direct an episode for us, and about two weeks before he was going to shoot, his agent called up and said, 'He's booked somewhere else.' We said, 'We have a deal, we hired him; we have an option on his services,' and his agent said, 'Well, he can't do it because he has to do something else.' We pushed the guy and asked, 'Look, is this pressure from Paramount?' and finally the person said, 'Yes, they won't let him do it.' They whacked us from every possible side for at least two years, and after we made it clear that we weren't going to go anywhere, there were still occasional pot shots in our direction, mainly from the corporate guys at Paramount.

Were you disappointed that the studio only ordered the pilot at first and not the series?

There were three or four guys at Warner Business Affairs who adamantly insisted that we could not do the show for the money. So they said, 'Before we can give you any kind of a serious deal, prove to us that you can do this thing and make a pilot first.' Our understanding was that if we made the pilot and brought it in under budget, they'd say, 'You get the series.' Well, we did the pilot and brought it in under budget — not a lot under, but somewhat — and they said, 'We've got *Time Trax*† going ahead; why don't you hold off on the series until we air the pilot first?' That was not what we understood the situation to be, and we were all bothered by it, because they'd pulled the football away at the last minute and said, 'Let's get the ratings first.'

So we had to wait for the ratings, and at that point, I did something stupid. I knew the *Deep Space Nine* pilot was going to be coming out after ours, because of what I knew from folks over at Paramount, and from knowing our airdate schedules. Stupidly, I said on the net, 'We're shooting to air this thing on this week,' which was the first that anyone had said about it. Less than a week later, suddenly everything changed over at Paramount, and *DS9* was going to be out two to three weeks before us. This falls under the category of, 'Joe, shut your damn mouth once in a while!' because they had enough time to pump a little more money into it and get it ready in time, while we didn't have that flexibility, either in time or money. Their show aired first, and when *B5* came along, everyone said, 'Oh, they're just copying *Deep Space Nine*!' which made me want to chew off my left arm and swallow it.

When you put together a group of writers for the first season of *B5*, did you bring in people you'd worked with before, or people you respected and wanted to work with?

---

* Who directed a number of episodes of TNG, DS9 and Voyager.
† Created by Harve Bennett, and featuring a future cop (Dale Midkiff) tracking down temporal fugitves in the 20th century, Time Trax *lasted one season in 1993.*

It was a combination of both. I'd worked briefly with David Gerrold on *Ghostbusters* and he was a lot of fun to work with. Dorothy Fontana was someone I don't believe I'd worked with prior to that, but I knew of her reputation. Larry was my story editor, and he'd come through the Filmation days with me, and everything subsequent to that. So I tried to find a cadre of people who could do the job. I went to them and basically said, 'Here are the stories I want you to write.' In all but one or two cases, the stories were based on assignments; I assigned stories and outlines and premises, which I never took credit for, because I didn't believe in doing that. Wherever they needed information filled out about what the arc was going to be, I gave them whatever they needed to know to write the script.

How careful were you about rewriting scenes in other people's scripts?

When you're working on a series of any kind, ultimately it has to go through your brain. It has to match what your ideas for the show are, so it's not a reflection on the writer. For a freelancer in particular, you come in, you get the information, and then you go off and write it, so you aren't there to see everything that goes before and everything that comes after it. So knowing where Londo was going to go, for example, and what I wanted him to do, I would go in and add scenes or change them to put them in line with my overall plan, but again, I never tried to put my name onto those scripts. A lot of people will rewrite scripts so they can put their name on them, but I don't believe in doing that; I don't believe in arbitration, and I never said where some of these things came from. In 'There All the Honor Lies' by Peter David, 'the moment of perfect beauty' scene between Sheridan and Kosh, that was mine, but I really didn't like to talk about that at the time, because it would have been bad form.

Were there any events during the production of *Babylon 5* that took you completely by surprise?

The only one that really knocked me askew for quite a while was Claudia [Christian]'s decision to leave. She's said in print that her story was over, which is absolutely not true, because in the last script that we shot, Ivanova was given the command of *Babylon 5*. So if she says she had nothing to do, well, look at how much Sheridan had to do, having been given that assignment. I had a whole arc planned that would have tied her in with the telepaths and with things that were happening back home, and I had to shunt all that aside. Every character had their window in the show where they shined. Garibaldi's was season four and part of season one. For Sheridan, it was season three more than anything else. Season five was to be Londo, G'Kar and Ivanova, so that was probably the biggest event that threw me.

It took me several episodes to wrap my brain around it again, because I also lost my notes at the same time — the maid threw them out at a convention. I was in Blackpool[*], and the convention screwed up the hotel situation, and the hotel moved my stuff from one room to the next. For anyone who's ever been in my office, as you

---

[*] *For Wolf 359, a massive UK B5 convention held after production wrapped on season four.*

sat facing my desk, behind you was a bookcase. In that bookcase was a black note-book, which had ten pockets containing three-by-five cards with the plans for each season. For five years, the whole thing sat there, and if anybody wanted to stand up, turn around and grab it, they'd see the whole five-year story right there, but nobody ever thought to look! Each season, I'd pull out those cards, lay them out and start inter-weaving things, so I could begin sifting all the top plots. Well, I had those cards with me in Blackpool, because I was working on putting them together, and it was a good chance to do them during the convention. And these were written years before; I generally knew what was there because I'd glanced over them a few times, but real-ly hadn't sat down to chew on them. But they were tossed out by the cleaning staff, so I had to reconstruct a lot of that. I'd say in general terms, 'Londo becomes emper-or and has to deal with the following problems...' but there's a difference between that statement and breaking it out episode by episode, in terms of the actual progres-sion. And that was the same weekend we lost Claudia, so as a result, I was somewhat unmanned, and the first part of season five starts slower than I had wanted it to. I extended the telepath arc further than I had meant to because I needed to keep some-thing going while I got my land legs again. It's like the long distance runner who's made it almost all the way, and then someone tosses a Styrofoam cup in front of you ten yards from the finish line and throws you off your stride.

Wasn't it John Copeland who suggested that you look at losing Ivanova as a posi-tive rather than a negative?

My problem is, I tend to be very linear in my thinking and if something causes me to jump the tracks, I go crashing off the edge of the cliff. Eventually, I'll find my way back to the tracks again, but initially, it helps to have the voice of reason say, 'Look, we've had to make adjustments before, and we'll adjust now!' John was the one to say, 'This could open up some creative possibilities for you; what does this give you that you didn't have before?' I grumbled and cursed and squabbled about it, and then started thinking, what *does* this give me? What opportunities does this present? What it made me realise was that at the end of the fourth season, every-one was pretty much on good terms. Londo and G'Kar were getting along, the war with Earth and the Shadow war were over, and everyone was being friendly with each other. I'd originally figured that most of the conflict would come from the out-side, *à la* the Byron situation, where Ivanova would have gotten close to the telepaths[*], causing a division between her and Sheridan. But now, it was a chance to bring the conflict closer to the inner circle by bringing in someone whose loyal-ty was suspect, or whose ideology might not be the same as our characters. And then it struck me like a lighting bolt: there were a lot of folks back home on Earth who didn't rise up against the government and had legitimate reasons for not doing so, and I wanted to make my new character[†] one of them. Once I made that deci-sion, everything else fell into place. It also gave me another aspect of Sheridan to play with over the course of the season. So Ivanova's departure opened up doors that weren't even visible before.

---

[*] *Ivanova was to have had a relationship with Byron, leader of the telepaths. With Claudia Christian gone, Lyta Alexander (played by Patricia Tallman) ultimately fulfilled this role.*
[†] *Tracy Scoggins joined the cast as Elizabeth Lochley, EarthForce captain, and Sheridan's ex-wife.*

You wrote and shot *Babylon 5*'s final episode, 'Sleeping in Light', at the end of season four, when renewal looked uncertain, and then put it on the shelf. In retrospect, would you have done anything differently if you had written it at the end of season five?

Obviously if Ivanova hadn't been available, I would have had to adjust accordingly, but I'm not sure who I would have put there, or if I would have just left that seat empty. That's the only real change I would have made. Bear in mind, even though we shot it in season four, we were still editing it in year five because I didn't want to deliver a finished episode and have it leak out. We kept it in the Avid [digital editing system], so I literally could have cut Ivanova out. It would have been possible, and we were actually long on some shots and had to cut a lot out to make it all fit, but I thought, am I being spiteful, am I cutting off my dramatic nose to spite my annoyed face? So I left her in.

What prompted you to make a cameo in that episode, literally turning off the lights as you left *Babylon 5*?

I deliberately refrained from appearing in any other episode that would air before I finished the story, because that would break the reality of it. But this was the very last episode, so at that point, it didn't matter if the reality was broken, because the writing process was done. When I looked at the scene where someone shuts off the lights at the end, there was a lot of symbolism there, and no one was more qualified to shut the lights off.

After *Babylon 5*, you immediately went into production on the spin-off series, *Crusade*, which was a much less pleasant experience for you. When did you get the first inkling that the show was going south?

It was after episode five. We'd had minimal notes from TNT, pretty much along the lines of the Warner Bros notes we had in our first season of *Babylon 5*, so things were going pretty swimmingly. Then, out of nowhere, they shut us down so they could look at the show. That wasn't a small sign, it was more like an explosion going off on the set. They had seen everything we'd done from start to finish, they had actually seen the finished cuts, but it was like they suddenly saw the show for the first time and thought, 'Oh my God, what is this?' So my first thought was, something is going on here to which we are not privy. As things became more egregious over time, I kept saying to anyone who would listen to me, 'There's something going on here that we're not privy to and they're using it as a reason to beat us up!' It was only after I had left that I ran into TNT executives who had been working there at the time, who said, 'We're sorry about what happened.' I asked them under promise of confidentiality what had happened, and it came down to two things. They had done a multi-year audience survey, and finally got the results in, right around the time we were shooting episode five. The survey said that the TNT audience did not like, or want, or respond to SF. Secondly, the *B5* season five reruns had started on TNT, and they discovered that when *B5* came up, the TNT audience left and the *B5* audience came in. When the episode ended, the *B5* audience left and the TNT audience came back in again, literally, so it had no effect in building the shows that followed it. What I was told is that when they saw those figures come in, they decided that they wanted to get out of the contract and use that money to buy repeats of *Law & Order*, which their survey indicated would be a good buy for them. It you look at the trades for that time, they were kind of surprised when TNT came in on this bidding war and nailed the *Law & Order* repeat rights. Everyone thought their budget for the year had been allocated, so where was this money coming from? By sheer coincidence, the money they paid is equal to what they were going to pay for a full season of *Crusade*.

So buying just thirteen episodes of *Crusade* freed up a lot of money.

Plus, they didn't want tö have to pay for the first thirteen! By trying to say it wasn't the show they ordered, they were trying to get out of paying anything, and stick Warners with the bill. That was the purpose of the notes that came through. They could say, 'We gave them notes, and they wouldn't do them.' No, because they were egregious and wrong and I *couldn't* do them, but at the time, I knew none of this. And as one TV person told me after the fact, 'Had you done every single note that they asked you for, they would have found some other reason to get out of that contract.' They were trying to paper their way out of the deal, which makes me even gladder that I stood up when I did. If I'd done what they asked, and compromised what the show should be, even more than it was already compromised in a thousand smaller ways, it would have been for nothing. If you're going to sell your soul, you should at least get something out of it.

Is it true that you wrote the first-season cliffhanger with Gideon getting shot in 'End of the Line', because you were shopping *Crusade* to the Sci-Fi Channel, who may not have been interested in keeping Gary Cole in the lead?

Not true. There were similar things at work, but that was not it. There was a possibility of the show going to the Sci-Fi Channel, but my concern was more the fact that I had a suspicion that Gary Cole, who took on the show for TNT because it was a fairly large network, would not want to do a Sci-Fi Channel thing. It was a much smaller network, and that would tag him to a certain extent as being one thing or another. So that was part of it, and I also wanted a nice jeopardy. If he came back the next year, I figured (A) the jeopardy would work, and (B) I had some plans for Gideon and the Apocalypse Box [the mysterious oracle that advises Gideon on his quest]. The only clue that I can give you for what I had in mind is if you look at the episodes where we had the Apocalypse Box speaking, the person doing the voice is Gary Cole. So we were going somewhere with that. The Apocalypse Box would have been used to save his life, but the two would have been merged in a very unfortunate way.

Do you have any interest or plans to tie up the *Crusade* storyline at some point?

To some extent, a lot of those threads are being dealt with in the Techno-Mage novels[*], particularly the third one, which brings a lot of that stuff into the foreground. There's some in volume two, but there's even more in volume three. If *Rangers* does continue, there will be some measure of overlap by virtue of the fact that this starts two-and-a-half years after the events of [*B5*'s penultimate episode] 'Objects at Rest'. If *Rangers* went on for three years, keeping to our timeline, we would run smack dab into the events of *Crusade*.

Speaking of the new spin-off, *Legend of the Rangers*, did you deliberately set out to create a very different tone from either *B5* or *Crusade*?

Without question. It's a big universe, and the tone of a story set in Southern California will not be the same as a story set in Afghanistan, because the environment is different. So there's no logic to my trying to maintain the same tone in different parts of the universe. Beyond that, I was looking to do a story about the Rangers and about younger characters, and to try and have fun with it. What I initially wanted to do with *Crusade*, before things got kind of bogged down (A) in the plague and (B) in notes, would have been a lot more fun, but if I'm not having fun, the characters don't have fun. If I have to suffer, they have to suffer! So *Rangers* is more of a fun show.

LEGEND OF THE RANGERS

After the cancellation of *Crusade*, it looked like the *Babylon 5* saga had reached an end, at least on television, until the Sci-Fi Channel saw the viewing figures for *B5* repeats and approached Straczynski about a follow-up. *Babylon 5: Legend of the Rangers* takes place in the year 2265, about three years after the events of 'Objects at Rest'. In the first two-hour movie, 'To Live and Die in Starlight', David Martel (Dylan Neal) is given command of the *Liandra*, a battle-scarred ship that is supposedly haunted. Joining him on his new mission is Dulann (Alex Zaharas) his Minbari first officer, weapons/tactical expert Sarah Cantrell (Myriam Sirois), and a relatively young crew complement. Also making an appearance is former Narn ambassador G'Kar (Andreas Katsulas), who becomes an advisor of sorts on their first mission. For Straczynski, the opportunity to write 'To Live and Die in Starlight' for the Sci-Fi Channel couldn't have come at a better time. 'There is a sense of a bad taste in the mouth left by *Crusade*,' he notes, 'which this will hopefully help to wash away. Left alone to my own devices, this is the kind of show we can do.'

[*] *A trilogy of* Babylon 5 *novels, written by Jeanne Cavelos.*

Which is evident by the presence of G'Kar, who's become the elder statesman of *B5*.

It's always very easy for me to write G'Kar. The hard part is making him shut up once in a while. There's this door in my head marked 'G'Kar', and when I open it up, I just walk away and he does all the work, and I come back after an hour and close the door again. There's a certain dignity and eloquence, but yet loonyness that he brings. He's completely free of all expectations. He can be deadly serious, and then turn right around and give that line about 'I wouldn't live anywhere else,' and then turn around and say, 'Kiss kiss, love love; gotta go, bye!' and give an air kiss as he walks out the door. He can be hysterically funny, but then he can turn around and be profound, so that kind of complete liberation makes him a fascinating character to write.

After finishing the *Rangers* movie, you went into production almost immediately on *Jeremiah* for the Showtime channel and MGM. How did your involvement with that project arise?

They chased me for months, and I kept saying no, because I couldn't see what the story was. This has been in development for about five years, and they couldn't get it from the back burner to the front. Finally, they said the important three words, which are 'total creative freedom', so I said, 'let me do something with it.' I took the bare bones of the concept and the two main characters, plus the post-apocalyptic environment, and that's all I really used. I said okay, what if everyone over the age of puberty was wiped out, and it's now fifteen years later? Everyone who was then in their early teens is now twenty-seven, maximum. You could ride the ashes of the old world for a good long amount of time, but eventually, you will run out, so you either keep on going down and you bottom out, or you get to rebuild. This cusp right here is where the cool stuff happens. I didn't want to do a big post-apocalyptic show about everything falling apart, because it's been done. I wanted to do one about rebuilding, where there's a strand of hope at its core, and they loved the idea. I did the pilot script, and suddenly it went from the back burner to a go order for twenty episodes.

Are you planning a long-term story arc for the series?

Yeah, in fact, I keep forgetting that I haven't told Sam[*] parts of it yet! I'll say, 'By the way, did I mention...?' and he'll say, 'No, you didn't; where did that come from?' and he'll have to go and adjust. The first two episodes are somewhat independent because you want to introduce people who might have missed the two-hour pilot to the world and what the roles are, the same as we did on *Babylon 5*. You want to establish the rules of the game, and you have to be fair about them and see that they are consistent. Once we've done that in the first handful of episodes, we'll start laying in elements of the arc, so by the end of the first season, we end on a high note that might tell you where we could go for the second season.

---

[*] *Sam Egan, whose credits include* The Outer Limits, *is an executive producer on* Jeremiah, *and Straczynski's right-hand man on the series.*

Jeremiah was originally a comic book series. How much of that did you use as source material?

I have to be honest, because people are going to check the books and see what we're doing, so if I lie about it, it's going to be obvious. I really found the book to be kind of obtuse, and wasn't sure how well it would work for an American audience, so I just pared it down. The whole idea of a virus that wipes out everyone over the age of puberty, they never did that. It was a race war, and I said, 'No, no,' so I went through and took the two characters Jeremiah and Kurdy, and kept the names and the car that they drive around in, and the fact that it was after a major apocalypse. That was pretty much it.

While on the subject of comics, how do you manage to find time to write them on top of all your television work?

I try and work on whatever is cooking at that particular time. I put these various pots on to simmer, and I never quite know when they're going to come to a boil. When they do, I just write it down. I wish I'd been better about it of late, because the necessity of prepping *Jeremiah*, writing a bunch of episodes and now producing the first two hours have been so egregious that I fell way behind on the Joe's Comics* stuff. I got up to *Midnight Nation* #9 recently, but there's a two- or three-month gap between

JEREMIAH

Having spent more than a decade in the *B5* universe, Straczynski is now hard at work on a very different world. *Jeremiah* is a new post-apocalyptic drama, loosely based on the award-winning graphic novel series by Belgian comic book creator Hermann Huppen. *Jeremiah* is set in the future where a decade or so earlier, a deadly virus had wiped out the entire adult population, sparing only those who hadn't reached puberty. Now in their twenties, the survivors of the pandemic include Jeremiah (Luke Perry) and Kurdy (Malcolm-Jamal Warner). Jeremiah is on a quest to find a place called Valhalla, which may provide some hope for the survivors. He eventually finds himself falling into a reluctant partnership with Kurdy, as they encounter other young adults who have formed rival social groups. It is Jeremiah who tries to orchestrate peace between these warring factions, and keep the deadly virus from returning. 'What I wanted to do is a post-apocalyptic series about hope,' claims Straczynski. 'It's about the birth of a new world out of the ashes of the old. It's a story about beginnings, not endings, and that gave me the venue I needed to explore both sides of the equation, to be dark in some episodes and light in others.'

* *Joe's Comics is Straczynski's line of titles published by Top Cow, and includes* Rising Stars, Midnight Nation *and the graphic novel* Delicate Creatures.

issues which I wasn't happy about, and which is entirely my fault. I just didn't antici-pate quite how big the show was going to be when I first got on to it. I do try to com-partmentalise, but it's also a question of where the inspiration is.

But for a lifelong comic book fan, getting to write *The Amazing Spider-Man* must be a dream come true.

No question. The teenage Peter Parker was me. I got beat up a lot and that kind of shit, but it's a chance to really have some fun with someone that I grew up with as a character. It's been a great chance to play with an icon, and you can't beat that.

Any plans for the future?

It's hard to answer that, only because I've never sat down to make a big master plan. I go where the story is. I turned down *Jeremiah* three times until they gave me those three important words, and then I suddenly got interested. I go where the story is, and if I don't see a good story, I'll just stay home and knit. Oddly enough, there's anoth-er series I have in development for the Sci-Fi Channel, called *Polaris*. I just signed the deal for two one-hour scripts and a bible, and they want to fast-track it, so I've got to figure out how I'm going to work it all in. They want to do forty-four hours to start off with. I was meeting with the guys at the Sci-Fi Channel about *Rangers*, and they said, 'We'd love to have you do something else for us; do you have anything in mind?' Having not planned to pitch anything — I was just going there for a status meeting — I said, 'What about...?' and they suddenly sat forward and said, 'We can sell that.' Afterwards, I told my friends, 'I inadvertently sold a series!' So I may find myself in the middle part of next year with three series on the air, which is bizarre. I hadn't planned to take over the world, it just happened. In some ways I've changed and in some ways I haven't. The way I haven't changed is I still go where the story is. I do not want to stay in television forever. I do want to get out of it in a reasonable amount of time. Before it chews me up! ∎

ROBERT TAPERT

Robert Tapert has come a long way since he and his college friends, including Sam Raimi and Bruce Campbell, made themselves a little horror movie called *The Evil Dead* back in 1983. That film launched Raimi as a director, the inimitable Campbell as an actor, and Tapert as a producer, professions they are all still in today, though they now enjoy a somewhat higher profile! When, after working with Raimi on several features, Tapert made a foray into TV, he couldn't have imagined the success that was to come. It's fair to say that *Hercules: The Legendary Journeys* was largely responsible for reviving TV fantasy, and it certainly made a household name of its star, Kevin Sorbo. A season later, lightning struck again when *Hercules*'s spin-off series, *Xena: Warrior Princess*, single-handedly reinvented the action heroine genre, providing international recognition for a Kiwi actress named Lucy Lawless. For nearly a decade Tapert, as executive producer, was the chief motivating force on *Hercules* and *Xena*, supervising virtually every aspect of both series. While not strictly a writer, he provided countless story ideas, directed many of *Xena*'s more memorable episodes, and logged millions of frequent flyer miles commuting between offices in LA and the production base in New Zealand. Tapert also made head-lines when he married Lawless, whose real-life pregnancy was incorporated into *Xena*'s fifth season. Unfortunately, the ever-changing syndication market in America meant the demand for fantasy began to wane, and both *Hercules* and *Xena* were brought to a close after six seasons apiece. Tapert is now in the process of pitching several new projects, and based on his love of fantasy and action-adventure, it seems inevitable that lightning will strike a third time...

When you and your old schoolfriend and partner Sam Raimi were approached about producing a series of *Hercules* TV movies, most of your work together had been features. How difficult was it to make the transition?

It wasn't very hard, because what we did, which was different back then, but which everyone now follows in line with to some degree, was to bring more of a feature film mentality to television in terms of action and special effects. We opened the door in that regard to a whole host of imitators. Things that you couldn't imagine being on the small screen previously were allowed to go forward because of what *Herc* and *Xena* set up originally.

How enthusiastic were you about doing a series of movies based on the Hercules myths?

As a producer, to have four two-hour movies* was incredibly appealing. I have to say that once we were doing *Hercules*, I was very enthusiastic because I like mythology. Originally, we had wanted to do Conan but the rights weren't available, so we tackled Herc, and the further we got into it, the more enthusiastic I became.

Considering Kevin Sorbo is now forever associated with Hercules, it's interesting to note that you originally approached Dolph Lundgren for the role.

The road is filled with a hundred pitfalls, and whether it was Dolph Lundgren or somebody else instead of Kevin, I don't know that the show would have worked, because I don't think Dolph has the everyman appeal that Kevin Sorbo does.

Speaking of casting, is it true that you asked Charlton Heston to play Zeus in the first film?

We literally begged and begged and begged him to be Zeus! He kept putting us off, saying we should go to Mickey Rooney, who's a totally underrated actor in his mind, and he wouldn't do it. So we shot the first two-hour movie, *Hercules and the Amazon Women*, with another actor as Zeus and showed it to the studio, who said, 'It's great, but we need a star to play Zeus!' At that point, the casting director was able to muscle forward and get Anthony Quinn's agents to take notice. So we went back and re-shot all the scenes with Zeus from *Hercules and the Amazon Women* with Anthony Quinn, and it worked out great.

When *Hercules* was ultimately picked up as a weekly series, what sort of changes did you have to make in the format you'd just established?

We knew there were some things we liked, such as the chemistry between Hercules and Iolaus [Michael Hurst], the 'hero with a quest' theme, and trying to figure out why he went out and did what he had to do.

ROBERT TAPERT

Date/Place of Birth:
1955, Michigan, USA

Home Base:
Los Angeles, California, USA/New Zealand

Education:
Michigan State University

First TV Work:
M.A.N.T.I.S.

TV Career Highlights:
M.A.N.T.I.S., *Hercules: The Legendary Journeys*, *Xena: Warrior Princess*, *Young Hercules*, *Jack of All Trades*, *Cleopatra 2525*

* *A fifth movie,* Hercules in the Maze of the Minotaur, *was later added.*

We felt we had told a certain story with the five two-hour movies, that kind of wrapped themselves up, and going on to a series, we felt we had to set up the initial situations that forced Hercules to go on his quest. Basically at the end of the two-hour movies, Hercules was reunited with his dad, he was happily married to Tawny Kitaen [who played Herc's wife, Deianeira] and living the big family life. So the first thing we did is set him off on a quest. We killed off his family in the teaser of the series and put him on the road with Iolaus.

Is it fair to say that John Schulian, the show's original head writer, had a lot to do with creating the unique tone of the series?

Yes it is. John brought something to the character of Hercules that was invaluable in the series, which was Herc's likeable, self-deferential quality. John put something in the character that gave him a certain nobility, so I don't want to in any way detract from John's contribution.

Then what would your contribution have been as producer at that point?

I think I was pretty instrumental in guiding stories up until they go to script, and keeping the hero in the forefront of those stories. I'm also very good at post-production — editing, sound, music. But that said, John found the dialogue to put in Kevin's mouth, and although Kevin sometimes had a little problem with it, it gave him a certain common man nobility. I think the quintessential John Schulian story, even though he didn't take credit for it, was an episode in the first season called 'The Gladiator', which guest-starred Tony Todd. Bob Bielak wrote the script and got the story credit, but that was a hundred per cent Schulian episode. I hate to say this because it will end up in print, but Bob always had a tremendously difficult time with story. Eventually, whether it was John or myself, you had to give him a 'beat sheet' and explain each step and then he could write it, but he really had a tough time telling the story. So that quality *Hercules* had in 'The Gladiator', with Tony Todd as the athlete who didn't know if he could go on, that was all Schulian. John was very instrumental early on, because I think the other writers had a great deal of difficulty finding the characters' voices for the first thirty episodes.

When did *Hercules* actually begin to hit its stride in terms of the writing?

When Alex and Bob* came aboard. *Hercules* was an incredibly difficult show to write, because he's the guy who goes in and fixes other people's problems, and it's often very hard to figure out 'how does this affect Hercules?' That was the difference between Herc and Xena, which made Xena easier to get into darker, tougher stories: she was a different kind of hero than Hercules. It was tough to write *Hercules* stories that were meaningful to the character. The truth is, I really liked the first thirty-five episodes of *Hercules* a lot, but then it got really scattershot. After the first season and a half, it became much more hit and miss, so in my book, seasons three and four were a little scratchy.

---

* Joining in season four, the writing duo of Alex Kurtman and Roberto Orci eventually became the show's head writers. When Hercules *ended, they spent a short time working on* Xena's *fifth season, before moving over to* Jack of All Trades.

What were Alex and Bob able to bring to the table?

Kevin loved them, which really made a huge difference. We were able to make the stories about Hercules's quest, and it seems odd to say this, but we were able to give Kevin more to do. Herc lost his nerve, Iolaus was dead, so Herc took off on the road and went to the Norse lands, he questioned whether he'd done right in his life... we were able to get into all of that. Alex and Bob could write those stories, and they could also write zany comedies, which I'm a great lover of.

Taking a step back, you introduced Xena in a three-episode arc at the end of *Hercules*'s first season. Did you see the character's spin-off potential right from the very beginning?

I didn't know we *could* spin it off, because there wasn't a time slot for it originally. But by the time we'd edited the first episode of the arc, which was 18 January 1995, *Hercules* and its companion piece *Vanishing Son** had both been on TV for one week. It was very easy to see the drop off in audience figures between *Hercules* and *Vanishing Son*, and that there was a possible window there. The studio had seen a rough assembly of that first episode with Xena, and were already saying, 'You should come up with a new series.' My partner Sam [Raimi] was actually working on a *Jason and the Argonauts* thing, but for years and years I had wanted to do a female action hero, and now the door was open.

Going back to the Dolph Lundgren/Hercules comparison, Lucy Lawless wasn't your first choice for Xena, was she?

It just happened. What's odd is that even back when we were doing *Hercules and the Amazon Women*, our final choices for the part that Roma Downey played [Queen Hippolyta] were Roma, Vanessa Angel, Elizabeth Hurley and Lucy Lawless. Those were the four people that read, and we decided to go with Roma Downey, even though she was the smallest person, because she gave the best reading. So we'd cast Roma instead of Lucy in *Hercules and the Amazon Women* [though Lawless was cast as Lysia, Hippolyta's henchwoman], and Lucy went off to do her Kiwi travel show or something. Then we cast her as Lyla in an early *Herc* episode ['As Darkness Falls']. Vanessa Angel was originally supposed to play Xena in the three-episode arc of *Hercules*, but she never made it down to New Zealand, due to illness, and in a last-moment replacement, Lucy came in to fill the role. It really was at the last minute, like 31 December at 11:59, that she stepped in to take over. If Vanessa Angel had been Xena in the three-episode arc, I don't think we would ever have had a spin-off. Casting Vanessa in the first place was a request from the studio, because she was in the *Weird Science* TV series at the time, and when I told them we were going to do this three-episode arc, they said, 'It would be great if you could use the girl from *Weird Science*!'

How did the character change between her appearance in *Hercules* and the first episode of *Xena: Warrior Princess*?

* A cross between The Fugitive and Kung Fu, Vanishing Son was introduced, like Hercules, in several TV movies, but only lasted thirteen episodes as a series.

I knew how it was going to end in *Hercules*, meaning that she was going to die. After the studio said, 'Hey, maybe we will do the series!' I sat down and did a very rough outline for what I wanted out of that series, who Xena was and what she had done, and it was always going to end up with her dead. The odd thing was, I think R. J.[*] and I had many similar ideas, but his ideas about Xena's past were different from mine — I thought she was a much worse person! When we sat down together, R. J. had a much stronger sense of who Gabrielle was, and for the first ten or twelve episodes, his love of that character really came through. Once he saw Lucy in some of the completed episodes and how we were approaching it, we started widening out what we thought the scope of the character was. She was originally more of a Clint Eastwood-like character with a dark past, set on the road to reform herself.

At that point, you had *Hercules* and *Xena* on the air at the same time. Was it difficult to treat both of your 'children' equally all the time?

I think *Xena* was so new, by having a tough woman with a dark past as the lead, that it made it easier to tell stories, as opposed to maintaining a Butch Cassidy and the Sundance Kid-type relationship between Herc and Iolaus, and sending Hercules on mythological adventures. It seemed that the stories sprung to life more easily for Xena than they did for Hercules. For instance, I was driving in my car one day and heard on the radio that a baby had been found in a garbage can, and they were arresting the woman who had abandoned it there. I thought, 'I know how to tell that as a *Xena* story!' I called R. J. and bounced it off him, and we assigned the story to Steve [Sears], that Xena once had a child and had given it away in order to protect it. You just can't do that with Hercules! So we were able to take news headlines and human drama and very easily stick them into the *Xena* characters.

Your old friend Josh Becker[†] once said if you ate a bad pizza, you'd come in the next day with all sorts of wild ideas, some of which would eventually become *Xena* episodes.

There were a lot of wild ideas, and we did incorporate some of them, and it's true that a lot of those ideas seemed to work better on *Xena*. It drove Kevin crazy eventually, because he felt he was the slighted child. On *Hercules*, the things I was able to contribute were the off-the-wall things, like having Aphrodite be a surfer and into extreme sports, although we dropped that actually. When we first introduced her [in 'The Apple'], I remember pitching that idea to Schulian and the writer, and them thinking I was out of my mind. With Herc, it was hard to find the source of inspiration for stories that were uniquely his. We were always looking for it, and when Alex and Bob came in, they really bought a sensibility that was good for the show. Also, Kevin felt that they were a hundred per cent dedicated to *Hercules* and making it as good as they possibly could.

A good example of the difference between the two shows is the idea of doing a musical episode, which worked beautifully on *Xena* with 'The Bitter Suite',

[*] R. J. Stewart *co-created* Xena: Warrior Princess, *and was head writer and executive producer for most of the show's six-year run.*
[†] *Who also directed a number of* Xena *episodes.*

but your *Hercules* episode, 'And Fancy Free', was a bit disappointing.

I put thousands of hours into that *Xena* musical! I really wanted to direct it, and I actually storyboarded the whole thing before realising that everything was going to fall apart if I directed it at that juncture. It was literally two weeks before we started shooting when I brought in Oley [Sassone, the eventual director], so it was incredibly labour- and time-intensive. Chris [Manheim] and Steve [Sears] were just lost. We would sit in a room for hours and hours, going over the lines to make sure the prose leading up to the first verse and song worked right. We worked with the songwriters over the intent of the songs, and I forced them all on this wild ride. You normally can't put that much time into an episode, because eventually everything else will suffer. Look, I didn't want to do another musical in any way, shape or form, and the next one* we did arguably didn't work. It was only once Alex and Bob came aboard that I dared to push that issue, because R. J. wanted no part of a musical again, even if it worked. The writer is really behind the eight ball when you do a musical, because much less of it is ultimately in their hands or down to their decisions. You're driving camels through small openings, and sometimes they work and sometimes they don't.

Was it difficult juggling the dramatic episodes of *Xena* with more overtly comedic episodes?

Part of that was in knowing who our audience was. Because it spanned so many different people and age groups, it made our approach to the show slightly schizophrenic. We went from having comedy within a drama to doing solid all-dramas or all-comedies, as opposed to mixing them, as we'd done in the first season and a little bit of the second. We started to do the third season as either comedy or drama; some were still mixed I suppose, but those were never the audience's favourites. It was only in the fifth season that we did some bad comedies that just didn't work, and dramas that didn't work, and the whole thing stuttered along.

At what point did you discover that part of your audience had taken an interest in the so-called 'gay' subtext between Xena and Gabrielle?

Before the end of the second season. When we did 'The Quest', we never assumed that we were playing the subtext. R. J. did titillation, and we had done comedy like the teaser in 'Altared States' in the first season [in which Xena and Gabrielle are seen swimming together], where we set the audience up, but it was never really done to say that they were in any way romantically linked. R. J. and I had been in Europe, where women walk down the street hand in hand and kiss each other, but it's not in a romantic sense. When we'd come back from Europe, and had shot eight episodes into the second season, Lucy got injured. So we did the Joxer episode 'For Him the Bell Tolls', and then 'Intimate Stranger', and we changed the ending of 'Ten Little Warlords', or maybe it was the other way around, but anyway, we extended the Xena in Callisto's body arc. Somewhere in there we shot the Xena in Autolycus's body

---

* *'Lyre, Lyre, Hearts on Fire' was a rock musical in Xena's fifth season.*

episode, 'The Quest', with that kiss with Gabrielle, that leaning into Autolycus' body, but we still didn't in any way really think that Xena and Gabrielle were lovers. And then there was the hot tub scene in 'A Day in the Life'. Well, that was our way to get two good-looking women without their clothes on! We were past naïve in thinking that it wouldn't be perceived 'that' way, but there was a tremendous amount of feedback from that point on. It probably coloured our thinking, but through 'The Quest' and even 'A Day in the Life', it was never really what we thought.

There seems to have been a difference of opinion within your production team between some of the writers who thought the subtext was fun to play with, and say, your producer Liz Friedman, who thought you shouldn't put your feet in the pond and then play it safe.

That may be her rewriting history. Let me just say, she was horrified at 'Altared States', that we would get away with that, because Liz was there when the studio made it absolutely clear, no question, that these two women *liked guys*. When we started *Xena*, there was a big concern about how the show was going to be perceived; that guys would not tune in to see ass-kicking women warriors. That they would somehow be seen as lesbians, that was the largest fear that the studio and the syndicators had, and we went out of our way to make sure we didn't in any way portray Xena and Gabrielle as lovers. For the first seven or eight episodes, it was a constant 'old boyfriend, new boyfriend', Ares showed up somewhere in there, so we did everything we could to

WRITING AROUND THE PROBLEM

The production teams on both *Hercules* and *Xena* had to pull out every trick at their disposal when their respective stars suffered serious injuries. Lucy Lawless was taping a comedy sketch in America for *The Tonight Show* when she fell off a horse and fractured her pelvis. With their leading lady laid up for several weeks, the writers had to come up with a number of Xena-free episodes, including the Joxer (Ted Raimi)-heavy 'For Him the Bell Tolls' and a hastily expanded body-swap story arc involving Callisto (Hudson Leick). The effects of Kevin Sorbo's injury proved to be longer in duration. During *Hercules*'s fourth season, the actor was rushed to hospital with a burst aneurysm, and even after his return, his shooting time was limited to a few hours a day. The result was such episodes as 'Porcules' (in which Herc is turned into a pig), 'Yes Virginia, there is a Hercules' (with Sorbo making a brief appearance in the final scene) and some wacky Herc-free episodes featuring supporting actors Michael Hurst (Iolaus), Robert Trebor (Salmoneus) and Bruce Campbell (Autolycus). As the old adage goes, the show must go on; even in Pre-Hellenic mythological times.

paint that picture. But after 'The Quest' we started getting such positive feedback from the gay community. And we had done a couple of gender-bending episodes along the way, with 'Miss Amphipolis' and a few others. To me, that was more racy, but from that point in time on, Liz might have thought she wanted to push the lesbian angle. The flip side of the coin to that is what R. J. always thought: that it was very important to never shatter the guy's fantasy of having sex with those two women!

It was R. J. who wrote the infamous hot tub scene in 'A Day in the Life', which he meant as a homage to the classic westerns, where the heroes would be taking a bath after a hard day.

That's right, and people read into it. My feeling was, I'm always for getting two women naked in a bathtub, because I'm a red-blooded guy. It was just one of those things where it then found a wider acceptance within the gay community. So that was good, and being something of a liberal, I thought, as did R. J., that since Xena and Gabrielle were now looked upon as icons by the gay community, it would be wrong to totally dash that hope, or dismiss it. Being in the right place at the right time had presented an opportunity, and it would have been wrong *not* to use it to accept greater sexual tolerance, for lack of anything else.

Oddly enough, you caused more of a controversy when you took on the subject of religion in *Xena*'s fourth season.

We did, and it just proves that religion is a very hot topic. There's a show I still want to do — and I can't sell it, so I'll tell you about it. A bunch of people came to me and said, 'We want to do a gladiator show!' I said, 'How the hell do you do a gladiator show? Do people get killed in the ring every week?' They said, 'We want to find a way to do it so that it's like big-time wrestling, with different characters, you know...' and I said, 'That totally sickens me!' But going back into those somewhat esoteric theological things that excite me, I know how to set Rome and the arena against the background of all the different religions of Christianity and Judaism. We could do a real '*Touched by an Angel* meets *Gladiator*', but I've had no luck in selling it. What's weird is, I said, 'Let's tell it as *Melrose Place* in the Christian holocaust,' although nobody's going to bite on that. But I do believe that there is a huge 'want to see' amongst television viewers for religiously challenging or religiously reaffirming drama. I don't mean goody-goody stuff, but stories to make people think a little bit.

The feedback you got from some of your viewers on *Xena* would suggest otherwise.

I don't believe that reaction. I got in trouble with a certain group over that episode ['The Way', which dealt with aspects of the Hindu faith], but Indians as a whole really liked that episode, they didn't have the same problems. Personally, I like a lot of the fourth season, where it was Xena and Gabrielle wondering, 'What the hell is my goal on Earth, and is this the right path that I should be walking?' All of that was very interesting to me. As far as the online response, I can't really believe much of what is said there. It's just a small sample; every time I've gotten research indications back, the people who post on Internet websites are not your normal viewing audience. If I had listened to them, I would have made Xena and Gabrielle lovers. They would have won by sheer determination, and that would have been wrong for all the other people who watch the series. Even so, a large amount of people said, 'Oh, that's that gay show!' so whatever happened, it was still perceived among crazy bigots as being a gay show.

You mentioned Lucy's injury earlier. It's interesting to look back at how the stars of *Hercules* and *Xena* both suffered major injuries that affected production of the series, and how your writers were able to deal with it.

Funnily enough, the *Xena* situation was less troubling to me than the *Hercules* one, which I eventually solved by bringing in Bruce Campbell. The Kevin Sorbo situation had a far longer-lasting effect, meaning he was simply not able to work, and it was hard to keep him the star of the show. He didn't want to talk about it or publicise it in any way, shape or form, because he thought it would affect his ability to get feature film work.

That must have caused a lot of problems, having an action star whose action output is severely curtailed.

It did. That's why we did episodes like 'One Fowl Day' and 'Porcules' and all those things. 'Okay, we've got Kevin for two hours on set,' so that was scrambling early on to try and cover ourselves.

Of course the other major life-changing event on *Xena* was the one you were responsible for, namely Lucy's pregnancy. Was it tough to find your footing direction-wise in the fifth season?

It's easy to look back and say, 'I should have, would have, could have.' In my mind, and I've said this before, there were a couple of major failings in that season, and there was also a tremendous run in a row of either weak, or too nutty and kooky stories. From the middle of November with our China episodes, through 'Life Blood' and 'Kindred Spirits', there was a tremendous run of shitty episodes. Those corresponded to Xena's baby being born, and the reasons for that are many... but I did like the beginning of the season!

I liked 'Animal Attraction' and then 'Anthony and Cleopatra' and the end of the season was good. And I never had any problem with 'Motherhood' except that Xena was supposed to throw the chakram outside through the window at Gabrielle not knowing it was her who was threatening Eve [Xena's daughter], but it didn't get shot that way. I liked the first four episodes and the last five, and in the middle there's 'Seeds of Faith', which is one of my favourite episodes.

At the beginning of *Xena*'s fifth season, you'd lost Steve Sears, who'd gone off to produce *Sheena*, and R. J. was busy with *Cleopatra 2525*. Then you had Bob and Alex come in, which didn't seem to work very well, so it seems the constant change in writers could have been part of the problem.

It was, but not in the way anyone thinks it was. I think Alex and Bob are good writers, and I think they would have gotten *Xena*. They also took some episodes that were weak and made them better in that stretch. Without getting myself in a bunch of trouble, I'm not going to say anything, but I think the guys are good writers, and they did what they could. I forced them to do 'Lyre, Lyre' and 'Fishsticks', but it was only because they were there that Kevin would come back to do 'God Fearing Child' [an episode of *Xena* shot after *Hercules* had ceased production].

Many of the writers you brought in for season six of *Xena* seemed a bit disappointed that you and R. J. basically had stories for most of the episodes in mind right from the very beginning.

We had a pretty good handle on a lot of the stories we wanted to do. After season five, I was just going to take the bull by the horns, so in the sixth season, I put my stamp on the final episode and did massive rewriting on a lot of scripts down in New Zealand prior to shooting. That really started in the fifth season, from 'Anthony and Cleopatra' on.

JACK AND CLEO

When Hercules ended after six seasons, Tapert was asked to come up with a replacement. The result was two half-hour action-adventure shows that would be shown back to back: *Jack of All Trades*, starring Bruce Campbell as a 19th century swashbuckler and *Cleopatra 2525*, a post-apocalyptic SF drama. Stylistically, the two shows couldn't be more different, which proved to be their downfall. Halfway into the season, *Jack* was cancelled, and *Cleopatra* was expanded into an hour, but eventually got axed as well. Looking back, Tapert says the experiment was a mistake. 'I should never have tried to do two half-hours,' he reflects. 'They were totally incompatible. Alex Kurtman and Bob Orci, the co-executive producers on *Jack*, strongly wanted to make it less of an action show and more of a witty barb show, which became a compatibility problem. Looking at who watched *Cleo* and *Xena*, it was an entirely different audience from those who liked *Jack*. *Xena* and *Cleopatra* played heavily to a minority and ethnic audience, and Jack was way too fast-talking and "white bread", for lack of another term. So I made the mistake in not making *Cleo* an hour and forsaking doing business with Bruce Campbell. Had I done that, it may have had a slightly better chance.'

Were those fundamental or cosmetic changes?

All of the above. They were character changes, they were ways of making everybody's goals understandable — not that I always succeeded — and I think Lucy and Renee [O'Connor, as Gabrielle] were more watchful of exactly how they were going to play things. For better or worse, they were very wary of portraying their characters in ways that were untrue to them.

Was that caution justified?

Yes it was. I'm going to hang Emily [Skopov] with this, even though she just got dealt the cards. She got two episodes to do where Xena was not Xena, therefore Lucy wanted a lot of changes in what was written, to protect her as a hero. It was 'Heart of Darkness', and then 'Return of the Valkyrie', where Xena has amnesia. Emily got dealt a tough hand there, so there were quite a few changes made to motivation; what the characters were doing and why.

So it simply became the nature of the stories you were handing your writers.

We only had 'x' amount of episodes for the sixth season, and there were some very definite things we wanted to do. There were stories I wanted to tell, and I also wanted to make sure that Xena and Gabrielle's relationship was protected through the sixth season. Again, there are some things I wish I'd done differently towards the end, but until you shoot twenty-two episodes in a season, nobody understands the time pressures involved in that.

What were you trying to accomplish in that season?

We wanted to clear things up with Eve, Xena's daughter and her past, and their relationship with the Amazons and how that played into Gabrielle and the Amazons. And then we wanted to play the little mini-arc about Gabrielle killing the wrong kid early on, which revisited a theme from years gone by, but I still thought it was worth following through. So I'm glad we did that, and we reserved our god arc, and we did some comedies that were actually funny again. I really liked 'Old Ares Had a Farm', which is one of those episodes I can watch many times. I liked the chances we took with 'You Are There'; whether it worked or not, it made me laugh.

One of the episodes that never reached fruition in season six was a musical written by Missy Good that fell through at the eleventh hour. Was that disappointing?

At the time it died, I just had to move on to put all my attention on the finale, so I didn't have time to think about it. Looking back, I chased the idea of doing that musical, trying to work it out and secure the rights to a bunch of songs, and overall, it hurt the quality of the season enders. With the two finales, I wish I had more time in the story phase to get everything I wanted working better, so yes, it was upsetting. I wish I'd found a way to do that musical, and more importantly, having thrown in the towel, I wish I had thrown it in months earlier. It would have been as wild and crazy as any of our episodes have ever been. It's unfortunate that it went away, and I saw what it was going to be in my own mind, but whether or not it would ever have come to fruition is a whole other thing.

Despite those production problems, those last half-dozen episodes turned out very well.

You know why? Because I love that show, and I think R. J. loved that show, and by that time, everyone knew it was coming to an end and gave it 150 per cent. I made a mistake in one of the episodes, the one that Mr Becker did*; I wish I hadn't done that. I went back to answer what happened to Gabrielle, and that was a wasted episode. I wish I hadn't wasted it, because I had another really good story I wanted to tell. The truth is, we were looking to explain what happened to Gabrielle between 'Sacrifice' and 'Family Affair', which I thought was one of the large unexplained things in the series, but the truth was, I should never have bothered. I had wanted to do a tough drama about Gabrielle's family doing an intervention and trying to save her from being with Xena and dying. So that was a whole different story, of them trying to set up Xena to be captured in order to save Gabrielle from what they thought was certain death.

Did you and R. J. know from the beginning of the season how it was going to end?

Let's put it this way: I knew how Xena was going to end from the time she was in a three-episode arc on *Hercules*. She was going to die. So, there was no question that Xena was going to die at some point. The only question was, were we going to do a couple of, not theatrical movies, but either direct-to-video or high-budget mini-series for television? When that didn't come through, Xena's fate was sealed.

Knowing that you were going to direct the final two-parter yourself, were you able to put aside a little extra money for a big finish?

I didn't have that much extra money! Yes, those episodes were expensive for the costume and set dressing, but I didn't get any more time than most guys get for shooting two episodes. It wasn't more expensive or more extravagant than the musical episodes, or the Chinese episodes. Unfortunately, in the fifth season, the studio cut our budget pretty severely, and we'd done a lot of big episodes all season long.

Were you taken aback by the angry reaction to Xena's death?

We went out of our way to make it an episode that was going to have a tearjerker

---

* 'Soul Possession' was a comedic episode, in which a 'lost' Xena scroll was discovered, bridging the gap between Gabrielle's apparent death in season 3's 'Sacrifice', and her return in season 4's 'Family Affair'.

ending, so the fact that people cried and were upset wasn't a surprise. I never know really who the fan base is. If I go by what I'm told, it's families of four with incomes of under $40,000 and no college education that watch *Xena*. There was a group of people who didn't like the ending, but many of them are the same people who haven't liked the show since the second season, so I really don't know what to say about it. I got more heartfelt mail from nine year-olds for killing off Iolaus in *Hercules* than I did from killing off Xena, but yes, I know there is a negative reaction. It took me a little while to understand the vehemence of some of the people, but once I understood who they were, it became easier to understand.

But people really don't like change, do they?

They hate change, they really do. There's a strange thing, and I can't believe I'm saying this, but I think the show got a little bit hurt, after we went from Universal to Studios USA, by not having a studio or executives that were very strong, who would really challenge us. They want *Walker, Texas Ranger*; they want to know that every week, the good guys are going to win. Of course, left to our own devices, we never wanted to tell the story that everyone was comfortable with every week. I think that's what made *Xena* interesting: we were allowed to have the characters change, as opposed to just making everybody comfortable. Now maybe that helped the show and maybe it hurt it, but there was nobody at the studio, whose opinion

XENA'S OFFSPRING

Before the arrival of *Xena: Warrior Princess*, action heroines on television were few and far between. There was the original *Sheena* TV series way back when, and the occasional female cop show, but that was pretty much it. When *Xena* quickly became an international success, broadcasters began casting around for other properties featuring sexy action heroines. There was *Relic Hunter*, about a sexy globetrotting archaeologist *à la* Indiana Jones. You had *Queen of Swords*, a sexy Zorro-like Spanish adventuress. *VIP* had former *Baywatch* babe Pamela Anderson fronting an entire group of sexy security agents. *Black Scorpion* was a, yes, sexy Batman-type super-heroine, complete with a cool car and a rogue's gallery of colourful super-villains. And *Sheena* returned, this time played by another *Baywatch* alumnus, Gena Lee Nolan; this new version was co-created by former *Xena* writer/producer Steve Sears. Even the creators of *Xena* tried to capitalise on their own success. Their next attempt at the genre was an unsold pilot called *Amazon High*, which ultimately became part of a *Xena* episode. And a year later, there was *Cleopatra 2525*, a futuristic action-adventure with no less than three heroines kicking ass and saving the world.

I really believed in, saying, 'You know what guys, you're straying too far from what the audience's comfort level is!' There were a couple of things we screened for people in audience focus groups and doing research, and they said, 'Well, all the episodes seem the same.' I've been told that they say that about all action-adventure shows, though I always thought we mixed it up pretty well. But partway through the fourth season, as the numbers started to decline, we decided to find out what had gone wrong. I think the audience as a whole had a real misconception of what they were viewing.

Are you saying you needed someone who could look at the series more objectively?

There was nowhere to get any answer. If you asked, they'd say, 'The show is in syndication, and you can't judge anything from one week's ratings.' I've been told that a hundred times, so I said, 'Well, if all the centaur episodes rate high and all the Amazon episodes rate high, can I assume that the audience likes centaurs and Amazons?' They said, 'It's not a large enough sample, and viewing patterns in syndicated TV are such that you just never know what people are tuning in to see, and what you're up against or why they're watching this episode.'

Was it difficult for you to see your show, which was once so big for the studio, suddenly losing its support?

It was a very bitter pill to swallow and still is. I've gotten myself in trouble with Studios USA by saying I don't believe they had any idea or any ability to exploit the two franchises of *Hercules* and *Xena*. I think they totally dropped the ball, and it's not a Universal thing, it was a Studios USA thing. When we got traded from Universal, none of the execs who were responsible for the series went along with it, so everybody at Studios USA were just Johnny-come-latelys and would only back the glory of it. And then there was another management change, so very quickly, nobody had any vested interest in *Hercules* or *Xena*'s continued success or building a franchise, because it wouldn't be their personal triumph or glory.

Is there the possibility of another *Xena* adventure in the future, either a TV movie or feature film?

I don't think the door is sealed to doing a long-form production. I think it's actually set up as a want-to-see, but right now, it's really in Studio USA's court. Sometime in the future, since they hold all the copyrights and all the rights to the series, they have to decide if they ever want to do a feature and treat it properly, but I've sealed the door to doing anything shoddy; that's what I believe.

Is the TV industry moving away from fantasy at the moment, and if so, are you taking note of that fact in the kind of projects you're developing?

No, I like fantasy, and I like action, therefore I'm at loggerheads with the industry right now. There are a few shows coming up that have fantasy. The WB has announced they're doing *Oz* based on Frank Baum's books, but I think the industry as a whole looks at fantasy as a freak and doesn't know where to place it.

When you look back at your work on *Hercules* and *Xena*, what did those two shows contribute to the genre, and to television as a whole?

Without those two shows, *Hercules* leading to *Xena*, I don't think you would have *Buffy* and *Witchblade*, and I don't think you would have had *Relic Hunter* or *Sheena* or *Queen of Swords*. *Xena* convinced people that you could make a show with a woman action hero in the lead, and have it be successful. I think the genre of sword and sandals was basically revitalised a little bit, and — to be totally vainglorious — I don't know that they ever would have made *Gladiator* if *Herc* and *Xena* hadn't shown that there was life back in that genre. ∎

JOSS WHEDON

oss Whedon is a third-generation television scriptwriter, possibly the first one. As he tells the story, he never intended to follow in his father's footsteps: he started his career as a snobby film student who never watched television and intended to write movies, until he found out how much TV writing paid. Ultimately, he did both, working as a scriptwriter on *Roseanne* and the TV series *Parenthood* before selling his script to the 1992 *Buffy the Vampire Slayer* movie. For several years, he was a film writer and a script doctor, doing uncredited touch-ups on *Twister*, *Speed* and *Waterworld*, and writing drafts of projects such as *X-Men*, *Toy Story*, *Titan A.E.*, *Disney's Atlantis* and *Alien Resurrection*. But Whedon came into his own with the television incarnation of *Buffy*, which has, over the past few years, grown from a cult classic into a cottage industry. As the original creator of the Buffy character, Whedon — now a writer, director and executive producer of the *Buffy the Vampire Slayer* TV show — has a hand in virtually all of its spinoffs, including the WB series *Angel*, a line of comic-book tie-ins, and an upcoming animated series and BBC TV show. Speaking to Tasha Robinson of *The Onion A. V. Club* just before the début of the sixth season, Whedon talks about the *Buffy* phenomenon, his bitterness over his movie career, and the fans who share in his worship of his creations.

So, after her death at the end of season five, how are you bringing Buffy back?

Aw, I'm not supposed to tell.

I'm teasing. I know you get that a lot.

Yeah, it's the first thing everybody asks, including my developers. And the answer is, I can't say, because that's why you watch the show. The one thing I can say is, I think we earn it. There's no Patrick Duffy in the shower, there's no alternate-universe Buffy. It's not going to be neat. Bringing her back is difficult, and the consequences are fairly intense. It's not like we don't take these death-things seriously. But exactly how she comes back, I can't reveal.

When your actors get questions like that in interviews, they always seem to

answer with horrific threats: 'I can't tell, Joss will rip out my tongue and feed it to wolves,' and so forth. Do they actually get these threats from you?

I'm a very gentle man, not unlike Gandhi. I don't ever threaten them. There is, sort of hanging over their head, the thing that I could kill them at any moment. But that's really just if they annoy me. They know that I'm very secretive about plot twists and whatnot, because I think it's better for the show. But anybody with a computer can find out what's going to happen, apparently even before I know. So my wish for secrecy is sort of pathetic. But they're all on board. They don't want to give it away, and a lot of times, they just don't know.

You're a third-generation television scriptwriter, possibly the first one. How did your family affect your career choice?

At first, I was like, 'I shall never write for television.' I was a total snob. I never watched American TV, I only watched, like, *Masterpiece Theatre*. And I was like, 'Television is lame-o, I am a film student, I shall never write for... They pay how much?' When I was just starting out, and I had no idea how I was going to become the brilliant independent filmmaker that I imagined myself to be, and I was staying with my father[*], I thought, 'Well, I'll try my hand at a spec.' You know, by selling a TV script, I could make enough money to sort of keep myself afloat. That was the first time I ever sat down and tried to write. I had always sort of written, but I had never studied writing, or thought of myself as a writer exactly. I always assumed I would write whatever I made, but I never really gave it much thought. Then I sat down and really tried to write a script and found the great happiness of my life.

Was that in college, or post-college?

Post-college. I started writing TV specs, and I was like, 'Writing is fun, and there are some good shows out there! I was being a snob!' So I wrote a bunch of specs, I didn't get any work, and finally I landed a job on *Roseanne*. And having walked, now, in the movie and TV world, I'm still a complete snob, but it's reversed. I feel like film is a ridiculous hell, and TV is the greatest place in the world.

Did you ever have a day job that wasn't related to media or TV?

JOSS WHEDON

Date of Birth
23 June 1964

Home Base:
Los Angeles, California, USA

Education:
Wesleyan University

First TV Work:
Roseanne

TV Career Highlights
Roseanne, Parenthood, Buffy the Vampire Slayer, Angel

---

* *Joss's father, John Whedon, wrote for* The Dick Cavett Show, Alice *and* Benson *in the 70s and 80s, while his grandfather, Tom Whedon, wrote for the likes of* The Donna Reed Show *and* Leave It to Beaver *in the 50s and 60s.*

I worked at a video store. Actors wait tables, directors work at video stores. I did research for the American Film Institute, for the guy who was doing their Life Achievement Awards. Those were my two big, exciting gigs. I landed a job pretty young. I was, like, twenty-four when I started. I turned in my first script on my twenty-fifth birthday. And I looked much younger. When they found out I was twenty-five, it was like, 'Oh, you're no Boy Wonder. You're over.'

Roseanne was your first actual writing job. Did you quit that when you sold the original _Buffy_ movie script?

I wrote the _Buffy_ script because I had way too much free time. I was on _Roseanne_ for a year, and in the first half of that year, I wrote five scripts. I was a staff writer, the lowest thing you can be. And one of my father's older writer friends actually asked me, 'Have they let you start to write a script yet?' I was like, 'I'm on my fourth.' Because there was such chaos, and almost nobody else there could do it. It was great. It was like this vacuum of power, and I got sucked up. I got so much responsibility. But then my stuff kept getting rewritten, and in the second half of the year I just wrote one. I got shut out by the producers, basically. And I wasn't writing. I was coming in late, leaving early, and writing my screenplay instead, because they weren't using me, and it was driving me crazy, because I don't want money for nothing. So I

BUFFY THE MOVIE

Anyone who's seen the original 1992 feature _Buffy the Vampire Slayer_ has probably wondered how such a forgettable film could be made into a successful, often inspired TV series. The answer: just keep the name, the basic concept and discard everything else. In the original film, shopping-addicted high school cheerleader Buffy (Kristy Swanson) discovers that she is actually the 'Slayer', a warrior that is selected from each generation to battle vampires. With the help of a mysterious gentleman named Merrick (Donald Sutherland), Buffy learns to confront her destiny as the Slayer, much to the surprise of her slacker boyfriend Pike (Luke Perry). She also finds herself battling the ancient vampire lord Lothos (Rutger Hauer) and his minion Amilyn (Paul Reubens). Well, it seemed like a good idea, as the television series eventually proved, but the original _Buffy the Vampire Slayer_ is basically a misguided mess. Flatly directed by Fran Rubel Kuzui and badly miscast (one gets the feeling that Sutherland was working from a different script to his co-stars), the film bears virtually no resemblance to its TV counterpart. Thankfully, writer Joss Whedon had the advantage of hindsight when he revived the concept years later, knowing just which dramatic pitfalls to avoid.

said, 'I quit.' There was nothing for me to do there. So I had written *Buffy*, I hadn't sold it. I quit because I wanted to work harder, and I got a job on *Parenthood*, which ran for about thirteen episodes. Which was a good show — good staff, good cast — that got eaten up by the network. So I had that experience, and after that I waned on TV and wanted to work more in the movies. And, after all the studios had [adopts booming, jocular voice] 'Loved it and passed on it!' [producer] Fran Kuzui started nosing around *Buffy*, and that started to take off.

What about your *Boy Meets World* direction credit? When did that happen?

[Laughs.] That never happened. [The Internet Movie Database] says I directed a very special episode of *Boy Meets World*, and I laughed so hard. I've never seen the show, but apparently it's on the Internet that I directed one. Boy has never met world. Let me put it this way. The episode of *Boy Meets World* that I never made, I'm still prouder of than *Alien Resurrection*.

How closely were you involved with the making of the Buffy movie?

I had major involvement. I was there almost all the way through shooting. I pretty much eventually threw up my hands because I could not be around Donald Sutherland any longer. It didn't turn out to be the movie that I had written. They never do, but that was my first lesson in that. Not that the movie is without merit, but I just watched a lot of stupid wannabe-star behaviour and a director with a different vision than mine — which was her right, it was her movie — but it was still frustrating. Eventually, I was like, 'I need to be away from here.'

Was it a personality conflict between you and Sutherland, or was he just not what you'd envisioned in that role?

No, no, he was just a prick. The thing is, people always make fun of Rutger Hauer [for his *Buffy* role]. Even though he was big and silly and looked kind of goofy in the movie, I have to give him credit, because he was there. He was into it. Whereas Donald was just... He would rewrite all his dialogue, and the director would let him. He can't write — he's not a writer — so the dialogue would not make sense. And he had a very bad attitude. He was incredibly rude to the director, he was rude to everyone around him, he was just a real pain. And to see him destroying my stuff... Some people didn't notice. Some people liked him in the movie. Because he's Donald Sutherland. He's a great actor. He can read the phone book, and I'm interested. But the thing is, he acts well enough that you didn't notice, with his little rewrites, and his little ideas about what his character should do, that he was actually destroying the movie more than Rutger was. So I got out of there. I had to run away.

What was Paul Reubens like? He seems to be the actor people remember most from the movie.

[Adopts weepy, awed voice.] He is a god that walks among us. He is one of the sweetest, most professional and delightful people I've ever worked with. [Normal voice.] He was my beacon of hope in that whole experience, that he was such a good guy, and so got it. I mean, most of the people were sweet. Most of them were actively out there trying... They were good people. Paul was a delight to be around, trying to make it better. He actually said to me, 'I'm a little worried about this line, and I want to change it. I realise that it'll change this other thing, so if that's a problem...' I'm like, 'Did I just hear an actor say that?'

How early on did it occur to you to re-do *Buffy* the way you'd originally intended?

You know, it wasn't really my idea. After the première of the movie, my wife said, 'You know, honey, maybe a few years from now, you'll get to make it again, the way you want to make it!' [Broad, condescending voice.] 'Ha ha ha, you little naïve fool. It doesn't work that way. That'll never happen.' And then it was three years later, and Gail Berman actually had the idea. Sandollar [Television] had the property, and Gail thought it would make a good TV series. They called me up out of contractual obligation: 'Call the writer, have him pass.' And I was like, 'Well, that sounds cool.' So, to my agent's surprise and chagrin, I said, 'Yeah, I could do that. I think I get it. It could be a high-school horror movie. It'd be a metaphor for how lousy my high-school years were.' So I hadn't had the original idea, I just developed it.

You joke a lot in interviews about how you wanted to write horror because you experienced so much of it in high-school. Did you have an unusually bad high-school experience, or was it just the usual teen traumas?

I think it's not inaccurate to say that I had a perfectly happy childhood during which I was very unhappy. It was nothing worse than anybody else. I could not get a date to save my life, but my last three years of high-school were at a boys' school, so I wasn't actually looking that hard. I was not popular in school, and I was definitely not a ladies' man. And I had a very painful adolescence, because it was all very strange to me. It wasn't like I got beat up, but the humiliation and isolation, and the existential 'God, I exist, and nobody cares' of being a teenager were extremely pronounced for me. I don't have horror stories. I mean, I have a few horror stories about attempting to court a girl, which would make people laugh, but it's not like I think I had it worse than other people. But that's sort of the point of *Buffy*, that I'm talking about the stuff everybody goes through. Nobody gets out of here without some trauma.

You describe yourself as an isolated, solitary kid, and then you moved into writing, which is often a solitary profession. Did you have problems adapting to an environment where you have to work closely with large crowds of people for long hours every day?

You know, I had a lot of brothers, and then boarding school, thirteen to a room. I definitely need my alone time. And when I'm writing, I'm happiest. My greatest joy is being alone with a story. But on the other hand, I enjoy people. I enjoy directing, making the show, and the people I work with are smart and funny. As long as I keep balanced, I'm okay. I need to spend more time alone than most people I know, and it's hard to. When you're producing a show, you're never alone. So to find the time to write, to really get away from everybody, it's difficult. It's difficult to find a balance. But it's not like I can't be around people, like this insane recluse with a big beard.

Has your film degree come in handy, or did you walk out of school with a lot of useless abstract knowledge?

I walked out with unbelievably essential knowledge. I happened to study under the people that I believe are the best film teachers ever. Film hasn't existed that long, so I say that with a certain amount of confidence. The teachers at Wesleyan were brilliant, the most brilliant people I've been around, and there is not a story that I tell that does not reflect something I either learned, or learned but already knew, from my professors. In terms of production, the place was useless. In terms of connections, I suppose you could go there, but it wasn't the fast track to becoming a hotshot producer. But my. It was just an undergraduate degree, but I'm talking about an education, the most valuable thing I ever learned. Oddly enough, I never studied writing. I studied almost everything except writing.

And you never took any sort of outside classes or looked into any kind of formal writing training?

I'd been around scripts my whole life. I'd seen my father's scripts, I knew the basic format, and I understood the basic style, the language, the rhythm. But in terms of whether I had any kind of structure or character, it was a crap shoot.

Did you ever go to your father for writing advice?

I never actually said, 'Father, what do I do?' But he has given me some great advice. In fact, I've actually said to my writers, 'You know, my father said to me once.' and then stopped and said, 'I can't believe that came out of my mouth, who said that?' The best piece of advice he ever gave me — he's written sitcoms exclusively — was, 'If you have a good story, you don't need jokes. If you don't have a good story, no amount of jokes can save you.' I'm not really that interested in jokes. I like the more dramatic stuff. But that tenet of 'the story is god' is the most important thing I could have learned.

How did you pick up the practical skills you needed to direct?

Some of them just by watching, and some of them by doing. I just watched a lot of movies, and I had an idea of what I wanted to convey visually. My first experience was really bad. It was the presentation by which we sold [the TV version of] *Buffy*, and it was dreadful. I had a terrible crew that I could not communicate with, and I was a first-time guy who didn't know what he was doing, surrounded by old veterans who didn't know what they were doing. So I was hoping somebody was going to know what they were doing at some point, to sort of help me out there. I look back and see the mistakes I made, but I also know that visually, I always knew what I was trying to say and how to convey it. I just didn't know how to get the crew to make that happen. As soon as I started working with my permanent crew on *Buffy*, we had a great DP and a great bunch of people with whom I could communicate really easily, I realised, 'Okay, I guess I can do this.' Because there was a period where I was like, [whining] 'Oh, I just wanna go home and write movies, this is gonna make me miserable,' and Fox was like, 'We just want him to go home and write movies.'

When you saw the completed *Buffy* movie, it wasn't the film you wanted to make, and several years later, you recreated it as a successful franchise. Do you ever have similar thoughts about *Alien Resurrection*? Do you ever want to go back and 'fix' it?

Oh, yes, I have. Ohhh, yes, the fantasies. I've never had a worse experience in my life, and I've often thought of doing a lecture series on how to make movies based on just showing that movie, because I think they literally did every single thing wrong. The production design, the casting, there wasn't a mistake they left unturned. So I've often thought about it, because we'd been in talks about *Alien 5*. I love sequels, I love franchises, and I love big epic stories that go on and on. I used to love summer movies, before every single one of them was crap. So, yeah, I've thought about doing what I'd originally thought in *Alien 5*. And, after I found out on the Internet that I was making it, just after I directed *Boy Meets World*. [Laughs.] I thought about what I would do, what I would want to do with that franchise. And I was like, 'You know what? I think maybe I'd like to work on something that nineteen people don't own and control.' We have so many executive producers on *Buffy* — and they leave me alone, they're great, but I think I'd like to do something that isn't just somebody else's. Having said that, I'm now considering doing the *Iron Man* movie. But that's just because it's got that cool shiny suit. *Alien 5* was a longer shot. I mean, you have a body blow to recover from there.

Were you on the set for that, watching them take your script apart?

No, I wasn't involved at all. I only went to the set once or twice. I'd been on movie sets, and I tend to stay away from them, because people want rewrites. They see the writer, and they're like, 'Wouldn't it be cool if my character.' 'Gotta go, bye!' So I went once or twice, and I went after the première of *Buffy* [the series]. And the producer guy they had saw me, and said, 'Hey, I went to the première of your show, and it was so weird. I said, "Hey, they're playing it the way he writes it!"' I was like, 'And what are they doing here?' That was my first sign that there might be trouble. I literally didn't see any of it again until I saw the director's cut, during which I actually cried.

Just over what they'd done to your script?

It was a single manly tear rolling down my cheek. About an hour into the movie, I just started to cry. I said, 'I can't believe this.' I was heartbroken.

How much of your writing made it into the final versions of *Twister* and *Speed*?

Most of the dialogue in *Speed* is mine, and a bunch of the characters. That was actually pretty much a good experience. I have quibbles. I also have the only poster left with my name still on it. Getting arbitrated off the credits was un-fun. But *Speed* has a bunch. And *Twister*, less. In *Twister*, there are things that worked and things that weren't the way I'd intended them. Whereas *Speed* came out closer to what I'd been trying to do. I think of *Speed* as one of the few movies I've made that I actually like.

What about *Waterworld*?

[Laughs.] *Waterworld*. I refer to myself as the world's highest-paid stenographer. This is a situation I've been in a bunch of times. By the way, I'm very bitter, is that okay? I mean, people ask me, 'What's the worst job you ever had?' 'I once was a writer in Hollywood...' Talk about taking the glow off of movies. I've had almost nothing but bad experiences. *Waterworld* was a good idea, and the script was the classic, 'They have a good idea, then they write a generic script and don't really care about the idea.' When I was brought in, there was no water in the last forty pages of the script. It all took place on land, or on a ship, or whatever. I'm like, 'Isn't the cool thing about this guy that he has gills?' And no one was listening. I was there basically taking notes from Costner, who was very nice, fine to work with, but he was not a writer. And he had written a bunch of stuff that they wouldn't let their staff touch. So I was supposed to be there for a week, and I was there for seven weeks, and I accomplished nothing. I wrote a few puns, and a few scenes that I can't even sit through because they came out so bad.

It was the same situation with *X-Men*. They said, 'Come in and punch up the big climax, the third act, and if you can, make it cheaper.' That was the mandate on both movies, and my response to both movies was, 'The problem with the third act is the first two acts.' But, again, no one was paying attention. *X-Men* was very interesting in that, by that time, I actually had a reputation in television. I was actually somebody. People stopped thinking I was John Sweden on the phone. And then, in *X-Men*, not only did they throw out my script and never tell me about it; they actually invited me to the read-through, having thrown out my entire draft without telling me. I was like, 'Oh, that's right! This is the movies! The writer is shit in the movies!' I'll never understand that. I have one line left in that movie. Actually, there are a couple of lines left in that are out of context and make no sense, or are delivered so badly, so terribly... There's one line that's left the way I wrote it.

Which is?

'It's me.' 'Prove it.' 'You're a dick.' Hey, it got a laugh.

It's funny that the only lines I really remember from that movie are that one and Storm's toad comment.

Okay, which was also mine, and that's the interesting thing. Everybody remembers that as the worst line ever written, but the thing about that is, it was supposed to be delivered as completely offhand. [Adopts casual, bored tone.] 'You know what happens when a toad gets hit by lightning?' Then, after he gets electrocuted, 'Ahhh, pretty much the same thing that happens to anything else.' But Halle Berry said it like she was Desdemona. [Strident, ringing voice.] 'The same thing that happens to everything eeelse!' That's the thing that makes you go crazy. At least 'You're a dick' got delivered right. The worst thing about these things is that, when the actors say it wrong, it makes the writer look stupid. People assume that the line… I listened to half the dialogue in Alien 4, and I'm like, 'That's idiotic,' because of the way it was said. And nobody knows that. Nobody ever gets that. They say, 'That was a stupid script,' which is the worst pain in the world. I have a great long boring story about that, but I can tell you the very short version. In Alien 4, the director changed something so that it didn't make any sense. He wanted someone to go and get a gun and get killed by the alien, so I wrote that in and tried to make it work, but he directed it in a way that it made no sense whatsoever. And I was sitting there in the editing room, trying to come up with looplines to explain what's going on, to make the scene make sense, and I asked the director, 'Can you just explain to me why he's doing this? Why is he going for this gun?' And the editor, who was French, turned to me and said, with a little leer on his face, [adopts gravelly, smarmy, French-accented voice] 'Because eet's een the screept.' And I actually went and dented the bathroom stall with my puddly little fist. I have never been angrier. But it's the classic, 'When something goes wrong, you assume the writer's a dork.' And that's painful.

Have you done any other uncredited script work?

Actually, my first gig ever was writing looplines for a movie that had already been made. You know, writing lines over somebody's back to explain something, to help make a connection, to add a joke, or to just add babble because the people are in frame and should be saying something. We're constantly saving something that doesn't work, or trying to, with lines behind people's backs. It's almost like adding narration, but cheaper. I did looplines for *The Getaway*, the Alec Baldwin/Kim Basinger version. If you look carefully at *The Getaway*, you'll see that when people's backs are turned, or their heads are slightly out of frame, the whole movie has a certain edge to it. I also did a couple of days of looplines and punch-ups for *The Quick and the Dead*, just to meet Sam Raimi.

Have you ever been asked to doctor a script that you thought was doomed from the start?

I've never taken a gig like that. There have been different situations. Like, *Speed*, I loved the idea so much that I was very anxious to come in and rewrite the characters. But I loved the plot. *Toy Story* was the greatest opportunity in the world, because it was a great idea, with a script I didn't like at all. When you know the idea is solid. I've been pitched ideas, or seen scripts, where I've been like, 'You don't need me. You need to [shouting] not make this.' There have been some terrible ones. But the thing is, for a script doctor, the best thing in the world is a good idea with a terrible script. Assuming they'll let you play with it, which they did on *Toy Story*. Because you have the solid structure, and you can work the story into it.

How was your experience working on *Atlantis* with Disney?

The only reason my name is on that movie is that I was the first guy on it, about eight years ago. I wanted to write musicals, and I thought it was going to be a musical. So I started working with them, because they wanted to do *Journey to the Centre of the Earth*, plus *Atlantis*, plus *The Man Who Would Be King*. That was their idea, and I wrote the first treatment for that, but I didn't have anything to do with the movie since. The movie they made has nothing to do with that treatment, but I'm happier having my name on that movie than on *Titan A.E.*

Apart from the problems with getting respect and avoiding rewrites in film, what kind of differences do you find between writing for TV and writing for film?

Well, you also have the overload of, 'I'm not doing ninety minutes, or two hours, of writing, this year. I'm doing twenty-two,' or in my case, forty-four. You have a huge amount of pressure, constantly having to get it out there. It certainly creates discipline. I think every filmmaker should have to work in television. First of all, films wouldn't all be two and a half hours long, because you really learn about what you need when you're limited to forty-four minutes. It's just a great, great training ground, to constantly be working. What you trade is the ability to control every piece of the frame, to really make everything work exactly the way you want. Yes, I have a great crew, we've been together so long, the cast gets it, the writers are superb. But you sacrifice a certain precision: you have to get this, you have to get that. But you also have a higher chance of doing your best work and getting it out there, because there are fewer executives and stars and ridiculous people between you and getting it done when it airs in two weeks and you have to shoot it. I've been described as Ed Wood, and I've been assured that this is a compliment, because of the amount of work we have to get done in so short a time. Especially with *Buffy*, which is a very hard show to make, because we have the action and the special effects, and we have to be very careful about the performances, making it all work. So you get that overload thing.

How about comic books? How does that compare?

Well, I get to be alone more, and the characters never say, 'Oh, I don't think I'd say that in boldface,' or 'I don't think I'd wear this.' They just sort of do whatever I tell them. It's different but similar, and there's a little more leeway. It's fun.

Do you prefer one of the three over the others?

At the end of the day, I would probably rather be making movies. I love television, because you get to see more of the characters than you'd ever see in the movies. You get to see a hundred hours, seventy-five hours of a drama, and you just keep learning about the characters. That's really exciting. But at the end of the day, movies are my area. I would love to write a novel, I would love to write an opera. More than anything, I want to write a musical. So I'm happy if I'm writing. I love to direct, I love to edit, I love to produce, I love all of it. But as long as I'm writing, I'm happy.

I attended your Q&A session at a comics convention last year, and many of the people who got up to ask questions were nearly in tears over the chance to get to talk to you. Some of them could barely speak, and others couldn't stop gushing about you, and about *Buffy*. How do you deal with that kind of emotional intensity?

It's about the show, and I feel the same way about it. I get the same way. It's not like being a rock star. It doesn't feel like they're reacting to me. It's really sweet when people react like that, and I love the praise, but to me, what they're getting emotional about is the show. And that's the best feeling in the world. There's nothing creepy about it. I feel like there's a religion in narrative, and I feel the same way they do. I feel like we're both paying homage to something else; they're not paying homage to me.

Does knowing that you have fans who are that dedicated put extra pressure on you, or does seeing the show as something outside yourself make it easier to deal with?

You don't want to let them down. The people who feel the most strongly about something will turn on you the most vociferously if they feel you've let them down. Sometimes you roll your eyes and you want to say, 'Back off,' but you don't get the big praise without getting the big criticism. Because people care. So. Much. And you always know that's lurking there. It does make a difference. If nobody was paying attention, I might very well say, 'You know what, guys? Let's churn 'em out, churn 'em out, make some money.' I like to think I wouldn't, but I don't know. I don't know me, I might be a dick. Once the critics, after the first season, really got the show, we all sort of looked at each other and said, 'Ohhh-kay...' We thought we were going to fly under the radar, and nobody was going to notice the show. And then we had this responsibility, and we got kind of nervous. You don't want to let them down. But ultimately, the narrative feeds you so much. It's so exciting to find out what's going to happen next, to find the next important thing in the narrative, to step down and say, 'That's so cool.'

Are you ever surprised by your fans' passion for the show?

No. I designed the show to create that strong reaction. I designed *Buffy* to be an icon, to be an emotional experience, to be loved in a way that other shows can't be loved. Because it's about adolescence, which is the most important thing people go through in their development, becoming an adult. And it mythologizes it in such a way, such a romantic way — it basically says, 'Everybody who made it through adolescence is a hero.' And I think that's very personal, that people get something from that that's very real. And I don't think I could be more pompous. But I mean every word of it. I wanted her to be a cultural phenomenon. I wanted there to be dolls, Barbie with kung-fu grip. I wanted people to embrace it in a way that exists beyond, 'Oh, that was a wonderful show about lawyers, let's have dinner.' I wanted people to internalise it, and make up fantasies where they were in the story, to take it home with them, for it to exist beyond the TV show. And we've done exactly that. Now I'm writing comics, and I'm getting all excited about the mythology. We're doing a book of stories about other slayers, and I'm all excited about that, and it's all growing in my mind, as well. I think she has become an icon, and that's what I wanted. What more could anybody ask?

FRAY

For every generation, there must be a slayer, and 200 years in the future, her name is Mel Fray. That's the premise of *Fray*, a new SF/horror comic book mini-series created by Joss Whedon. Mel, a small-time street thief, discovers that she is the current slayer, just as the forces of darkness discover they have a new enemy to deal with. 'Writing Fray has been delightful,' claims Whedon, 'because instead of hours and hours of production and actors and props to deal with, I just hand it to Carl Moline [the book's penciller], and all of those things come back to me beautifully done, so in a way, it's more fun. It's also been fun to open myself up to different ways of storytelling. With *Fray*, I decided to adopt a very dense kind of straightforward, first-person method, and I want to be true to that even while I'm exploring other ways in other books. I thought, I'll do something new, that's in the *Buffy* universe so I don't have to create a whole new universe for my first foray into comics, that will therefore be of interest to the fans, but not interfere with anything.'

Do you ever feel a responsibility to society, to use your massive power for good?

Yes and no. I mean, I've always been, and long before anybody was paying any attention, very careful about my responsibility in narrative. How much do I put what I want to put, and how much do I put what I feel is correct? People say, 'After Columbine, do you feel a responsibility about the way you portray violence?' And I'm like, 'No, I felt a responsibility about the way I portrayed violence the first time I picked up a pen.' I mean, everybody felt... It's a ridiculous thing to ask a writer. But you feel it, and at the same time — and I've said this before — a writer has a responsibility to tell stories that are dark and sexy and violent, where characters that you love do stupid, wrong things and get away with it, that we explore these parts of people's lives, because that's what makes stories into fairy tales instead of polemics.

That's what makes stories resonate, that thing, that dark place that we all want to go to on some level or another. It's very important. People are like, [whining] 'Well, your characters have sex, and those costumes, and blah blah...' And I'm like, 'You're in adolescence, and you're thinking about what besides sex?' I feel that we're showing something that is true, that people can relate to and say, 'Oh, I made that bad choice,' or 'Oh, there's a better way to do that.' But as long as it's real, then however politically correct, or incorrect, or whatever, bizarre, or dark, or funny, or stupid — anything you can get, as long as it's real, I don't mind.

Speaking of sex and reality, the Tara-and-Willow relationship has been controversial from several angles, with one side of the spectrum accusing you of promoting a homosexual agenda while the other side accuses you of exploiting lesbian chic.

You just have to ignore that. I actually went online and said, 'I realise that this has shocked a lot of people, and I've made a mistake by trying to shove this lifestyle — which is embraced by, maybe, at most, ten per cent of Americans — down people's throats. So I'm going to take it back, and from now on, Willow will no longer be a Jew.' And somebody was actually like, [adopts agitated whine] 'What do you mean she's not going to be a Jew anymore?' I was like, 'Can we get a 'sarcasm' font?' But, you know, the first criticism we got was, 'She's not gay enough. They're not gay enough.' We were playing it as a metaphor, and it was like, 'Why don't they come out? They're not gay enough!' And eventually we did start to say, 'Well, maybe we're being a little coy. They've got good chemistry, this is working out, why don't we just go ahead and make them go for it?' And, of course, once you bring it out in the open, it's no longer a metaphor. Then it's just an Issue. But we never played it that way.

Ultimately, some people say 'lesbian chic,' I say, 'Okay, whatever.' Those criticisms don't really bug me. You look at shows like *Ally McBeal* and *Party of Five*, which both did lesbian kisses that were promoted and hyped for months and months, and afterwards the characters were like, 'Well, I seem to be very heterosexual! Thank you for that steamy lesbian kiss!' Our whole mission statement was that we would bury their first kiss inside an episode that had nothing to do with it, and never promote it, which I guess caught people off-guard at The WB. The reason we had them kiss was because if they didn't, it would start to get coy and, quite frankly, a little offensive, for two people that much in love to not have any physicality. But the whole mission statement was, 'We'll put it where nobody expects it, and we'll never talk about it.' I mean, there are people who are genuinely concerned — are we falling into a pattern that other shows are falling into? It's very possible. The WB was like, 'We have gay characters on all our shows. Why didn't you tell us you were making characters gay?' 'Well, I don't watch your other shows. I didn't know.' I'm sort of not really aware of what's going on out there. So the accusations of, 'You shouldn't have a gay character on your show,' those people are just — they should just be tied to a rock. 'Whatever, you dumb people.' Not that I feel strongly. But the other ones, 'Oh, you just do that because it's sexy'... Well, the writers, and the men and women on the set, are like, 'Yeah, it is pretty sexy!' I mean, so were Buffy and Angel. If it's not sexy, then it's not worth it. Like those two guys in *Thirtysomething* sitting in bed together, looking like they were individually wrapped in plastic. They did a scene with two guys in bed, and it was a big deal, on *Thirtysomething*, and it was the most antiseptic thing I've ever seen in my life. They were sitting ramrod-straight, far away from each other, and not even looking at each other. I was like, 'Ahhh, sexy!'

One aspect of your fans' dedication is that they become very threatened by perceived changes in the show, like Giles becoming a lesser character as Anthony Stewart Head moves to Britain, or the show itself moving from the WB to UPN.

Change is a mandate on the show. And people always complain. [Agitated voice.] 'Who is this new guy, Oz?' 'Where'd that guy Oz go?' They have trouble with change, but it's about change. It's about growing up. If we didn't change, you would be bored. The change as far as Tony Head is concerned, the man has two daughters growing up in England, and he'd like to live there. The kids [on *Buffy*] are old enough now that they don't really need a mentor figure, and this is a period in your life when you don't really have one. So it made sense for him to go back, and he chose to be on the show as a recurring character. But change is part of the show, and people always have a problem with it. But I think it's why they keep coming back.

How do you think the move to UPN will affect the series?

I don't think it'll affect it one iota. Any change that happens in the show will happen naturally because the show evolves. UPN has never said, 'Skew it this way, do this thing,' and they never will, because I'm not going to do it. I've had an unprecedented amount of control over the show, even for television, considering the show is a cult show. From the very start, The WB left me alone. You know, they collaborated, they didn't disappear, but they really let me do what I wanted. They trusted me. And UPN is on board for letting me do the show the way that works. I don't think anything will change. I mean, there'll be wrestling. But tasteful wrestling. Wrestling with a message behind it.[*]

I've got a quote here from a recent interview with James Marsters, who plays Spike on *Buffy*: 'Joss likes to stir it up. He likes a little chaos. He likes to piss people off. He likes to deny them what they want. He loves making people feel afraid.' Do you agree with that?

First of all, if you don't feel afraid, horror show not good. We learned early on, the scariest thing on that show was people behaving badly, or in peril, morally speaking, or just people getting weird on you — which, by the way, is the scariest thing in life. In terms of not giving people what they want, I think it's a mandate: don't give people what they want, give them what they need. What they want is for Sam and Diane to get together. [Whispers.] 'Don't give it to them. Trust me.' [Normal voice.] You know? People want the easy path, a happy resolution, but in the end, they're more interested in... No one's going to go see the story of Othello going to get a peaceful divorce. People want the tragedy. They need things to go wrong, they need the tension. In my characters, there's a core of trust and love that I'm very committed to. These guys would die for each other, and it's very beautiful. But at the same time, you can't keep that safety. Things have to go wrong, bad things have to happen.

RIPPER

As if Joss Whedon didn't have his hands full between *Buffy*, *Angel*, the comic book work and an upcoming *Buffy* animated series, he's also developing a new spin-off series with Anthony Stewart Head continuing in the role of Rupert Giles, now back in his native England. The proposed six-part spin-off, now dubbed *Ripper*, would be produced as a co-production with the BBC. Long-time *Buffy* fans will doubtless recognise 'Ripper' as Giles's college nickname, during the days when he was heavily involved in mystical (and on at least one occasion, demonic) activity. The series follows on from Head's desire to cut back on his involvement with *Buffy*, which is shot in LA, in order to spend more time with his family back in the UK. To that end, Giles is seen returning home in the show's sixth-season opener, following Buffy's death. It appears that his life won't be returning to normal anytime soon, as he gets involved with various monsters in his native land. 'I want to make a show that's very quiet, very adult,' Head has revealed, 'dealing with ghost stories, family metaphors and monsters representing what's wrong with us. Giles's show is a little more adult, with some genuine horror to it.'

---

* *UPN is well known for its wrestling shows, which even led to a crossover of sorts between the WWF and* Star Trek, *when The Rock appeared in an episode of UPN's* Voyager.

What's your method for balancing humour and drama when you're writing the show?

We get bored of one, and then switch to the other. I thought we got very dramatic last year, and I was like, 'We need more jokes this year!' Every year the balance falls one way or another. You've just got to keep your eye on it. All of my writers are extremely funny, so it's easy to make [*Buffy*] funnier. The hard part is getting the stuff that matters more. Our hardest work is to figure out the story. Getting the jokes in isn't a problem. We wanted to make that sort of short-attention-span, *The Simpsons*, cull-from-every-genre-all-the-time thing. 'You know, if we take this moment from *Nosferatu*, and this moment from *Pretty In Pink*, that'll make this possible. A little *Jane Eyre* in there, and then a little *Lethal Weapon 4*. Not *3*, but *4*. And I think this'll work.'

Does the writing itself come naturally to you, or do you have to set hours and force yourself to sit down and get it done?

It's like breathing. I'm not un-lazy, and I do procrastinate, but... Some of my writers sweat. The agony, they hate doing it, it's like pulling teeth. But for me, it comes easy. I love it. I don't rewrite, almost ever. I basically just sit down and write. Now my wife is making gestures about what a pompous ass I am. [Laughs.] And she's not wrong. But that's how it is. I love it. And I know these characters well enough that it comes maybe a little more naturally to me.

Have you gotten good at delegating, or do you really want to be doing all the writing yourself?

No, I have, and that was really hard for me. It was hard because I had such a specific vision, and nobody was seeing it. And so you have to do everything — props, costumes. Gradually, you surround yourself with people who do see it your way. I've worked for producers, and I know producers, who are true megalomaniacs, and need to write everything, and be responsible for everything, and get all the credit. And, although I am something of a control freak, if somebody does something right, I will not change a word. If the script works, if a costume is right, if an actor gets it, I'm not going to get in there just so I can have gotten in there. I've spent five years culling the most extraordinary staff, which I trust to share my vision and my experience. So if somebody gets it right, I leave it alone.

Do you think you'd ever be able to completely let go of a *Buffy* spin-off, leave it totally in someone else's hands?

It's possible. It's possible that I could. A while ago, I would have said, 'No.' But now I'm working on what will be four *Buffy* shows and three *Buffy* comics, and eventually you sort of go, 'Uh, maybe somebody else could do that other thing.' Would I be able to not have any hand in it at all? I think I just said 'yes' and meant 'no.' I don't want it to have my name on it if it doesn't reflect what I want to say. Because once you get to the position of actually getting to say something, which is a level most writers never even get to, and is a great blessing, you then have to worry about what it is you're actually saying. I don't want some crappy reactionary show under the *Buffy* name. If my name's going to be on it, it should be mine. Now, the books I have nothing to do with, and I've never read them. They could be, 'Buffy realised that abortion was wrong!' and I would have no idea. So, after my big, heartfelt, teary speech, I realise that I was once again lying. But I sort of drew the line. I was like, 'I can't possibly read these books!' But my name just goes on them as the person who created *Buffy*.

Are you ever worried about getting into a *Buffy* rut?

Yes. *Buffy* burnout big. I'm definitely eyeing some non-*Buffy*-related projects.

Besides *Iron Man*, are there any other scripts on the horizon?

I have a script idea that I'm just developing, one of the things I really want to do, but it's still embryonic, so I don't want to say anything about it. Though I'm sure you can read all about it now on the Ain't It Cool website.

And you'd direct that yourself if it ever actually became a film?

Yes. That's the next step. Part of the reason I made the TV show *Buffy* is because as a writer — even a successful one — in Hollywood, when you say you want to direct movies, they're appalled. They look like, 'Do you kill babies?' I mean, they're just shocked. 'What? You want to what?' 'I'm a storyteller. I want to tell stories. I want to direct.' 'Uh, I don't get it. You want to what?' And people actually said to me, 'Well, if you'd directed a video.' I'm like, just once, somebody please say to a video director, 'Well, if you'd written a script. If you just knew how to tell a story.' I mean, the percentage of video directors who have actually told stories. Not that all writers can direct, or should, or want to. I'm sure a lot of writers want to direct because they're bitter, which is not a reason to direct. I want to speak visually, and writing is just a way of communicating visually. That's what it's all about. But nobody would even consider me to direct. So I said, 'I'll create a television show, and I'll use it as a film school, and I'll teach myself to direct on TV.'

You still have some unproduced scripts floating around Hollywood. Do you have any interest in directing those yourself?

Well, there are a couple that I've sold, that have been through rewrites and hell and whatnot, and I've given up on them. I've moved on emotionally. I liked the scripts, and I wish they'd been made into movies, but I'm done with them. I want to do the next thing. There's one that I wrote that I never sold to anybody that I might think about. But really, why go back to the old stuff?

Has your cult success in TV sparked any interest in having other directors revive those scripts?

You'd think it would. Every now and then I hear a little buzz about them. But no. The two worlds, although people can move between them easily, they don't have much to do with each other. I'm still nobody. They're starting to notice me now, so that could change. But nobody in Hollywood seems to be saying, 'Hey, let's go talk to that Sweden guy.' When you get to, like, Stephen King level, then they want to film your sweatsocks. 'You wrote down a phone number? I'll option it!' But I'm not at that level.

How much involvement will you have with the *Buffy* animated series?

A great deal of involvement. We've got a bunch of scripts together, written by the *Buffy* writers, who know the characters and are the best writers I know. I expect my involvement to taper off as the show moves forward, but I'll still have control.

Given that the original *Buffy* and *Angel* are, as you've said, dark shows with sexual content, how will that translate to a Saturday-morning cartoon?

They're also shows with teen angst, empowered girls, funny little monsters, and lots of jokes. The writers are constantly making jokes we could never use [on the live-action show] because they're too silly, or abstract, or *Simpsons*-esque, and the cartoon is kind of our release valve for that. It's Buffy: Year One. Obviously, there's not going to be dark sexuality, because it's for kids. It's not for babies, but it's for kids. It's sort of Buffy: Year One, the untold stories, which is Willow loves Xander, Xander loves Buffy, Buffy sort of has a crush on this vampire guy who's a little bit older, Giles is in the library, Cordelia's a bitch, and it's going to stay year one as long as we can. Unlike the series, it's not about change. It's a chance to tell all of the high-school stories that we couldn't tell because they were only in high-school for two and a half years. Stories like the driving test, and having to eat cafeteria food, and all the little minor stuff that we can blow up into real stories. It's a very silly show. We refer to it as *Simpsons* Beyond.

Is it actually going to be called Buffy: Year One?

No, that's just the mandate for the series, in reference to Frank Miller's [graphic novel] *Batman: Year One*. *Buffy the Vampire Slayer: The Animated Series* is, I think, long enough.

Now that you've actually appeared in an episode of *Angel*, do you have the acting bug? Are you going to write yourself into more scripts?

I do and I don't. I've always had it, and I think it's part of being a writer and a director. It's knowing how you want things to be played. But I don't have the face — that's the problem — and I don't want the giant ego. I don't want to become Kevin Costner, singing on the soundtrack to *The Postman*. The acting bug, I mostly got the worst from doing our weekly Shakespeare readings.

Weekly Shakespeare readings?

Some of the writers and the cast and some friends from both shows come to the house on Sundays to do readings of plays. And it's incredible. I'm working with actors I know are great, and a lot of the writers have long careers in theatre. Some of them are carrying spears and saying 'Yes, sir,' and others have the big monologues, but we do it in shifts every week, and it's really tremendous.

How do you decide who gets what role?

Based on what people want, did they have a big role last time, were they really great. Some people get more big roles, some people don't want them. Some people are terrified by the prospect and refuse to come. I try to shift it around, try to make everybody do spear-carrying duty. It's extraordinary. More than putting on makeup for three hours and dancing around like an idiot, that really gives you the feeling of being inside a piece, really acting. It gives you perspective, which is good to have. It's not good that I should think of myself as a TV star, because I'm not. But it is good to be in touch with what an actor goes through, because it makes you better.

What would you like to be working on right now that you don't have time for?

My movie. I really want to get rolling on it.

What would you like to be doing just in general that you don't have time for?

Well, everything. The things that people do when they don't write. Playing games, sports maybe. Drinking and sex are things I've heard a lot about.

If you had *Buffy* to do over from the start, this time knowing how popular it would get, would you do anything differently?

Not in terms of popularity. I mean, there were certain things on the show that I learned the hard way, but not really. I love the show, and I love the people. I love the stories we told. I mean, I'm angry about every single edit, and line, and costume change, and rewrite, but that's part of the business. So ultimately, I wouldn't change anything. ∎

ROBERT HEWITT WOLFE

What would you do if somebody offered you the opportunity to create a new SF series loosely based on concepts by Gene Roddenberry? Well, if you were Robert Hewitt Wolfe, you'd say yes. The result is *Gene Roddenberry's Andromeda*, a futuristic action-adventure show, starring Kevin Sorbo (*Hercules: The Legendary Journeys*) as Dylan Hunt, a starship captain trying to bring order to a galaxy wracked by chaos. Wolfe was the perfect candidate to bring a new Roddenberry universe to life, as he had spent the past several years telling stories in the *Star Trek* milieu. After realising while he was at college that he really didn't want to be an electrical engineer, Wolfe switched to film school, originally aiming to write features. Work wasn't forthcoming, so when he got the opportunity to pitch for a TV show, he jumped at the chance. He successfully sold a story to *The Next Generation* during its sixth season — the holodeck-Western, 'A Fistful of Datas' — and was quickly drafted in to work on the new spin-off series, *Deep Space Nine*. It was the beginning of a long and productive run, which covered five seasons and included more than three dozen episodes to which he contributed. With *Andromeda*, executive producer Wolfe has now been able to make an elaborately plotted genre series of his own. This interview was conducted during production of *Andromeda*'s second season, as Wolfe was overseeing the final half-dozen scripts in development, as well as trouble-shooting the countless last-minute problems that crop up during shooting. In other words, business as usual...

How did you become a television writer after going to school to study electrical engineering?

I originally went to UCLA as an electrical engineering major, and did that for a year. Then one night, three weeks after spring break, I was in a dorm room at three o'clock in the morning with four other guys, working on physics problems, when I realised that I didn't want to do that for the rest of my life. That's what engineers do to a certain extent; they do math problems all day. So I left the engineering department. I'd always wanted to work in films, and frankly, I got into electrical engineering because at the time, when so many of the effects were still physical FX, I thought it would be a cool way to come into the special FX field. But as I realised that there was a film department at UCLA, and that I could actually study film to get into film, I started drifting in that direction, although I had a bunch of other majors by the time I finally got into film school. You couldn't get into the film school at UCLA until you were a junior; you had to apply at the end of your sophomore year, so I'd done a year or so dabbling around campus, and then got into film school, and got my bachelor's degree in film. I then got my master's degree in screenwriting, because I couldn't get any work, so I got a fellowship to go back to school, and it was a way of getting paid to write.

I did that for two more years, and then started banging my head against the wall for a while, until I finally got a pitch at *The Next Generation*, because my agent represented one of the other writers there. But I'd never written any television at all; I'd never even written television specs because I'd always been emphasising feature stuff. But I got in, and I eventually sold them 'A Fistful of Datas' as a pitch, and they hired me to write the episode. They liked what I did, and hired me as a freelancer to write another episode, 'Q-Less' for *Deep Space Nine*. They liked that one too, so they hired me on staff.

When the producers on *TNG* or *DS9* found a writer who 'got' the show, wouldn't they often try to put them on staff?

That's basically it: I showed them that I was on their wavelength, and they hired me on staff. That was Michael Piller's theory — he liked to try people out as freelancers, then hire them. I did that myself with Zack Stentz and Ashley Miller on *Andromeda*.

So when you wrote 'A Fistful of Datas' for *TNG*, that was really on-the-job training?

Basically yes, that whole six year process was; it was all on-the-job training for writing in television, so *Star Trek* was sort of my post-graduate studies, as it was for a lot of people. There are some very good writers who have come out of *Star Trek*, and working for Ira Behr and Michael Piller on *Deep Space Nine* was a really great educational experience for me, and René [Echevarria] and Ron [Moore]. It's a testament to the education that we all got while working for them. One of the things I'm most proud of about *Deep Space Nine* is that me, Hans [Beimler], Ira, René and Ron are all either

ROBERT HEWITT WOLFE

Date/Place of Birth:
1964, Waterbury, Connecticut, USA

Home Base:
Los Angeles, California, USA

Education:
UCLA; UCLA Film School

First TV Work:
Star Trek: The Next Generation 'A Fistful of Datas'

TV Career Highlights:
Star Trek: The Next Generation, Star Trek: Deep Space Nine, Futuresport, Gene Roddenberry's Andromeda

running or co-running a show right now[*]. We're all either the number one or number two guys on our own show. Hans did *The District* for a year, and before that, he was on *Profiler*, always as the number two guy, and now he's on *The Chronicle*. So we've all done really well, and I think that's a testament to the quality of the writing on *DS9* and the quality of the people we worked for.

Do you feel that much of the success of the writing on *DS9* was due to Ira Behr as head writer and executive producer?

That's absolutely right. Michael was completely there for the first year, but then he went off to start working on *Voyager* pretty rapidly thereafter, and even in the first year, Michael relied on Ira a lot. I think Ira was the head writer for five and a half of the seven years on the show, and was definitely there and a very strong presence for the other year and a half.

When did the two of you realise that you could write together?

I can't remember the first time we actually started writing in the room together. We always talked a lot about story, and obviously everything I did in season one went through him when I was working as a staff writer. He gave me very thorough notes, and we talked a lot about specific scenes, and I think that continued throughout the second season. But that was to be expected, because I was a staff writer and he was co-

RON MOORE

Ronald D. Moore was a devoted *Star Trek* fan who spent the better part of a decade exploring the final frontier, after his spec script 'The Bonding' led to a job as story editor on *The Next Generation* during its third season. Moore not only established himself as the show's resident Klingon writer, but also proved to be quite adept at telling stories on a big canvas — as seen by his work on the two-hour *TNG* finale 'All Good Things' or the feature films *Star Trek Generations* and *Star Trek: First Contact*. When *The Next Generation* ended, Moore moved on to *Deep Space Nine*, where he proved equally prolific over the next several seasons. A brief but less satisfying stint on *Voyager* followed, as well as the script for *Mission Impossible 2* (written with fellow *Trek* writer Brannon Braga). Moore then joined the staff of the tongue-in-cheek supernatural cop show *G Vs E* for the last half of its one-season run. Meanwhile, he was also developing a series based on the *Dragonriders of Pern* novels, but that project was shelved just as cameras were set to roll. Moore is currently writing about aliens once again, as a producer on *Roswell*.

[*] *Moore is currently co-executive producer on* Roswell *(see box), while Echevarria recently took over as executive producer on* Dark Angel *(see page 85). Behr has been working on several projects (see page 237), while Beimler is a producer on the* The Chronicle.

executive producer, and I was working for him. I think there was a point where we actually sat down and started writing some scenes together. I can't remember which script it was on, but I know it really started to coalesce more with him. I don't have a chronology of scripts in front of me, but I know we did a lot of work together on 'The Jem'Hadar'; we also did a lot of work together on 'The Wire', even though my name is on 'The Wire' and his name is on 'The Jem'Hadar'. But we still weren't in the room working on it together every day. And then we did — it was either 'The Collaborator' or 'Second Sight', anyway, it was one of those two, because it needed rewriting, so we were rewriting in the same room together all the time. I'd rather say it was 'The Collaborator', because that one actually worked by the time we were done with it. I'd hate to say we figured out that we could work really well together on what was ultimately not a very good episode! But we enjoyed working together, and then as he started being executive producer, obviously it helped me tremendously as a writer. When Ira was head writer and executive producer, he didn't have a lot of free time — something I now know all about! What was nice for him, I think, was that together, the two of us were able to write something very quickly. We could do all the writing work we needed to do in the morning before lunch; we were *blindingly* fast together when we needed to be, and I think that was a big help to both of us.

Did you pretty much write with one person sitting at the computer and the other pacing back and forth?

It was usually me at the computer, because frankly Ira can't type! He'd sit next to me or pace back and forth and look over my shoulder and talk to me, and that was how it all worked out. That was how we worked, although other writing teams do it differently. Neither of the writing teams on my staff ever work in the same room together, which has always mystified me, but I think for me, the best way to do it is to have one person sitting at the typewriter and somebody pacing around. What's the point of having a writing partner if you have to be in the room by yourself?

On *DS9*, would you and Ira write scripts from stories that the whole staff had come up with together, as a group?

Usually, or it could be stuff that just Ira and I would sit down and talk about. We could come up with ideas for scripts, and then do them together. Sometimes an idea would come up in the room with the rest of the staff, or sometimes there would be a pitch from a freelancer that we would shepherd; no two scripts would ever be developed the same way.

Do you find that you're more comfortable writing by yourself or with a partner?

It's apples and oranges. There are some things that are really great about writing with someone else, especially someone you really enjoy writing with. In some ways, you get a lot more done per hour, because you don't have an excuse to goof off. There's usually only a limited amount of time when the two of you can work together, so you'd better get it done. And then there are some things that I don't like as much about it, because it's not a hundred per cent yours, and you have to make compromises with the other writer... so there are strengths and weaknesses to it. I love writing with Ira, but I also like writing by myself. I'm writing with Hans right now on a spec feature script. Part of the problem is that we never have any time to get together, but it's fun, and we're having a good time.

Were there certain aspects of writing for *DS9*, specific characters perhaps, that appealed to you in particular?

It was just a great show to write for, and I liked everything about it. That was something like five years and thirty-odd episodes. I really loved all the characters, they were all fun to write for. I thought Sisko was a really cool and interesting character, but also a difficult one, which made him even more fun to write for. Plus you just knew that Avery [Brooks] would always do some really cool stuff with whatever you wrote for him, so that was nice. Although I liked writing for all the characters, I suppose I had a particular affinity for Dr Bashir, because Sid [actor Alexander Siddig] and I are almost exactly the same age, although I'm not half-British, half-Sudanese, but we're both lanky proportioned guys. I've always had an affinity for Bashir, so when I turned thirty, we did an episode about him turning thirty, that kind of thing. But I also identified a little bit with Jake Sisko, being an officer's son myself, so it made that character interesting and fun to write. And then that whole universe was really cool and exciting too. There wasn't a single character on that show that I didn't enjoy writing for.

When you decided to leave the series at the end of season five, did you feel that you'd run out of stories to tell?

That was pretty much the case, and it was a tremendously difficult decision. It was probably one of the harder decisions I've ever had to make in my life. I had a contract for year six, and I could certainly have been there for year seven, but I guess I felt like I'd done all I could do for the show. I didn't want to be writing for the show and not enjoying it, or be tired and not giving it my best effort, because I thought that would be doing the show a disservice. It wouldn't have been fair to Ira or the other writers for me to be 'half' there. To grow further as a writer, I felt that I needed to move on.

Did you literally wake up one morning and think to yourself, 'I don't have any more ideas'?

It wasn't that I didn't have any more ideas — I did come back and write for them again in year seven ['Field of Fire']. It was just a growing realisation that I didn't want to be going through the motions. It wasn't that I couldn't have done it, and in fact, I talked with Ira about it for a long time, and one of the things I said was, 'I'll do this if you want me to, if you really need me here, I'll be here.' And he basically said, 'If you need to go, you need to go,' so it was a slow dawning thing. It wasn't like I woke up one morning and said, 'Oh my God, the well is dry...' You don't have that luxury of drying up when you have a mortgage!

That last season five episode you wrote was 'Call to Arms', during which the cast recorded a special 'goodbye Robert' scene. Did that surprise you?

That was a really cool thing for them to do. It was really moving, and I also got dragged off the show bleeding in that episode!* It was really nice, and everybody was terrific about it. Ira was very understanding, and the cast was great, and I really enjoyed working there.

Some people might think going off to write the TV movie _Futuresport_ may not have been the best career move you could have made after leaving _DS9_.

The truth of the matter is, I went off and did a lot of different things. One of the main things I wanted to do was the feature I was working on for Fox, which is a great script, but has never been done, for various and sundry reasons. The feature world is a huge crap-shoot, and the proportion of things that get developed and actually get made is very skewed when compared to television. I had really wanted to pursue that specific

---

IRA BEHR

Few people had more of an influence in shaping _Deep Space Nine_ than head writer and executive producer Ira Steven Behr. A relative newcomer to SF before his work in the _Star Trek_ franchise, Behr's previous non-genre credits included _Once a Hero_, _The Bronx Zoo_, _Fame_, _Brett Maverick_ and _Jessica Novak_. He joined the _Next Generation_ staff during season three, working on 'Yesterday's Enterprise,' 'Captain's Holiday', and 'Qpid' before moving on. Behr found the show's format restrictive, but was interested in Michael Piller's offer to join _Deep Space Nine_, which promised a bit more inter-personal conflict and edgier stories than were possible on _TNG_. That decision turned out to be a judicious one. After Piller's departure, Behr took over as head of the writing staff, quickly placing his own distinctive stamp on the series and its characters. Over _DS9_'s seven-year history, he was credited on more than fifty episodes, either as solo writer, or with long-time collaborators Robert Hewitt Wolfe and Hans Beimler. Following the end of _DS9_, Behr began developing his own projects, including a possible genre series called _ESPers_, and the sitcom _Bob Alexander_, starring Jason Alexander (_Seinfeld_), though the latter proved very short lived.

---

* _Wolfe is seen as an injured crewman limping past Dax and Worf. The 'goodbye' scene, recorded just for Wolfe and presented to him on a videocassette, featured the main cast, each holding up a sign reading '(sad)' as they said farewell._

feature, and *Futuresport** was just a rewrite job that I got offered. It's the *Citizen Kane* of futuristic sports movies I suppose, but it's never going to be much more than that. But frankly, we did think that we could have made a pretty cool series out of it, a way of doing a show about fame and sports and all that stuff; that whole culture of over-identification with athletes, and the difficulties involved in that. If it was going to be made into a series, we wanted the show to be about the guy who blows out his knee and can't play anymore, the union strikes, the referee strike, the behind-the-scenes negotiations; I think that's a very rich and interesting field. The movie turned out pretty well, but like I said, I only came on it as a rewrite job, and then kept rewriting it and rewriting it. I was hired to do one rewrite, and then they kept hiring me back to do more things. But they never really hired me on as a producer, always just a writer, so I wasn't really able to supervise it once it was in production. I think it could maybe have been better, but who knows?

Didn't you also work on something called *Splicers*?

That was the feature I was just talking about, which never got produced. I've had some interest, and I've sold it twice, the second time to Fox. I own it again now, so if you want to buy it, it's for sale! It's a cool project, but it's very expensive. I had some people looking at it last week, and they really liked it and they were very interested, but they were in the business of making $30 to $50 million movies, or even less, but certainly not $100 million, which is probably what the minimum cost would be to make *Splicers*. That's part of the reason why it's been very difficult to get it started and launched. It's a *Spartacus*-y kind of thing. It's about genetically engineered soldiers who are slaves, and the truth is, when I wrote it, there were five movies about enhanced soldiers that came out on the spec market at the same time. One of them was *Universal Soldier*, and then there was *Rogue Trooper* [based on the *2000AD* comic strip], *Tail Gunner Joe*, *Soldier* and mine. So *Universal Soldier* got made, and in the next go round, mine was in development at Fox, and *Soldier* was in development at Warner Bros and they made *Soldier* first. Even though they're very different stories on a total-ly different scale, I think that was part of the reason why Fox decided not to go through with it. Getting a feature film made is a really long, difficult and uphill strug-gle, and it just didn't work out for *Splicers* this go round, but now there's only me, *Tail Gunner Joe* and *Rogue Trooper* left, so maybe it will be my turn the next time.

Is it true that you can be a successful feature writer in Hollywood and never get a movie produced?

Two of our freelancers on *Andromeda* this year, John Parry and Eric Oleson, are both very successful feature writers, neither of whom have had anything produced. Their first produced credits will be episodes of *Andromeda*, despite the fact that John Parry has been a working screenwriter in Los Angeles for eight years, and Eric Oleson has been doing it for two or three years, and yet neither of them has had anything on screen. They're 'overnight success' stories — eight years and three years. So it's not

---

* *Futuresport (1998) starred Dean Cain (Lois and Clark) and, in a supporting role, Wesley Snipes (who also produced). The hoped-for series was never commissioned.*

anecdotal, there really are people who work for ten or twenty years as feature writers and never get a screen credit.

When you began work on developing *Andromeda*, how much did you actually have to work with in terms of notes and concepts left behind by Gene Roddenberry?

I had a big pile of notes, but very few of them were specific to this project. The central concept was pretty simple, but he hadn't written a lot of things down. It was more like, 'What other things would I do for a starship show?' So that was very thin; there was almost nothing there. There was a great deal of general material, but the truth of the matter is, by the time you go through it and distil it all down, the things of Gene's are the central premise of a man restoring civilisation after being asleep for a long time — which was a theme he revisited several times — the character of Dylan Hunt, and the central idea of a sentient starship. There was a ton of other material, and I tried to put in fun little references to a lot of the other stuff he'd done at various points in time, but by and large, that's really what was there. All the other characters, the nature of the universe, the type of technology we use, the back story of the Commonwealth and the specificity of the civilisation (for example, the fact that Dylan's mom was from a heavy gravity world), none of that was there. It was just those very broad concepts. It was basically a springboard, but those are also the most essential elements of the show. In some ways, this show is more Gene's than *Deep Space Nine* was. In *Deep Space Nine*, we had a background and universe that he created and nothing else, including the themes or principal characters. None of those were Gene's. In this show, the principal theme, the main character, the main drive of the show and the nature of the ship, those are all Gene's. The background is not, so it's sort of the opposite situation. Basically, Gene had an acorn, which I lovingly grew into an oak tree, but it's Gene's acorn.

Both Dorothy Fontana and Michael Piller, who were interviewed for this book, had their own comments on Gene Roddenberry's utopia-like vision of the future. Did you try to use part of that vision in *Andromeda*?

I think Gene was not a simple guy; he was a complicated man. I never met him myself, but I read a lot of his stuff, and specifically in regard to *The Next Generation*, he wanted to portray a more evolved civilisation, one with less conflict and with a better fellowship of man, for lack of a better term. The man developed six television shows, although only two of them really saw the light of day, so he did a lot of different things. You can look at the original *Star Trek* series and what he was trying to do there, and what he was later trying to do in *The Next Generation*, and I think they're two very different things. I think Dorothy is seeing the original series Gene, and Michael was probably seeing the *Next Generation* Gene, but that doesn't make either of them wrong. In some ways, I think it's harder to write *The Next Generation* because of the inability to use character conflict as a principal engine for the show. I didn't have to worry about that in *Andromeda*, because the situation was so different. It wasn't about the Commonwealth at its height, with a lot of people trying to do a lot of really good things. It was about all kinds of screwed up people trying to do good things, so it was a different paradigm.

On *Andromeda*, we've shown that the original Systems Commonwealth did have some warts. I guess I'm not comfortable with a utopian kind of simplicity. I don't think there's been an ideal government or organisation, ever. Even the most ideal organisations can make mistakes, so I don't think it's fair to portray the perfect little fantasy government. Okay, we're going into political theory here, but my feeling is, you can have a very good government, but you have to work really hard to have it. To imply that you have a perfect government, and that you don't have to work *really* hard to keep going, is not a good message to send, I think. To a certain extent, it inspires hope to say that there could be a government like the Federation, but if I had an issue with *The Next Generation*, it was the idea that maintaining that level of perfect utopia didn't seem to be a huge effort for them. I think it should have required a lot of work, and we should have been more realistic about it. We should be inspiring people to work to get to that future, to embrace the goal, but also embrace the work you need to do to get to the goal.

THE FIRST DYLAN HUNT

Gene Roddenberry will forever be known as the creator of *Star Trek*, but many of his other forays into SF television weren't nearly as successful. In 1973, he created the pilot called *Genesis II*, about a scientist named Dylan Hunt (Alex Cord) who awakens from suspended animation in a post-apocalyptic 2133. Earth's scientists have banded together as the peace-loving group Pax, while mutant Tyranians attempt to rebuild pre-war nuclear technology. The pilot wasn't picked up. A year later, Roddenberry tried again with a reworking of the same concept called *Planet Earth*, starring John Saxon in the lead, but that didn't lead to a series either. Ironically, the notion of Dylan Hunt, awakening from suspended animation in the future, became a core concept of *Gene Roddenberry's Andromeda*. 1974 also saw the screening of *The Questor Tapes*, starring Robert Foxworth (in a role reportedly written for Leonard Nimoy) as a human-like android trying to track down his mysterious creator. And in 1977, there was *Spectre*, featuring Robert Culp and Gig Young as a pair of occult investigators. A forerunner to *The X-Files*, it may have been a few decades ahead of its time. Recent years have seen a renewed interest in Roddenberry projects, thanks to *Earth: Final Conflict* and *Andromeda*. A third series, *Gene Roddenberry's Starship*, remains unproduced.

How did you go about assembling your writing staff on *Andromeda*?

Basically, I got a huge stack of scripts to read. A lot of them were given to me by Tribune and Fireworks [*Andromeda*'s co-production companies], while others were given to me by various agents. I'd met Matt [Kiene] and Joe [Reinkemeyer] a couple of times before, so I knew their work, but I looked at it again and thought they had a certain intelligence and a certain focus on this sort of high concept show, but could still explore character, so they were a fairly easy choice. I'd never met Ethlie [Ann Vare] before, but Tribune had worked with her and recommended her to me. So I read some of her scripts, and thought she was a very smart writer with a lot of energy. The shows she had worked on were of varying degrees of quality, but her scripts always read as very smart. I thought it was very important to have a woman on the staff; when three of your main characters are women, it's good to have that perspective. So we had our staff, the four of us were working together, and then we invited Zack [Stentz], who I knew as a journalist, and Ashley [Miller] in to pitch. They were one of our first pitches, and they sold us something like four great stories in one go, so we assigned 'D-Minus Zero' to them and they did a really nice job on it. I had been saving a space for a young writer or writing team that delivered on a freelance script and they definitely delivered, so we brought them in.

Do staff writers each have their own areas of speciality within the series?

Yes, but I think you'd also be foolish to stereotype writers. On *Star Trek*, to say that Ron Moore could only do Klingon shows for example, would be a disservice to Ron, and to the show if you locked yourself into that. Yes, it becomes evident that certain writers have an affinity for certain characters or certain types of story, but I also believe that good writers always want to push themselves and try new things. To use that same example, sometimes it's fun to get another writer to do a Klingon story so you get a different feel for that episode, or to have Ron write an outright comedy like 'In the Cards'. I thought he did a great job with that episode, and it wasn't the kind of show you would usually associate with him. Not every show that René did had to end with somebody crying! On *Andromeda*, 'A Rose in the Ashes' was not a very successful episode, but it was a successful Dylan script, so to say Ethlie writes Beka stories the best, yeah, maybe, but she also writes good Dylan shows, and she writes well for all of the characters. Just because Matt and Joe have ended up writing a lot of shows featuring our genetically enhanced race, the Nietzscheans, because they enjoy that culture, it doesn't mean that anybody else on the staff shouldn't be writing Nietzschean shows, or that Matt and Joe should only be writing those shows.

Did you apply some of the lessons you had learned from *Star Trek* to *Andromeda* in terms of creating a staff, breaking stories and so forth?

That was a model, yes. I think Ira is a terrific show runner, and so is Michael. I wanted to apply some of the lessons I learned on that show about how to run a staff, how to break stories and how to keep the writing going on a reasonable schedule, so you don't get into crises. That was one of the things we did really well on *Deep Space Nine*. We were almost always ahead of shooting, and almost never delivered a script any later than the first day of pre-production, and usually far in advance of that, so that was one of my goals on this show too. We did twenty-six episodes a year on *Deep Space Nine*, and we only do twenty-two episodes on *Andromeda*, so my feeling was if we could deliver that on *DS9* with twenty-six episodes, we had no excuses not to do it with twenty-two! That was one of the things I set out to do, and I think we've been able to accomplish it as a staff.

Is it difficult for freelancers to 'get' *Andromeda* at this point, after only a season or so?

There are four writing entities on the staff, and twenty-two episodes a year, so each of us usually writes four or five episodes a year. If you do the math, that only leaves maybe three or four episodes a year to freelance out. Last year, we had the one for Walter [Jon Williams], the one for Steve [Barnes], so we freelanced out two episodes. This year, by the time all is said and done, we'll have freelanced out three — two to the same guy, because he definitely got the show — and we actually brought another writer in house to get ready for the writers' strike which then didn't happen, so Emily [Skopov] did two. We don't need freelancers all that much, and it is a hard assignment. SF shows in general are tough to nail, and it's tough to nail a show that's only been on the air for a year, because you don't see all that much of it. But we've had pretty good luck with our freelancers. Ashley and Zack started out as freelancers, and John Parry who we used this year did a nice job. Eric Oleson, who we also used this year did a really nice job. And Walter brought a lot of cool ideas to the show he did, 'All Great Neptune's Ocean'. He'd never done a screenplay, so for somebody who'd never written for television before, I think he did some good stuff. I think that episode was a failure much more because of some other technical problems, I don't think the script was all that bad. There are still some very nice scenes in it. And then Steve did a nice job coming in on 'The Sum of Its Parts', which again, was a very tricky episode, but the script was nice, so we've had good luck with our freelancers.

Did you find that some freelancers would dust off their old *Star Trek* pitches and bring them to you?

Constantly, and we said no. We would explain to them why that was not going to work, and they'd try again. I think people have seen a lot of *Star Trek*, and especially a lot of *TNG*. I've had people bring in *TNG* pitches to us; they used to bring in *TNG* pitches to *DS9* and we'd turn them down because that was a very different show. It's not unusual, I'm sure the people on *Law and Order* get dusted-off *Murder, She Wrote* scripts!

Should TV pitches have an expiration date so they can't be recycled over and over again?

If that were true, *Andromeda* wouldn't have had 'Angel Dark, Demon Bright', because that was a recycled show, one I'd wanted to do on *Deep Space Nine* but had never been able to. If you work them through, some shows can be moved from place to place, but a lot of people don't do the work. They don't file the serial numbers off; they don't take the time to make it an *Andromeda* episode. I think some ideas can work on pretty much any show if you tailor them to that show, while some ideas are so specific to the tone of the show you've created them for, there's just no getting around that.

Do you sit down with your staff at the beginning of a season to map it all out?

Not really. What we do is have a bunch of overall meetings about the kinds of stories we want to do. We try and get four or five stories in place as building blocks for the season, but there's enough chaos in television that I don't think it's smart to figure out where you're going to be a year ahead. You can have general goals, but if you get locked into stuff like that, you can get into a lot of trouble. I think we knew where we wanted to go, but frankly, this year's season finale is not going to be the season finale that I thought it was going to be a year ago, for a variety of reasons. We did sort of know what we thought the last episode of the season was going to be, and where we were going, but that's not where we're going now! We know how the season is supposed to end, and we know all the big secrets, so we're trying to figure out the best way to get there, sometimes on a day-to-day basis. It just depends on the circumstances.

Will you ask the writers to specifically come up with, say, a story based around Trance, or a Harper story?

Absolutely, you'll look at the schedule and say, 'We've got thirteen episodes in the works right now, and none of them are about Trance, so let's find something for her.' But then we also get a situation where we obviously want to do a lot of stories about Dylan because he's our lead, so it's a balancing act. The majority of the shows are about Dylan, so it's really a matter of picking and choosing places to give the other characters 'B' stories, or even 'A' stories that are about them.

Did you sit down at the end of *Andromeda*'s first season and do a post-mortem of what worked and didn't work?

I think a lot of our re-tooling was done on the fly, so we'd reached a pretty good place by the last four or five episodes of season one. Frankly, the kind of things that we found were mostly production, not writing-based. But we found that we did best, with our alien make-up for example, when we had a very long run-up. So one of the things we did was decide in advance the three or four different alien species we would do this year, how we would do each of them, what they would look like, and where in the season we would give them their first roll-outs. That gave our opticals and FX and make-up people a lot more time to try to work these things out. Part of that is a budgetary thing; our budget is quite low for the kind of episodes we're doing, so the more time they have to work on these things, the better. We also found that although our first location shoot last year, which was 'Rose in the Ashes', was not very good, we were doing a lot better by the end of the year, and it was worth going out as much as we could.

So we really put an emphasis on stories that would take us outside, or explore different sets that we didn't build. We thought that opened up the show quite nicely. And then just emphasising certain relationships between the characters, and exploring ones that we had under-utilised, but that's basically one of the things you do at the end of every year. You say, 'Okay, which relationship did we not explore? Which relationship really worked, that we want to keep going back to? Which ones have we been ignoring that we want to emphasise some more?'

You really didn't have any attrition in your writing staff between seasons, did you?

That was definitely the goal. I spent a lot of time looking for writers who I thought could pull the show off, and frankly there are a lot of show runners and a lot of production companies and studios that believe in shaking up the staff. I strongly feel that continuity in a show is an important thing, especially with this kind of show, which has a very specific style. These kinds of shows are not easy to write, and there aren't a lot of people that can do them, so I don't believe in change for change's sake. I think it can be quite destructive. There wasn't a lot of shake-up on *Deep Space Nine* from season to season either. There was some, but if you look at the history of that show, Michael built the staff over time, so I guess that's the school I came from. If you've got people who can do the job, you stand by them.

Do you give your actors a lot of background information on their characters, or is it more or less on a 'need to know' basis?

I really don't feel that it does people a service to give them everything we know about their character, because my feeling is that everything we know about their characters is what is in the scripts up to that point, with one exception. Trance is the only character where I felt that the actress really needed as much information as I could give her, so I told Laura [Bertram] everything I know about Trance. The truth is, I think I tell the actors everything I do know about their characters at any given time, but trying not to give them stuff that may change. I think the only thing that matters is what's been on screen and what's in the scripts.

Is there a long-term plan for *Andromeda*?

Only in the vaguest possible sense. I definitely know where I want each of the characters to end up, but they may not end up there. Television is a chaotic medium, and things change. For example, I never would have thought in a million years that Dax would marry Worf; I don't think anybody on *Deep Space Nine* did, or that she would die. Frankly, I think we all felt that Terry [Farrell] would be on the show until the end. I actually argued against their relationship, but had I known that she was going to die, I would have argued for it. It all kind of worked out, but no one knew at the time. To a certain extent, there are some things you just can't plan for.

So you favour a more organic evolution for the characters?

Exactly, because otherwise things begin to feel forced. I think you run into the danger of feeling like the story is driving the characters, and the characters aren't always the same people at the end of two or three seasons as they were at the beginning of their first season; they may not act the same. It may not feel natural any more for them to do certain things, so if you get locked into a certain agenda, you run the risk of distorting the story you want to tell because you're forcing it, and you can't force things in story-telling.

If you'd planned all along that Little John was going to kill Robin Hood, say, and you get to season three and you're like, 'Little John wouldn't do that anymore!' because it's so clear that he's not that guy — if you do it anyway, the audience will feel betrayed. You're not playing fair; you have to make sure that the relationships are still appropriate to do that. You may even have been foreshadowing it three years ahead, but then get to a point where you realise it's just not going to happen. So then you realise that what you were really foreshadowing was that it was something that the character was *thinking* about, but he was never actually going to do it. There were things like that on *Deep Space Nine*, where we were foreshadowing X, and it turned out that X wasn't going to work, but it turned out great because we realised we were foreshadowing Y. I do feel like you need to let the story grow organically though. That's not to say you should have no plan at all, but that plan may have to change.

From a writing perspective, are things going relatively smoothly on *Andromeda*'s second season?

The process of writing television is never easy, but by now in the process, I've reached a certain comfort level and so have the writing staff, about what we feel we want the show to be, and the types of stories we tell well. We're more than halfway through the second season, but we're always learning. If the writing on a show is not constantly improving, you're not doing your job right. I think we had a pretty good idea what we were going to try and do at the beginning, but you experiment, you push a little bit here and there, and you see what works and what doesn't.

I think we also have a better feeling now, after some thirty-odd episodes, for what the actors can do. A lot of those things are still a mystery when you first come in. You hope that everything you write will be delivered beautifully, but in reality, you have new guest stars every week, and you never really know if they're going to pull off what they did in the room when you auditioned them. Television has a lot of committee processes, so sometimes we cast people who weren't my first or even second choice, because they were somebody else's first or second choices, and it's been a crap-shoot sometimes. With the central cast, we went through an exhaustive auditioning process, but even then, it's still difficult to know a hundred per cent what everyone can do. We've been very blessed and very lucky on *Andromeda* that we have a very talented cast that definitely delivers what we ask of them, and that gives us a great deal of freedom as writers to try difficult and interesting scenes.

Are you interested in working on non-SF shows in the future?

There are a lot of very good things about working on a show like *Andromeda*, and frankly, there are certain non-SF shows I would have no interest in writing for because they just don't appeal to me. There are some other ones that do, though... ∎

INDEX OF TV SHOW CREDITS

The following A-Z index of TV shows aims to provide a guide to the key series discussed in this book. The regular and main recurring cast are given for each show, and while the crew/production credits are not exhaustive, they cover the main writing/producing credits (and certainly include all the people mentioned in passing in the book). The credits of the interviewees themselves are picked out in bold type. The numbers in brackets refer to the season, eg (3) refers to season three.

Angel
1999-
Mutant Enemy Inc/Kuzui Enterprises Inc/Sandollar Television Inc in association with Twentieth Century Fox
Creator: **David Greenwalt, Joss Whedon**
Executive Producer: Gail Berman, **David Greenwalt**, Fran Rubel Kuzui, Kaz Kuzui, Marti Noxon, **Joss Whedon**
Co-Executive Producer: Tim Minear (3)
Consulting Producer: Howard Gordon (1), Jim Kouf (2-), Marti Noxon
Supervising Producer: Tim Minear (2)
Producer: Gareth Davies (1), Kelly A. Manners, Tim Minear (1), Marti Noxon (3-), Shawn Ryan (2), Tracey Stern (1)
Co-Producer: James A. Contner (1), Skip Schoolnik
Associate Producer: Robert Price
Writer (selected): Meredyth Smith (2)
Main cast: David Boreanaz (Angelus 'Angel'), Charisma Carpenter (Cordelia Chase), Alexis Denisof (Wesley Wyndham-Price), J. August Richards (Charles Gunn), Glenn Quinn (Allen Francis Doyle, 1), Elisabeth Rohm (Kate Lockley), Keith Szarabajka (Horst, 3)
See p148-161 **David Greenwalt:** Creator, Executive Producer, Writer, Director
See p212-231 **Joss Whedon:** Creator, Executive Producer, Writer, Director

Babylon 5
1993-8
Babylonian Productions Inc, Rattlesnake Productions Inc (pilot)
Executive Producer: Douglas Netter, **J. Michael Straczynski**
Producer: Robert Latham Brown (pilot), Richard Compton, John Copeland
Writer (selected): Peter David (1-2), Lawrence DiTillio (1-2), Kathryn M. Drennan (1), **D. C. Fontana** (1),

Neil Gaiman (5), David Gerrold (1), Christy Marx (1)
Director: John Copeland (4-5)
Production Design: John Iacovelli
Cast: Michael O'Hare (Jeffrey David Sinclair, 1-3/Valen, 3), Bruce Boxleitner (John Sheridan, 2-5), Jerry Doyle (Michael Alfredo Garibaldi), Claudia Christian (Susan Ivanova, 1-4), Mira Furlan (Delenn), Richard Biggs (Dr Stephen Franklin), Peter Jurasik (Londo Molari), Andreas Katsulas (G'Kar), Andrea Thompson (Talia Winters, 1-2), Bill Mumy (Lenier), Stephen Furst (Vir Cotto), Ardwright Chamberlain/Jeffrey Willerth (Vorlon Ambassador Kosh Naranek, 1-3/Vorlon Ambassador Ulkesh Naranek, 3), Jeff Conaway (Zack Allan, 2-5), Jason Carter (Ranger Marcus Cole, 2-4), Tracy Scoggins (Captain Elizabeth Lochley, 5), Patricia Tallman (Lyta Alexander, 1, 3-5), Walter Koenig (Alfred Bester, recurring)
See p180-195 **J. Michael Straczynski**: Creator, Executive Producer, Writer, Director (5)

Buffy the Vampire Slayer
1997-
Mutant Enemy Inc/Kuzui Enterprises Inc/Sandollar Television Inc in association with Twentieth Century Fox
Creator: **Joss Whedon**
Executive Producer: Gail Berman, Sandy Gallin, **David Greenwalt** (2-3), Fran Rubel Kuzui, Kaz Kuzui, **Joss Whedon**
Co-Executive Producer: **David Greenwalt** (1), Marti Noxon
Consulting Producer: Howard Gordon, **David Greenwalt** (4-)
Supervising Producer: David Fury, Marti Noxon
Producer: Gareth Davies, Jane Espenson, David Fury
Co-Producer: Marc D. Alpert, Jane Aspenson, James A. Contner, Gary Law, Kelly A. Manners, Marti Noxon, John F. Perry, Douglas Petrie, David Solomon
Writer (selected): Howard Gordon (2), Joe

Reinkemeyer (1-2)

Casting: Marcia Schulman (1)

Main cast: Sarah Michelle Gellar (Buffy Anne Summers), Nicholas Brendon (Alexander 'Xander' Lavelle Harris), Alyson Hannigan (Willow Rosenberg), Anthony Stewart Head (Rupert Giles), David Boreanaz (Angelus 'Angel', 1-3/4 recurring), Charisma Carpenter (Cordelia Chase, 1-3), Seth Green (Daniel 'Oz' Osborne, 2-4), Michelle Trachtenberg (Dawn Summers, 5-), Emma Caulfield (Anya Emerson, 4-), James Marsters (Spike aka William the Bloody, 2-), Alexis Denisof (Wesley Wyndham-Price, 3)

See p148-161 **David Greenwalt:** Executive Producer, Co-Executive Producer, Consulting Producer, Writer (1-3), Director (2-3)

See p212-231 **Joss Whedon:** Creator, Executive Producer, Writer, Director

Dark Angel

2000-

Cameron/Eglee Productions

Creator: James Cameron, **Charles H. Eglee**

Executive Producer: James Cameron, **Charles H. Eglee**

Co-Executive Producer: René Echevarria, Joe Ann Fogle

Consulting Producer: David Simkins

Supervising Producer: Patrick Harbinson

Coordinating Producer: Janace Tashjian

Producer: Rae Sanchini, Stephen Sassen

Co-Producer: Ron French, George A. Grieve, Stephen Tashjian

Associate Producer: Gina Lamar

Main cast: Jessica Alba (Max Guevara aka X-5 452), Michael Weatherly (Logan Cale aka Eyes Only), Jensen Ackles (Alec, 2), Alimi Ballard (Herbal Thought, 1), Richard Gunn (Sketchy), Kevin Durand (Joshua, 2), J. C. McKenzie (Reagan 'Ray' aka 'Normal' Ronald), Valarie Rae Miller (Cynthia 'Original Cindy' McEachin), John Savage (Colonel Donald Michael Lydecker), Martin Cummins (Ames White, 2)

See p78-87 **Charles H. Eglee:** Creator, Executive Producer, Writer

Doctor Who

1963-1989

A BBC Production

Executive Producer (selected): Barry Letts (18)

Producer (chronological): Verity Lambert (1-3), John Wiles (3), Innes Lloyd (3-5), Peter Bryant (5-6), Derrick Sherwin (6-7), Barry Letts (7-12), Philip Hinchcliffe (12-14), Graham Williams (15-17), John Nathan-Turner (18-26)

Associate Producer (chronological): Mervyn Pinfield (1-2), Peter Bryant (4)

Script Ed (chronological): Derrick Sherwin (6),

Terrance Dicks (6-11), Robert Holmes (12-15), Anthony Read (15-16), Douglas Adams (17), Christopher H. Bidmead (18), Anthony Root (19), Eric Saward (19-23), Andrew Cartmel (24-26)

Story Ed (chronological): David Whitaker (1-2), Dennis Spooner (2), Donald Tosh (2-3), Gerry Davis (3-4), Peter Bryant (4-5), Derrick Sherwin (5), Victor Pemberton (5)

Writer (selected): Robert Baker (8-10, 12, 14-17), Malcolm Hulke (4, 6-11), Louis Marks (2, 9, 13-14), Dave Martin (8-10, 12, 14-16), Terry Nation (1-3, 10-13, 17)

Main cast: The Doctors: William Hartnell (1-4), Patrick Troughton (4-6), John Pertwee (7-11), Tom Baker (12-18), Peter Davidson (19-21), Colin Baker (22-23), Sylvester McCoy (24-26)

Additional Cast: Roger Delgado (The Master, 8)

See p46-61 **Terrance Dicks:** Script Editor, Writer (6, 12, 13 credited as 'Robin Bland', 15, 18, 20)

Farscape

1999-

Jim Henson Television and Hallmark Entertainment

Executive Producer: Robert Halmi Jr, Brian Henson, David Kemper, Richard Manning (3), Kris Noble, **Rockne S. O'Bannon**, Rod Perth

Consulting Producer: Sue Milliken (3), David Willis

Supervising Producer: Justin Monjo (3)

Producer: Sue Milliken, Anthony Winley (3)

Co-Producer: Andrew Prowse (3)

Line Producer: Richard Clendinnen, Lesley Parker (3)

Main cast: Ben Browder (IASA Commander John Robert Crichton Jr), Claudia Black (Aeryn Sun), Virginia Hey (Pa'u Zotoh Zhaan, 1-3), Anthony Simcoe ('General' Ka D'Argo), Jonathan Hardy (voice of Dominar Rygel XVI), Gigi Edgley (Chiana), Lani [John] Tupu (voice of Pilot/PK Captain Bialar Crais, recurring), Paul Goodard (Stark, 1-2 recurring/3-), Wayne Pygram (Scorpius, recurring), Tammy McIntosh (Joolushko 'Jool' Tunai Fenta Hovalis, 3-)

See p14-27 **Rockne S. O'Bannon:** Executive Producer, Writer (1, 3)

Gene Roddenberry's Andromeda

2000-

Tribune Entertainment Company/Fireworks Inc

Creator: Gene Roddenberry

Developer: **Robert Hewitt Wolfe**

Executive Producer: Allan Eastman, Jay Firestone, Adam Haight, Majel Roddenberry (1)

Co-Executive Producer: **Robert Hewitt Wolfe**

Producer: Kevin Sorbo [uncredited], Keri Young

Writer (selected): Steve Barnes (1), Matt Kiene, Ashley Edward Miller, Eric Oleson (2), John Parry (2), Joe Reinkemeyer, Emily Skopov (2), Zack Stentz, Ethlie Ann Vare, Walter Jon Williams (1)

Main cast: Kevin Sorbo (High Guard Captain Dylan Hunt), Lisa Ryder (Freighter Captain Rebeka 'Beka'

Valentine), Keith Hamilton Cobb (Tyr Anasazi Out
Of Victoria By Barbarossa aka Nemo), Laura Bertram
(Trance 'The Purple One' Gemini), Brent Stait
(Reverend 'Rev' Bem aka Bohemian Far Traveller aka
Redplague), Gordon Michael Woolvett (Seamus
Zelazny Harper), Lexa Doig (Andromeda aka Shining
Path To Truth And Knowledge AI model GRA 112,
serial number XMC-10-182 aka Rommie)
See p232-247 **Robert Hewitt Wolfe:** Developer, Co-
Executive Producer, Writer

Hercules: The Legendary Journeys
1995-99
Renaissance Pictures
Executive Producer: Sam Raimi, **Robert Tapert**
Co-Executive Producer: John Schulian
Supervising Producer: Robert Bielak, Steve Roberts
Producer: Andrew Dettmann, Eric Gruendemann,
Daniel Truly
Co-Producer: David Eick
Associate Producer: Bernadette Joyce
Writer (selected): Alex Kurtzman, Roberto Orci
Main cast: Kevin Sorbo (Hercules), Michael Hurst
(Iolaus)
Additional Cast: Anthony Quinn (Zeus, 1-2)
See p196-211 **Robert Tapert:** Executive Producer,
Director

Lexx
1997-
Salter St Films
Executive Producer: **Paul Donovan**, Wolfram Tichy
Co-Producer: William Fleming
Line Producer: Stephen J. Turnbull
Writer (selected): Lex Gigeroff, Jeffrey Hirschfield
Main cast: Brian Downey (Stanley H. Tweedle), Eva
Habermann (Zev Bellringer, 1), Xenia Seeberg (Xev
Bellringer, 2-), Michael McManus (Kai), Jeffrey
Hirschfield (voice of 790), Tom Gallant (voice of The
Lexx)
Additional Cast: Nigel Bennett (Prince, 4)
See p62-77 **Paul Donovan:** Executive Producer,
Writer, Director

Mutant X
2001-
Tribune Entertainment Company
Executive Producer: Avi Arad, Jay Firestone, Adam
Haight, Rick Ungar
Creative Executive Producer: Seth Howard
Executive Consultant: **Howard Chaykin**
Producer: Jamie Paul Rock
Director (selected): T. J. Scott
Main cast: John Shea (Adam Xero), Tom McCamus
(Mason Eckhart), Forbes March (Jesse Kilmartin aka
Synergy), Doug O'Keeffe (Frank Thorne), Victoria
Pratt (Shalimar Fox aka Shadowfox), Lauren Lee
Smith (Emma Desalvo aka Rapport), Victor Webster

(Brennan Mulwray aka Fuse)
See p36-45 **Howard Chaykin:** Executive Consultant,
Head Writer

Neverwhere
1996
BBC/Crucial Films
Executive Producer: Polly McDonald, Chris Parr,
John Whitson
Producer: Clive Brill
Writer: **Neil Gaiman**
Director: Dewi Humphreys
Title Designer and Opening Sequence Director: Dave
McKean
Main cast: Gary Bakewell (Richard Oliver Mayhew),
Laura Fraser (Door), Hywel Bennett (Mr Croup),
Clive Russell (Mr Vandemaar), Paterson Joseph (The
Marquis De Carabas), Trevor Peacock (Old Bailey),
Freddie Jones (The Earl of Earl's Court), Tanya
Moodie (Hunter), Peter Capaldi (The Angel
Islington), Julie T. Wallace (Serpentine), Tamsin Greig
(Lamia), Stratford Johns (Mr Arnold Stockton),
Elizabeth Marmur (Jessica), Amy Marston
(Anasthesia), Sean O'Callaghan (Lord Rat-Speaker),
Earl Cameron (The Abbott of the Black Friars), Nick
Holder (Varney), Tony Pritchard (Hammersmith)
See p104-117 **Neil Gaiman:** Writer

Outer Limits, The
1995-
A Trilogy Entertainment Group and Atlantis Films
Production
Executive Producer: Pen Densham, Matthew
Hastings, Richard Barton Lewis, Grant Rosenberg,
Mark Stern, John Watson
Co-Executive Producer: Michael Cassutt (1), Sam
Egan, **Jonathan Glassner** (1-4), Grant Rosenberg,
Scott Shepherd (2), Brad Wright
Executive Consultant: Joseph Stefano (1)
Producer: Brent-Karl Clackson, Manny Coto, Justis
Greene, Scott Shepherd (1)
Co-Producer: Ron McLeod, Nora O'Brien
Associate Producer: Ben Brafman, Sally Dixon
Writer (selected): Alan Brennert credited as 'Michael
Bryan'
Director (selected): Peter DeLuise
Main cast: Kevin Conway (Control Voice)
See p118-131 **Jonathan Glassner:** Co-Executive
Producer, Writer (1-4), Director

Red Dwarf
1988-
A Paul Jackson Production for BBC North West (1-3),
A Grant Naylor Production for BBC North (4-)
Executive Producer: **Rob Grant** and **Doug Naylor** (5-
6), Paul Jackson, **Doug Naylor** (7-)
Producer: Ed Bye (7-), Hilary Bevan Jones (5), Justin
Judd (6)

Director: Ed Bye (1-4, 7-8), Andy DeEmmony, **Rob Grant** (5), Juliet May (5), **Doug Naylor** (5)
Main cast: Chris Barrie (Arnold Judas Rimmer, BSc, SSc), Craig Charles (Dave Lister), Danny John-Jules (Cat), Norman Lovett (1-2, 7-8)/Hattie Hayridge (3-6) (Holly), David Ross (2)/Robert Llewelyn (3-) (Kryten), C. P. Grogan (1-2 recurring)/Chloë Annett (7-) (Kristine Kochanski)
See p132-147 **Rob Grant:** Executive Producer, Writer (1-6), Director)
See p132-147 **Doug Naylor:** Executive Producer, Writer (1-8), Director

seaQuest DSV (1-2)/**seaQuest 2032** (3)
1993-6
Amblin Television Production in association with Universal Television
Creator: **Rockne S. O'Bannon**
Executive Producer: David J. Burke (1-2), Clifton Campbell (3), Carleton Eastlake (3), Patrick Hasburgh, **Rockne S. O'Bannon** (pilot), Steven Spielberg, Tommy Thompson
Supervising Producer: Lee Goldberg, Hans Tobeason
Producer: Steve Beers, Clifton Campbell, Oscar L. Costo (2), Carleton Eastlake (2), Gregg D. Fienberg (1-2), Patrick Hasburgh, Lawrence Hertzog (2), David Kemper (1-2), Philip Carr Neel, William Rabkin, Les Sheldon (1-2)
Co-Producer: Harker Wade (3)
Associate Producer: Peter Mavromates
Writer (selected): David Kemper (1)
Main cast: Roy Scheider (Captain Nathan Bridger), Stephanie Beacham (Dr Kristin Westphalen, 1), Stacy Haiduk (Lt Commander Katherine Hitchcock, 1), Don Franklin (Commander Jonathan Ford), Jonathan Brandis (Lucas Wolenczak), John D'Aquino (Lt Benjamin Krieg, 1, 3), Royce D. Applegate (Chief Manilow Crocker, 1), Ted Raimi (Lt J. G. Tim O'Neill), Marco Sanchez (Sensor Chief Miguel Ortiz), Kathy Evison (Lonnie Ellen Henderson, 2-3), Rosalind Allen (Dr Wendy Smith, 2-3), Edward Kerr (Lt James Brody, 2-3), Michael DeLuise (Tony Piccolo, 2-3), Peter DeLuise (Dagwood, 2-3), Michael Ironside (Captain Oliver Hudson, 3), Elise Neal (Lt J. J. Fredericks, 3), Michael Costello (UEO Secretary General Thomas McGrath)
See p14-27 **Rockne S. O'Bannon:** Creator, Executive Producer, Writer (pilot)

Star Trek
1966-69
A Desilu Production in association with Norway Corporation (1-2), A Paramount Production in association with Norway Corporation (2-3)
Creator: Gene Roddenberry
Executive Producer: Gene Roddenberry
Producer: Gene L. Coon (1-2), Fred Freiberger (3), John Meredyth Lucas (l-2), Gene Roddenberry

Associate Producer: John D. F. Black, Robert H. Justman, Edward K. Milkis, Gregg Peters
Story Consultant: Steven W. Carabatsos, **D. C. Fontana**, Arthur H. Singer
Executive Story Editor: **D. C. Fontana**
Writer (selected): Margaret Armen, Jerome Bixby (2-3), Robert Bloch (1-2), Harlan Ellison (1), David Gerrold (2-3), Stephen Kandel, Richard Matheson, Samuel A. Peeples (1), Theodore Sturgeon (1-2)
Main cast: William Shatner (Captain James Tiberius Kirk), Leonard Nimoy (Spock), DeForest Kelley (Dr Leonard H. 'Bones' McCoy), James Doohan (Montgomery 'Scotty' Scott), George Takei (Hikaru Sulu), Walter Koenig (Ensign Pavel A. Chekov, 2-3), Nichelle Nichols (Lt Uhura), Majel Barrett (Nurse Christine Chapel/Ship's Computer), Grace Lee Witney (Yeoman Janice Rand, 1)
See p88-103 **D. C. Fontana:** Story Consultant, Executive Story Editor, Writer (also credited as 'Michael Richards')

Star Trek: Deep Space Nine
1993-99
A Paramount Production
Creator: Rick Berman, **Michael Piller**
Star Trek Creator: Gene Roddenberry
Executive Producer: Ira Steven Behr (3-7), Rick Berman, **Michael Piller** (1-3)
Co-Executive Producer: Ira Steven Behr (1-2), Hans Beimler (7), Ronald D. Moore (6-7)
Supervising Producer: Ira Steven Behr (1), Hans Beimler (6-7), James Crocker (1-2), René Echevarria (7), Peter Lauritson (4-7), David Livingston, Ronald D. Moore (3-5)
Co-Supervising: Hans Beimler (5), René Echevarria (3-6)
Coordinating Producer: Robert Della Santina
Producer: Hans Beimler (4), Peter Allan Fields (2), Peter Lauritson (2-3), Steve Oster (4-7), **Robert Hewitt Wolfe** (5-6)
Co-Producer: J. P. Farrell, Peter Allan Fields (1), **Robert Hewitt Wolfe** (4)
Associate Producer: Teri Potts
Creative Consultant: **Michael Piller** (3-7)
Story Ed: Peter Allan Fields
Writers (selected): Bill Dial, **D. C. Fontana** (credited as Dorothy C. Fontana) (1), David Gerrold (5), Joe Menosky, Jeri Taylor (2)
Main cast: Avery Brooks (Benjamin Lafayette Sisko), Rene Auberjonois (Odo), Nana Visitor (Major Kira Nerys), Terry Farrell (Jadzia Dax, 1-6), Colm Meaney (Chief Operations Officer Miles O'Brien), Siddig El Fadil (1-3) credited as Alexander Siddig (4-7) (Dr Julian Bashir), Armin Shimerman (Quark), Cirroc Lofton (Jake Sisko), Michael Dorn (Lt Commander Worf, 4-7), Nicole deBoer (Ezri Dax, 7)
See p162-177 **Michael Piller:** Creator, Executive Producer, Creative Consultant, Writer

See p14-27 **Rockne S. O'Bannon:** Story Editor, Writer
(1-2)
See p180-195 **J. Michael Straczynski:** Story Editor,
Writer (2-3)

Xena: Warrior Princess
1995-2001
Renaissance Pictures
Executive Producer: **Robert Tapert**, Sam Raimi,
R. J. Stewart
Co-Executive Producer: Liz Friedman, Eric
Gruendemann, Steven L. Sears
Supervising Producer: Steven L. Sears, Emily Skopov
Coordinating Producer: Bernadette Joyce
Producer: Michael MacDonald, Chris Manheim
Co-Producer: Patrick Moran
Line Producer: Chloe Smith
Directors (selected): Josh Becker (1), Oley Sassone (3)
Main cast: Lucy Lawless (Xena/Meg/Princess
Diana/Melinda Pappas/Priestess Leah), Reneé
O'Connor (Gabrielle/Janice Covington/Hope), Ted
Raimi (Joxer the Mighty), Kevin Smith (Ares, god of
War), Hudson Leick (Callisto), Bruce Campbell
(Autolycus), Robert Trebor (Salmoneus)
See p196-211 **Robert Tapert:** Executive Producer,
Director

X-Files, The
1993-
Ten Thirteen Productions, in association with 20th
Century Television
Creator: **Chris Carter**
Executive Producer: **Chris Carter**
Co-Executive Producer: R. W. Goodwin, **David
Greenwalt** (4), Glen Morgan, James Wong
Supervising Producer: Alex Gansa, Howard Gordon
Executive Story Consultant: Chris Ruppenthal
Main cast: David Duchovny (Special Agent Fox
'Spooky' Mulder), Gillian Anderson (Special Agent
Dana Scully), Mitch Pileggi (Walter Skinner), William
B. Davis (C. G. B. Spender 'The Cigarette-Smoking
Man'), Robert Patrick (Special Agent John Doggett,
8-), Jerry Hardin (Deep Throat, 1/2- recurring)
See p28-35 **Chris Carter:** Creator, Executive Producer,
Writer, Director (5-8)
See p 148-161 **David Greenwalt:** Co-Executive
Producer, Writer (4)

Also available from TITAN BOOKS

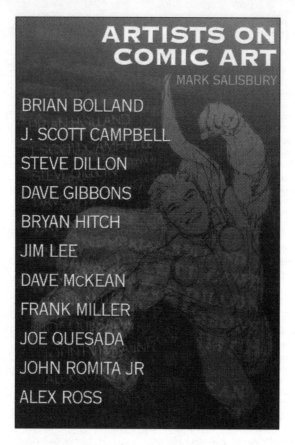

ARTISTS ON COMIC ART

MARK SALISBURY

BRIAN BOLLAND

J. SCOTT CAMPBELL

STEVE DILLON

DAVE GIBBONS

BRYAN HITCH

JIM LEE

DAVE McKEAN

FRANK MILLER

JOE QUESADA

JOHN ROMITA JR

ALEX ROSS

Artists on Comic Art
By Mark Salisbury

Journalist Mark Salisbury gets to grips with the lively creative genius behind the pencil and ink, presenting an unparalleled insight into the widescreen mind of the comic book artist, illustrated with scores of rare and previously unseen designs, sketches, breakdowns and thumbnails.

The hottest artists working in comics today are interviewed in-depth in the most comprehensive book on comics art and artists ever published, to reveal the secrets of translating comics script to graphic storytelling. Technique, style, layouts, approach, pencilling, inking... no facet of the artist's craft is left unexplored. Revealing, instructional, shocking and humorous, *Artists on Comic Art* has something for comics fans, budding artists and hardened professionals alike.

TO ORDER, CALL 01536 764646

Also available from TITAN BOOKS

The Complete Book of Scriptwriting
By J. Michael Straczynski

From J. Michael Straczynski (the creator of the TV SF phenomenon *Babylon 5*) comes a definitive, all-in-one guide to writing and selling screenplays, teleplays, theatrical plays, radio scripts and animation scripts.

How to structure your scripts, how to lay them out, a guide to the terminology used in the industry, tips on how to get your scripts seen by the people that matter: Straczynski deals with all the ins-and-outs of scriptwriting, step by step. As an added bonus, also included is the complete shooting script for the *Babylon 5* episode 'The Coming of Shadows'.

Worlds of Wonder: How to Write Science Fiction and Fantasy
By David Gerrold

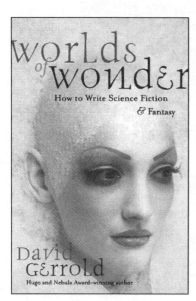

Worlds of Wonder: How to Write Science Fiction and Fantasy is a step-by-step guide for all budding sci-fi and fantasy writers, showing you how to turn your words into works of wonder. With the help of Nebula and Hugo award-winning *Star Trek* author David Gerrold, you'll gain insight into the craft as well as practise techniques that will immediately improve your writing.

Fun, accessible, and sparked by Gerrold's infectious enthusiasm, *Worlds of Wonder* is a must for SF and fantasy fans, as well as those who wish to succeed in these flourishing publishing genres.

TO ORDER, CALL 01536 764646

Also available from TITAN BOOKS

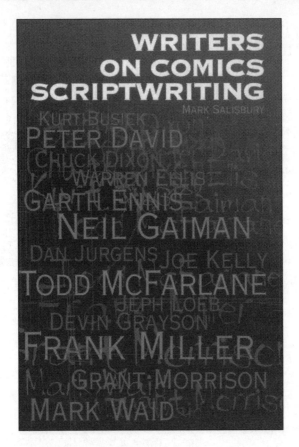

Writers on Comics Scriptwriting
By Mark Salisbury

Through a series of interviews with journalist Mark Salisbury, the biggest names in comics scriptwriting talk candidly and frankly about their profession, their approach to writing and the comics industry as a whole; revealing the mechanics of writing for comics and, in the process, a great deal about themselves.

Packed with personal information, contentious views and humorous anecdotes, this is both an exploration of the writer's craft and a who's who of the hottest comics' talent around today. The first ever book on comics scriptwriting and scriptwriters, this is a must for fans, professionals, would-be writers and anyone who's ever wondered exactly how the writer's mind works.